D1170831

INSCRIPTIONS OF ANCIENT NEPAL

VOLUME ONE : INSCRIPTIONS

INSCRIPTION

OF ANCIENT

NEPAL

D R REGMI

abhinav publications   NEW DELHI

First published 1983 in the
United States of America by
Humanities Press Inc
Atlantic Highlands
NJ 07716

ISBN 0-391-02559-7

Copyright 1983 by Abhinav Publications

All rights reserved. No part of this book may be reproduced
or transmitted in any form or by any means, electronic or
mechanical, including photocopying, recording or by any
information storage and retrieval system, without permission
in writing from the publishers.

Printed in India

PREFACE

The first collection of Nepalese inscriptions appeared in 1888 with the publication of Bhagwanlal Indraji's book 'Twenty-three Inscriptions from Nepal', in which 15 inscriptions of the ancient period with photocopies of the rubbings are published. They include 3 of Mānadeva (1, 2, 3), 1 of Śivadeva (5), 3 of Amśuvarmā (6, 7, 8), 3 of Jiṣṇugupta (9, 10, 11), 2 of Śivadeva II (12, 13) and 2 of Jayadeva (14, 15), 1 of Śivadeva I (S. 535) and the rest of unnamed kings. Bhagwanlal Indraji's was the pioneer work in this field.

Bendall had preceded Indraji. He visited Nepal in 1885 and published 3 inscriptions in his book 'A Journey of Literary and Archaeological Researches in Nepal and Northern India during the winter of 1884-85'. They were additional records. The inscriptions are one from Bhadgaon (Golmodhital), one from Sundhara, Patan and last, the stele of Gairidhara in Patan.

Bendall was followed by S. Levi who added more inscriptions in the third volume Le Nepal printed and published in 1902 in Paris. Levi reproduced the Changu Pillar inscriptions with more lines added to Bhagwanlal Indraji's but added 20 of his own. There are altogether 21 inscriptions in the book. Our inscriptions nos. 2, 3, 10, 25, 27, 46, 49, 57, 58, 61, 62, 63, 64, 75, 94, 106, 135, 139 and 143 are exclusively credited to Levi.

Bendall was shown utmost courtesy by the Government.

He had free access to the newly constituted Bir Library where he obtained a palm leaf copy of the manuscript of the old chronicle composed about the end of the 14th century. The chronicle, some leaves of which are reproduced in photos in two articles (attached to Journal of the Asiatic Society of Bengal 1903, pp. 1-32 and to H.P. Sastri's Catalogue of Palm leaf and Selected paper mss in the Darbar Library Nepal, 2 volumes, Calcutta, 1905, 1906), is a rare find for the early medieval period.

The chronicle (he designates three sections as V^1, V^2, V^3) as compared with the colophon dates of the mss available in H.P. Sastri's catalogue and others laid a sound basis for a correct history of the period of the country up to Jayasthiti-malla's time. But Bendall had failed to understand the importance of the chronicle in the light of the colophon dates. Colophons were much limited at the time the catalogue came out. But it cannot be denied that there was an element of unconsciously committed negligence. Bendall's History serves the purpose of introductory history as he also claims it to be so for that period. But the first section of this chronicle is much too complicated and erroneous.

After Bhagwanlal Indraji, the next historian of repute was Sylvain Levi who visited Nepal in the last days of Maharaja Bir Shumsher. Levi was fortunate enough to be allowed to stay longer than any other scholar. He was an erudite scholar of Sanskrit, vastly learned in orientology and possessed a thorough knowledge of the history of India, Tibet and China. While in Nepal he used his time and energy to collect rubbings of inscriptions available to him. He also obtained chronicles compiled by efforts of scholars of the early 19th century based on both Buddhist and Brahmanical traditions, which he used along with the inscriptions, to write his history of Nepal. But he did not know that he had ignored many inscriptions. S. Levi utilised Chinese sources no doubt. But this did not compensate the loss suffered on account of the negligence of locally available materials which with a little more effort could have been at his disposal. Even the account of Hiuen Tsand and Li I Piao he could not use in the proper direction as he was misguided by prejudices in favour of Tibet. He misread Tibetan history as narrated by Bu-ston, and could not find out the exact dates of Srong Tsang Gampo. Then he wrongly concluded that the epoch of the later group of inscriptions was to be sought in 595 A.D., some 48 years earlier to the actual date as it will appear later. His errors were, however, more due to his inability to trace related indigenous data of the period. The volumes Levi produced nevertheless bear the impression of a superb work of a man who was vastly learned in orientology. The 21 inscriptions though mostly incorrectly read are ably edited and presented with comparative notes full of references to standard classical texts. But as inscriptions are not the main source materials for Levi's chronology and history the books he wrote might be ignored for the present.

Levi while editing the inscriptions adds notes quoting chapters and verses from allied Indian classics, which had relevance with reference to the subjects mentioned in the many passages of the records. The treatment is masterly in so far as the same helps us to understand the terms and facts common to the inscriptions and literatures of both Nepal and India.

He has brought out wealth of materials, which on all accounts are valuable. But Levi has not been able to explain many classical Sanskrit terms as well as had failed to grasp the implication of non-Sanskritic words used except in a few cases. It so appears that Levi and others suffered from no official restrictions but then had no proper guides and if they failed to achieve anything substantial it was because conditions in Nepal were not ripe for a full scale research in the country.

None of these scholars could stay in Nepal for a long time. No one could go outside the Valley. But even their stay in the Valley was for a limited duration of time. They could hardly stay for more than a fortnight. There were no efforts made to prolong the stay and make an extensive and intensive search for the objectives. But their eyes also failed them. They could have marked the steles for rubbing as they walked and saw them. But they were not so watchful.

Prof. Tucci who came to Kathmandu in 1929 en route to Tibet did not find it possible to spend more than a few days and there was little time for him to divert his attention to the study of Nepalese historical sources. But Tucci's performance

was surely better while he conducted his tour of west Nepal
in 1954.

K.P. Jayaswal was the last of the old guards to come to
Nepal in quest of historical materials and for visiting sites.
As in the case of Bendall and Levi he was treated as a
state guest and got the same facilities. But his stay
was only for ten days and he could hardly do anything
but enjoy a glimpse. He could not discover any new
materials. Yet he wrote a book publishing the same with the
name 'History and Chronology of Nepal', which is based on
insufficient and unreliable materials. Nevertheless some of his
observations have attracted notice of scholars.

In the late forties the Bir Library collected rubbings of
inscriptions. This was the richest collection thus far made.
Some of our scholars utilised them in the next decade for
publishing in monthly magazines. However, the printed
items were much limited and Nepalese themselves hardly get
the credit for writing up till then.

Since early 1951 foreigners were allowed entry by the Government and Nepal was no longer a closed land. The Nepalese also were permitted to work in the field unhindered as the
foreigners as research scholars. If previously the Government
frowned upon such research activities, this was no more the case
when gates of freedom had been opened. In this period many
who had found the atmosphere uncongenial earlier but who
continued their taste for such work seized the opportunity to
collect suitable materials for history writing. I also tried the
the hard job along with others. But there were several handi-
caps, which few could overcome, the greatest being shortage of
money and materials. Physical labour alone could not do the
miracle. Resources were equally essential specially when one
had to plough a virgin soil.

As far as the search of inscriptions by the Nepalese themselves goes the names of two Nepalese, Baburam Acharya and
Mahant (monk) Naraharinath, come readily to notice. Both
were connected with a monthly in Sanskrit devoted specially
to historical writing. This monthly, however, ceased publication after a year and then M. Naraharinath on his own
published 3 magazines one after the other, the last of which
was Itihāsa Prakāśa, ill assorted but valuable. The various

issues contained only a few inscriptions of the Nepal Valley. But pages were filled with copies of texts of copper plate inscriptions and chronicles of 11-16th centuries from Jumla and other principalities in the far west and in early sixties Khardar Baburam Acharya was employed by the king to write a biography of Prithivinarayan Shah but he had to dictate his writing on account of blindness and old age. M. Naraharinath left his job unfinished to go to politics, and his material is not duly utilised in the field of paleographical research. There was little work done until R. Gnoli, an Italian scholar, brought out his collection.

Amongst the foreigners the names of Professors G. Tucci, R. Gnoli and Luciano Petech are prominent. All three writers are historians in their own way. Petech wrote about the early history of Medieval Nepal based on collections of ms colophons made by Pandits of the Bir Library. But R. Gnoli who has published quite a large number of ancient inscriptions is more relevant for us. R. Gnoli published all the data available to him, which included also those already published. His book 'Nepalese Inscriptions in Gupta Character' published with photostat copies of inscriptions is by far the largest collection of inscriptions published until 1958. Gnoli not only published new materials but corrected errors in the reading of the script made by Bendall, Indraji and S. Levi. He did not, however, visit sites but depended solely on the impressions collected by the Bir Library (now National Archives). If Gnoli himself had undertaken exploration he could have obtained more materials.

In the sixties the quarterly *Abhilekha Saṅgraha* brought out inscriptions, some old and some new, the former with improved reading. Later another quarterly 'Pūrnimā' continued the same laudable job. The sum total of the research appeared 18 years later in a separate book 'Lichchhavi Kālka Abhilekha' edited by Dhanavajra Vajracharya. The work was published by the Centre for Nepalese and Asian Studies, T.U.

The number of inscriptions published by Gnoli was 93. These included all the texts of inscriptions published by previous compilers. Gnoli's volume shows also new reigns such as of Rāmadeva and Gangadeva, which he misread as Gaṇadeva. More inscriptions of Śivadeva I and II and

Amśuvarmā and Jiṣṇugupta and his son Viṣṇugupta have found place in his work. Gnoli's collection also covered all inscriptions of Narendradeva, Śivadeva and Jayadeva. But his reading in some cases is defective and he has also left many lines unread, which he could have read with more effort as the rubbings clearly show them. But the 51 documents newly added are of real historical importance. Gnoli's collection in spite of limitations is an outstanding contribution to the literature on the subject.*

In Gnoli's collections there are several one word or 1 or 2 line inscriptions of no particular significance and so the number might be reduced to some extent. It also might be noted that the actual number of such inscriptions is much less than given in the compilation of Dhanavajra, a young researcher referred to in our text a little later as DV in abbreviated form, whose book has appeared in 1977.

Gnoli was followed by Thomas O. Ballinger who published photographs of 5 inscriptions but without reading anything except the dates.

The Na-bahil stone is the most important of them because it contains a charter of Amśuvarmā in the old era (500+   ). The photographs appear in Vol. 4 of the American Oriental Society published in 1958.

But Ballinger was not a historian and treats his subject casually and therefore the 5 inscriptions he brings out in the photographs might not have the importance of other compilations.

It must be said to the credit of Dhanavajra Vajracharya that though coming two decades after Gnoli's volume his collection stands foremost, in respect of the number of inscriptions, of all the contributions so far made in the sixties and seventies. It outbids Gnoli also as far as a few more important records go. We have already made passing reference to it and I think that this must be separately treated to realise its true import which we have done in the next few pages.

Dhanavajra's collection surely deserves fair treatment and therefore we are proceeding to make a wider reference to his

*Gnoli omits plates for inscriptions nos. 7, 24, 30, 31, 48, 49, 75, 79, 81, 82, all Gnoli's numbers.

work. But it is not the last volume on the collection of ancient inscriptions. Dhanavajra is followed by Hariram Joshi. Hariram Joshi's volume, however, contains just reproductions of the texts of 175 inscriptions, some published by R. Gnoli and others by Dhanavajra. He also published photographic copies of 65 steles. But it appears that Joshi did not try to correct Gnoli, and he also adopted texts published by Dhanavajra in the quarterly 'Pūrnimā', which the latter had later compiled into a book as he came out with a new volume Lichchhavi Kalka Abhilekha. The 'Pūrnimā' versions in many instances were erroneous, which Dhanavajra himself corrected in his forthcoming book. But Joshi by adopting what was published in 'Pūrnimā' seems to ignore the errors creeping in the texts published in that quarterly. This shows that his aim was just to collate the published materials. Thus Joshi's work might pass as one more compilation on the subject and not as a work of search and research. But for half a dozen new photographs he deserves the credit due to him. The performance on the whole may be important enough to draw close attention. If he had done his own reading the value of the work would have been really high.

As we have already said, Dhanavajra's collection is the latest work on the subject. It contains some new inscriptions not available in R. Gnoli. Although the collection goes without photostat copies of the rubbings yet the Nepali translation and explanations add a special importance to it. Dhanavajra's collection is exhaustive and shows considerable improvement on the reading of some inscriptions including mostly those of R. Gnoli, and is certainly by far the largest collection of Nepalese inscriptions so far published. Dhanavajra has published 190 inscriptions and this collection is impressive no doubt. But Gnoli's work with photographic plates has also its own special features. In fact Dhanavajra also has accepted a large number of inscriptions from Gnoli as they stood. Dhanavajra has improved on Gnoli's reading of some lines in so far as they go as regards many others. The collection, however, includes numerous one or two line inscriptions, which have no historical value as in the case of R. Gnoli. If minor one or two word or one line or two line inscriptions were not counted

the total number would be considerably less in the collections
of both Gnoli and Dhanavajra.

It is not my intention to disparage any attempt to include
in the publications one or two line inscriptions. This has
been the practice without exception since a long time and
Gnoli and Dhanavajra were not expected to follow any other
course. I have myself done it as I could not avoid the same.
But what I want to stress is the fact that the collection would
not have looked so large as it appears when everything is
assembled.

In spite of a large number of one or two line inscriptions
Dhanavajra has added quite a good number of inscriptions,
which are not available in Gnoli. Of course, he also availed of
many rubbings collected by the Bir Library, and it was important as many of such inscriptions had escaped the Italian
scholar's notice. Dhanavajra has also added on his own yet
more inscriptions.

As we go through Dhanavajra's collection it appears that
if there are new additions already enumerated many inscriptions given by Gnoli are also as great many without any
correction and some with minor correction and yet a few with
major corrections. Dhanavajra also has corrected dates in
some cases where they were wrongly read. But such instances
are not numerous. The inscriptions from Gnoli accepted with
minor corrections or no corrections number nearly 56, and
all are important ones. Such inscriptions belong to various
reigns extending from Mānadeva to Jayadeva but they appear
more in number since Gaṇadeva's reign. The inscriptions of
Dhanavajra over and above what Gnoli gives might be distri-
buted over a long period to different reigns.

Whatever it might be Dhanavajra's collection has the
largest number of inscriptions published thus far. To his
credit it should also be said that he gave a correct reading to
doubtful letters, which earlier had confused Gnoli. They might
be limited, but they have their own importance.

He has surely presented an epigraphic survey down to
details. But in this attempt Dhanavajra himself had committed
mistakes in reading though to a limited extent. He has also
left gaps in lines of a few passages, which required filling.
I have corrected the wrong reading as well as filled the gaps.

This fact apart, the translation in Nepali of the inscriptions as done by him is not as intelligible as it should be, Dhanavajra has tried to pass many Sanskrit words as Nepali, which is a source of confusion. The words used in the inscriptions came from classical Sanskrit and it was difficult even for a well versed Sanskrit scholar to understand them. This is the reason that makes Dhanavajra's translated passages unintelligible even to Nepalese readers. My translation into English though meant for people knowing the English language and with or without Nepali does not suffer from this defect. The translation conveys the exact meaning of the words used in the epigraphs as I understand them. But many words being obscure could not be rightly translated.

Dhanavajra's explanations offered to every inscription represent a fresh attempt to give fuller information about so many things connected with the theme of the record. He must get the credit for what he has done. However, numerous loopholes are traced there in the book, and he has also skipped over quite a few words which have important bearing on economic and political subjects. All these need elaborate treatment, which also I have done here, but such cases are limited in number.

The present volume was scheduled to come out quite early in the sixties. The inscriptions were collected since quite long long ago. But on account of the author's preoccupation with political and later with other academic activities, the author could not give close attention to the final phase of writing and there was a considerable delay in finalising the manuscript. Now it is ready and I am placing the same before the scholarly world.

The volume carries photographic plates of the inscriptions published here under different captions. Their number is much larger than that of R. Gnoli or Hariram Joshi. There are 80-90 more plates than in R. Gnoli's collection.

Altogether I have published 164 inscriptions, out of which a large number of smaller records with no historical significance also have got place to keep up with the usual practice. I have left 23 inscriptions given by Dhanavajra but added a few new ones. But those omitted or adopted are not historically important. However there is much scope for search as the new finds in the Changu and Pasupati area go to prove.

Now, a few words about the arrangement of the inscriptions.

The readers should refer to the contents for the identity of the number in the translated part allotted to inscriptions in the original Sanskrit.

And one thing more. There has been a mistake in the numbering of the inscriptions from 54 to 58. The readers should correct 58 to 54, and then 54 to 55 followed by 56, 57, 58 (original 54). I regret this mistake.

The readers are also requested to note that in the English translation the word *malla* has been translated as deer or goat or some other animal. This might mislead them. But it is not the intention of the author to translate *malla* as a particular animal as far as this is done in the translation text. The readers might refer the question to the special note volume (III), where the subject is dealt with in detail.

I should also like to submit that the word dūtaka coming at the end of the text before the date line has been translated in different possible versions, all of which might not be strictly correct. The exact meaning is found in the part of the book giving special notes, etc.

The book is divided into 4 sections: (1) the text, (2) the English translation, (3) the plates and (4) special introductory notes for every inscription in historical perspective. The fifth section is being published as a separate volume under a new caption 'Nepal as Known from Inscriptions'. The corrigenda and addenda find place at the end of the 4th section.

Lastly, I owe a debt of gratitude to all the scholars who have worked in the past on the subject, in particular to C. Bendall, Bhagwanlal Indraji, Sylvain Levi, J.F. Fleet, Baburam Acharya, M. Naraharinath, R. Gnoli, Dhanavajra, H.R. Joshi, S.M. Rajavamsi, M.P. Khanal, Pantha brothers and others for enabling me by their contributions to bring out this collection of Nepalese epigraphic records.

I regret that the photograph of the Dumja stone inscription is missing.

Kathmandu, Nepal   D.R. Regmi

CONTENTS

SYSTEM OF TRANSLITERATION

a (अ)   ka (क)   dha (घ)
ā (आ)   kha (ख)   na (न)
i (इ)   ga (ग)   pa (प)
ī (ई)   gha (घ)   pha (फ)
u (उ)   ṅa (ङ)   ba (ब)
ū (ऊ)   cha (च)   bha (भ)
ṛ (ऋ)   chha (छ)   ma (म)
é (ए)   ja (ज)   ya (य)
ai (ऐ)   jha (झ)   ra (र)
o (ओ)   ña (ञ)   la (ल)
au (औ)   ṭa (ट)   va (व)
aṁ (अं)   ṭha (ठ)   ś (श)
aḥ (अः)   ḍa (ड)   ṣ (ष)
               ḍha (ढ)   s (स)
               ṇa (ण)   ha (ह)
               ta (त)   kṣa (क्ष)
               tha (थ)   tra (त्र)
               da (द)   jña (ज्ञ)

GENERAL ABBREVIATIONS

Ben	Bendall
Bh	Bhaṭṭāraka
BLI	Bhagvanlal Indraji
CIII	Corpus Inscriptionum Indicarum (J.F. Fleet)
DV	Dhanavajra Vajracharya
Gn	R. Gnoli
HR	Hariram Joshi
L	S. Levi
M	Mahārāja
Md	Mahārājādhirāja
Pm	Parameśvara
Pbh	Paramabhaṭṭāraka

GENERAL ABBREVIATIONS

I. The Changu Pillar Inscription

(BLI I; Levi I (III, II, 2), Sans. Sandeśa I-6; Gn I; DV 2; and HJ 3)

Two pieces of a pillar, one large and one small, stand before the western door of the temple of Narayana at Changu, literally, a round about and swing like ridge—synonymous with Sanskritic Doládri carrying the same meaning, about 6 miles north-west of Kathmandu. The two are parts of one pillar. The pillar seems to have broken about the bottom, some 80 cm above the ground, where the remaining portion in the shape of a stump still faces the main door. There are only 4 damaged lines on the stump but the other piece which is the second main part of the pillar containing the inscription of Mānadeva is a little far removed from the stump, suggesting that it is now removed from the base and has found a new bottom which is enclosed with a tortoise shaped stone. This tortoise is a new device and it is not surprising that a small portion of this piece of pillar remains underground with more lines of inscription. This is sure in view of the part (c) where the ending seems to be abrupt. We have no doubt that the pillar stood over the stump which faces the western door of the temple, and it is broken at the point where the top of the stump is visible. The breakaway was further broken in two.

The inscribed space is 34 cm wide. The date is *Samvat 386 Jyeṣṭha śukla pratipadā rohiṇi nakṣatra*. This is the only inscription giving a *nakṣatra* for the whole period.*

The stump of the pillar. This is found on the original base

of the pillar just in front of Changu Narayana Temple. The
inscribed part covers 20 cm in width of space.   Although Gnoli
says that the characters 'seem to me to be later than those of
the preceding inscription',   he might be wrong. Perhaps this
is the broken portion of the same inscription.

The inscription appears to deal with the grant of a piece of
land by the same donor.

*Bhagwanlal Indraji has read the first 17 lines of Face II, 17
of Face B and 20 of Face III. All the verses are composed in
Śārdūlavikrīḍita metre.

(a) East

१   संवत् ३०० ८० ६ ज्येष्ठमासे शुक्लपक्षे प्रतिपदि १

२   [रो] हिशी नक्षत्रयुक्ते चन्द्रमसि मुहूर्ते प्रशस्तेभिजिति

३   [श्री] वत्साङ्कितदीप्तचारु विपुल प्रोद्धृतवक्ष स्थल:

४   [श्री] वक्षस्तनपद्मबाहु [विम] ल: सम्यक्प्रवृद्धोत्सव:

५   [त्रै] लोक्यभ्रमयन्त्रवर्त्तीवि [विध] व्यासङ्गनित्योव्यय:

६   [दो] लाद्रौ निवसञ्जयत्यनि [मि] षैरभ्यच्र्च्यमानो हरि:   १

७   [श्रीमत्] त्चा न यप्रतापविभ [वैर्या] यामसंक्षेपकृत्

८   [राजा] भूद्दृषदेव: इत्यनु [पम: स] त्यप्रतिज्ञोदय:

९   यो रेजे सवितेव दीप्तकिर [णै:] सम्यग्ध [तै:] स्वै: सुतै:

१०   [वि] द्वद्दिर्बंहुगर्ब्विंतैर्च [पलै:] शू [रै] र्व्विनीतात्मभि:   २

११   [त] स्याभूत्तनय: समृद्ध [विष्] य: संरव्वेष्वजेयोरिभि:

१२   [वि] ज्ञ: शङ्करदेव इत्यनुपम दिप्तिप्रद: सत्यधी:

१३   [सो] यं विक्रमदानमानवि [भवै] लंब्ध्वा यश: पुष्कलं

१४   –संयम्य ररक्ष गामभिमतैंभ्रूंत्यैंमृं गेन्द्रोपम: ३

१५   [त] स्याप्युत्तम धर्म्मकर्म्मयशस:⋯⋯⋯वि ढ्वार्मिक:

१६   [ध] र्म्मा [त्मा] विनयेप्सु रुत्त [मगुण: श्रीध] र्मदेवो नृप:

१७   [ध] र्म्मेणैव कुलक्रमागत⋯⋯⋯राज्यं महत्

१८   [स्फी] तीकृत्य नयेन्नृं पर्षिचरि [तै: सम्] भाव्यचेतो नृणाम्   ४

१९ [इ] जेस-पशुभिः सुरान ···गुणैः सम्पन्न मन्त्र्ब्रिद्धिभिः

२० [यज्ञैः कर्म्म] विशुद्धदेह हृदय इचन्द्रद्युतिः पार्त्थिवः

२१ [प] त्नी तस्य विशुद्ध वंश बिभवा श्रीराज्यवत्युत्तमा

२२ [प्रा] णा [नाम] भवत् [प्रिया] कुलगु [णैं] लंक्ष्मीरिवाग्य्रा हरेः ५

२३ ······रतैर्य्यशोंशुभिरिदंव्याभास्य कृत्स्नञ्जगत्

२४ याति स्म त्रिदिवालयं नरपतावुद्यानयात्रामिव

२५ प्रम्लाना ज्वर विह्वलाकुलज···नैकमन्दा तदा

२६ देवाहार विधि क्रिया स्वभिरता तद्विप्रयोगात्पुरा   ६

Lines 22-26 are missing in Gnoli's plates. Also in mine.
Bhagwanlal Indraji's plate has 17 lines and his text is also of
the same extent. Levi though he gave the text upto 26 lines
also misses the last 5 lines.

(b) North

१ देवी राज्यवती तु तस्य नृपते भर्य्यर्य्यभिधाना सती

२ श्रीरेवानुगता भविष्यति तदा लोकान्तरासज्ङिनी

३ यस्याञ्जात इहानवद्यचरितः श्रीमानदेवो नृपः

४ कान्त्या शारदचन्द्रमा इव जगत्प्रह्लादयन्सर्व्वदा   ७

५ प्रत्यागत्य सगद्गदाक्षरमिदन्दीर्घं विनिश्चस्य च

६ प्रेम्ना पुत्रमुवाच साश्रुवदना यातः पिता ते दिवम्

७ हा पुत्रास्तमिते तवाद्य पितरि प्राणैर्बृथा किम्मम

८ राज्यम्पुत्रक कारयाहमनुयाम्यद्यैव भर्त्तुर्गतिम्   ८

९ किम्मे भोगविधान विस्तरकृतै राशामयैर्बन्धनै

१० मायास्वप्ननिभे समागमविधौ भत्र्रा विना जीवितुम्

११ यामीत्येवमवस्थिता खलु तदा दीनात्मना सूनुना

१२ पादौ भक्तिवशान्निपीड्य शिरसा विज्ञापिता यत्नतः   ९

१३ किम्भोगैर्म्मम किं हि जीवितसुखैस्त्वद् विप्रयोगे सति

१४ प्राणात्पूर्व्वमहञ्जहामि परतस्त्वं यास्यसीतो दिवम्

१५ इत्येवम्मुखपङ्कजान्तरगतैर्नेत्राम्बुमिश्रैर्दृढम्

१६ वाक्पाशैर्व्विहगीव पाशवशगा बद्धा ततस्तस्थुषी   १०

१७ सत्पुत्रेण सहौर्द्धंदेहिकविधि भर्त्तुः प्रकृत्यात्मना ²²

१८ शीलत्यागदमोपवासनियमैरेकान्तशुद्धाशया

१९ [वि] प्रेभ्योपि च सर्व्वंदा प्रददती तत्पुण्यवृद्धयै धनम्

२० तस्थौ तद्धृदया सतीव्रतविधौ साक्षादिवारून्धती   ११

२१ पुत्रोप्यूर्ज्जितसत्त्वविक्रमधृतिः क्षान्तः प्रजावत्सलः

२२ कर्त्ता नैव विकत्थनः स्मितकथः पूर्व्वाभिभाषी सदा

२३ तेजस्वी न च गर्व्विand न च परां लोकज्ञतान्नाश्रितः

२४ दीनानाथ सुहृत्प्रियातिथिजनः प्रत्यर्थिनाम्माननृत्   १२

Lines 17-24 are missing in the photographs of Levi, Bhagwanlal
Indraji, Gnoli and my own.

(c) West

१   अस्त्रापास्त्र विधान कौशलगुणैः प्रज्ञातसत्पौरुषः ²³ ²⁴

२   श्रीमच्चारूभुजः प्रपृष्टकनक ह्लक्षणावदातच्छविः

३   पीनांसो विकचासितोत्पलदलप्रस्पर्द्धं मानेक्षणः

४   साक्षात्काम इवाङ्गवान्नरपतिः कान्ताविलासोत्सवः

५   यूपैश्चारूभिरूच्छ्रितैर्व्वसुमती पित्रा ममालङ्कृता   १३

६   क्षात्रेणाजिमखाश्रयेण विधिना दीक्षाश्रितोहं स्थितः

७   यात्राम्प्रत्यरि सङ्क्षयाय तरसा गच्छामि पूर्व्वान्दिशम्

८   ये चाज्ञावशवर्त्तिनो मम नृपाः संस्थापयिष्यामि तान्   १४

९   इत्येवञ्जननीमपेतकलुषां राजा प्रणम्योचिवान्

१०   नाम्बानृण्यमहन्तपोभिरमलैः शक्रोमि यातुम्पितुः

११   किन्त्वाप्तेन यथावदस्त्रविधिना तत्पादसंसेवया

१२   यास्यामीति ततोम्बयातिमुदया दत्ताभ्यनुज्ञो नृपः   १५

१३   प्रायात्पूर्व्वपथेन तत्र च शठा ये पूर्व्वदेशाश्रयाः

१४   सामन्ताः प्रणिपातबन्धुरशिरः प्रभ्रष्टमौलिस्रजः

१५   तानाज्ञावशवर्त्तिनो नरपतिः संस्थाप्य तस्मात्पुनः

१६   निर्भीः सिंह इवाकुलोत्कटसटः पश्चाद्भुवज्जिन्निवान्   १६

१७   सामन्तस्य च तत्र दुष्टचरितं श्रुत्वा शिरः कम्पयन्

१८   बाहुं हस्तिकरोपमं स शनकैः स्पृष्ट्वाब्रवीद् गर्व्वितम्

१९   आहूतो यदि नेति विक्रमवशादेष्यत्यसौ मे वशम् ²⁵

२० किं वाक्यैर्बहुभिर्व्²⁶थात्र गदितैः संक्षेपतः कथ्यते   १७

२१ अद्यैव प्रिय मातुलोरुविषमक्षोभार्णर्णवस्पर्द्धिनीम्

२२ भीमावर्त्तं तरङ्ग चञ्चलजलान्त्वज्झण्डकीमुत्तर

२३ संनद्धैर्धरवाजिकुञ्जर शतैरन्वेमि तीत्वां नदीम्

२४ त्वत्सेनामिति निश्चयाभ्ररपति स्तीर्ण्णप्रतिज्ञस्तदा   १८

२५ जित्वा मल्लपुरीन्ततस्तु शनकैरभ्याजगाम स्वकम्

२६ देशम्प्रीतमनास्तदा खलु धनम्प्रादाद् द्विजेभ्योक्षयम्

२७ राज्ञी राज्यवती च साधुमतिना प्रोक्ता दृढं सूनु [ना]

२८ भक्त्याम्ब त्वमपि प्रसन्नहृदया दानप्रयच्छ स्व [तः]   १६

(d) On the stump²⁷

१ ·············वर्षबन्ध²⁸···

२ ·········भट्टारक पूजा²⁹····

३ ···············खकम्प्रिङ्ग्रामप्रदेशे मानि ५० ४³⁰

४ ·············२० दोम्मान मानि २०³¹

1. Gn, DV read प्रीद्धत्र ।

2. श्री is omitted by L and BLI.

3. Gn omits विमल though the letters are clear. DV reads
    विविध । L and BLI रुचिर but the letter is clear.

4. BLI स्म-तृं ····प्र etc. Gn प्रव्टत्तोत्सव; L स्मत् पष्टत्तोत्सवः ।

5. L, BLI भ्रमयन्नवः व्यासङ्ग etc.

6. DV, श्रीमच्चारू वप; Gn, त्सा ।

7. DV, Gn, योरेजे ।

8. BLI, L, DV धृतैः ।

9. Gn,···· BLI, ह्यान्तै ।

10. Gn, भूपः, BLI, L, DV, [राजा] ।

11. BLI, Gn read प तिपदः etc.

12. DV, स्वसंयम्य । Gn········

13. Gn doubles म in मृग ।

14. Gn, BLI,……विद् after य ।
15. Conjectural reading of DV, [मपान्नेपाल] which may be right or wrong.
16. L, सत्वाशंभि:; DV, सस्यद्यभि: ।
17. BLI reads upto this.
18. L, भवत् कुलासु-र ।   19. DV, [सत्कर्मावि] ।
20. DV [नाध्या] ।   21. BLI, L, भागमंम ।
22. BLI, L, प्रकृत्या ।   23. L, गगैं: ।
24. BLI, L, सत ।   25. BLI, L, देश्यतसौ ।
26. BLI, L, व्विधातृ ।
27. Both Gn and HJ take it as a different record unrelated to the above I a, b, c. HJ 3, Gn 2.
28. Gn……… ष ……
29. Gn……… भट्टारक………
30. ………मानि ५०४ ।
31. ………दो-नमानि २० ।

II. Lazimpat Śiva Liṅga Inscription of Manadeva's Reign

(Gn IV; DV 3; HJ 4) Round the base (*Jalahari*) of a liṅga at Lazimpat, Kathmandu, at a locality called Dhobichaur (the washerman's lawn). The inscribed part is about 106 cm wide and 7.5 cm long. Date: *Samvat 388 Jyeṣṭha śukla 14.* The metre used here is *Vasantatilakā.*

१ सम्वत् ३०० ८० ८   शौर्य्येण नीतिसहितेन विजित्य सम्यक्
                           चक्रे[1]…………………… विशुद्धकर्मा[2]

२ जेष्ठमासे शुक्लदिवा १० ४   तस्याज्ञया   शुभमतेश्शुभवृद्धि-
                           लिङ्गम्भृत्ये न भक्तिमहता नरवम्मंनाम्ना[3]
                           प्रासादस्यानुरूपमिह प्र[कल्प्य][4]
                           चारुलिङ्गम्[5]

1. Gn leaves कें ।
2. Correctly read by DV.
3. Gn could not read भृत्य ।
4. Gn, नुरूप-हृ प्र··· The date Gn puts at the end as 1a and 1b.
5. Letters are damaged.

III. Trivikrama Image Pedestal Inscription at Lazimpat

(L II; Gn III; footnote with Levi's reading; DV 4; HJ 5) The panel of figures is not well preserved. The date figure is *Samvat 389 Vaiśākha śukla divā 2*, and the text is similar to IV. The inscribed part is 5 cm long and 54.5 cm wide.

१ ॐ संवत् ३०० ८० ९ मातुः श्रीराज्यवत्या हितकृतमनसः[1] सर्व्वदा पुण्य बृद्ध्यै राजा श्रीमानदेवः शुभविमलमतिः पात्रदानाम्बुवर्षी[2]

२ वैशाख शुक्ल दिव २ लक्ष्मीवत्कारमित्वा भवनमिह शुभं स्थापयामास[3] सम्यक् विष्णुं विक्रान्तमूर्त्तिं सुरमुनिमहितं सर्व्वलोकैकनाथम्

1. L could not read हितकृत etc upto सर्व्वदा ।
2. L's reading thereafter (म्भा)····पातदि-ताम्ब वाभुः ।
3. L reads the next line as दा-यित्वानुट्टह म्इह घ-स्था-यां for a part, which leaves many gaps but the other letters following are correctly presented. In the date portion दिवा २ is missing.

IV. Trivikrama Image Inscription of Tilaganga

(Gn III; DV 5; HJ 6) The base of an image of Viṣṇu Vikrāntamūrti (Trivikrama) lying in the field above the bed of the river Bagmati, where it is joined by a channel of water called river Tilagangā, a little further south of the Paśupati

sanctuary across the sandy bed. The inscribed part is about
60 cm wide and 6 cm long. Date: *Samvat 389 Vaiśākha śukla
diva 2.**

१   संवत् ३०० ८० ६   मातुः श्रीराजवत्या हितक्रुतमनसः सर्व्वदा पुण्य
                          वृद्धयें राजा श्रीमानदेवः शुभविमलमतिः
२   वैशाख शुक्ल दिव २   पात्रदानाम्बुवर्षी लक्ष्मीव त्कारयित्वा भवन मिह्
                          शुभं स्थापयामास सम्यक् विष्णुं विक्रान्तमूर्ति
                          सुरमुनिमहितं सर्व्वलोकैक नाथम्*

*The metre used here is *Sragdharā*.

V. Another Inscription on Śivaliṅga at Lazimpat

(DV 6; HJ 7) Around the base of a *Śivaliṅga* near a wall on
a small hill at Lazimpat, Kathmandu. The *Śivaliṅga* was set
up by Kṣemasundari, wife of Mānadeva. The date is *390
Jyeṣṭha śukla 7*. The inscribed part is 80.5 cm wide and 11 cm
long. The metre used here is *Śārdūlavikrīḍita*.

१   कान्त्या कान्तिमतः सुरानिह् महैर्विद्वत्तया पण्डितान्
     शूरञ्शूरतयार्थिनोपि वसुभिश्शुद्धैर्य्यशोभिन्नृ°पान्
२   दाक्षिण्येन च दक्षिणान रमयत्सव्वर्षिच सव्वैर्गुणैः
     यः श्रीमान्स विशुद्धकाञ्चनवपु श्श्रीमानदेवो नृपः   १¹
३   पत्नी तस्याब्जपत्रामल शुभनयना इलाघ्थसौभाग्यरूपा
     सञ्चित्य क्षेमसुन्दर्य्यनुपमगुणधीर्द्धर्म्मकार्य्यैक कार्य्या
४   श्रीमत्संस्थानरूपम्भवनमिह् दृढङ्कारयित्वानुरूपम्
     ऐशानंलिङ्गमग्य्रं विधिवदनुपमं स्थापयामास भत्तया   २²
५   संवत् ३०० ८० ज्येष्ठमासे शुक्लपक्षे दिव ७

1. marked as /
2. marked as //

VI. Śivaliṅga Inscription of Manadeva I near Budhanilakantha

(DV 7; HJ 9) This *Śivaliṅga* is placed a little more than a furlong from the shrine of Budhanilakantha in the north-west, some 500 ft up the hill, near a banyan tree, where the stream Visnumati flows down to the valley. The inscribed part round the jalahari is 87 cm wide and 13 cm long. The date is *Samvat 395 Prathamāṣāḍha 12*. The year symbol is clear.*

*The metre used is *Vasantatilaka* and then *Mandākrāntā.*

१ ··········स्त्वस्कृतेह् यस्मात् त्वत्तस्तसमाज्जगदविहतङ्जायते लीयते च
भक्तिप्राणैरमल मतिभिस्त्वम्मुनीन्द्रैरनिन्द्यैः देवैस्सेन्द्रैरपि च भगवन्स्तूयसे-
वन्द्यसे च

२ ·······कुमतिग्रस्तघोरान्धकारे नानाकारे प्रचुरनरक प्रेत तिर्य्यंक्प्रतिष्ठे ये
सेवन्ते न खलु भगवंस्त्वां जना भक्तियुक्ताः ते सेवन्ते जननमरणव्याधि
दुःखान्यभीक्ष्णम्[1]

३ [श्रीमानदेव] नृपतिः प्रणतो जगाद यत्स्थापनाजनितमस्ति यदत्र पुण्यम् त
त्सर्व्वलोकसहितस्य विवृद्धमूलम् दुःखक्षयाय भगवन्मम सर्व्वथास्तु

४ [संवत् ३००] ६० ५ प्रथमापाढे शुक्लदिव[2] १२

1. DV reads भीक्ष्णम् as I put it but म् is attached below क्ष्ण ।
2. DV reads 396; Rajavamsi reads 395.

VII. One-line Inscription of Tuṇḍāldevī

(Gn V; DV 9; HJ 11) One of the stones forming the front-line of the platform of the temple of Tuṇḍāldevī, Visalnagar, Kathmandu. The inscribed part is about 26 cm wide and 1.8 cm long. Date: *Samvat 397 Jyeṣṭha śukla diva 2.*

१ सम्बत् ३०० ६० ७[1] ज्येष्ठ मासे शुक्ल दिव २

1. Gn reads 9; whereas DV reads 7. The latter is correct.

VIII. Śivaliṅga Inscription near the Temple of Dakṣiṇāmūrti

(HJ 12; Gn VI; DV 10) Round the base (*Jalahari*) of a liṅga in the thicket of Patatole quarter in Deopatan, just west of the temple of Dakṣiṇāmūrti in Deopatan. The inscribed part is about 115 cm wide and 17 cm long. Date: *Samvat 399 Āṣāḍha śukla 10.*

१ संवत् ३०० ६० ६   महेन्द्र समवीर्य्यस्य कन्दर्प सघशद्युते: राज्ञ:

श्रीमानदेवस्य सम्य [र्पा] लयत: प्रजा:[1]

२ आषाढमासे   तत्पाद भक्तया विधिवद्रत्नसङ्घ्ने सर्व्वदा

रत्नेश्वर: प्रयत्नेन स्थापितोयं सुरोत्तम: भगवते

रत्नेश्वराय रत्नसङ्घ्ने दत्तं क्षेत्रं यथा

३ शुक्रदिवा १०   दुलङ्ग्रामप्रदेशे पञ्चानां शतानाम्भूमि: ४००[2]

खोपृङ्ग्राम प्रदेशे षण्णां शतानां भूमि: ६००

दुप्रङ्ग्रामप्रदेशे शतस्य भूमि १०० ह्यसिमङ्ङ्ग्राम

प्रदेशे द्वयर्द्धस्य शतस्य भूमि: २५०[3]

४   विलिविक्षप्रदेशे ५० तृतीयस्य भूमि: ३००

वाग्वतीपार प्रदेशे शतद्वयस्य भूमि: २०० बेम्पाया

मशीत्युत्तरस्य भूमि: १५० खैनष्पुप्रदेशे नवत्या

भूमि: ६०

५   वल-ल प्रदेशे शतद्वयस्य भूमि: २०० यूप ग्राम

क्षेत्र प्रदेशे शतद्वयस्य भूमि: २००[4]

1. metre अनुष्टुप 2. Gn खैपृङ्ग्राम 3. Gn नि: 150 4. Gn प्रदेशे ⋯⋯भूमि : 100 for the entire line.

IX. Paśupti Śiva Liṅga Inscription

(Gn X; DV 11; HJ 13) Base of a liṅga in the courtyard of a house to the west of the temple of Paśupati. The inscribed part is about 68 cm wide and 15 cm long. The date is *420 Jyeṣṭha śukla 13.*

१ [सम्वत्] ४०० २ ज्येष्ठमास शुक्लपक्ष दिव १० ३ श्रीमानदेव नृपते

श्चरण प्रसादात् य: सार्थवाह—रुधी: किल रत्नसङ्घ:

२ ············न: प्रभुसङ्घनाम्न: लिङ्गाश्रिता कृतिरियञ्जगतो हिताय*

प्रभुकेश्वरस्य क्षेत्राभिलेख्यं यथा प्रङ्प्रिङ्ग प्रदेशे············

३ ········[प्र] देशे [प] ञ्चाशतो भूमि: ५० पिण्डकं मानिका २० २

मेसिन्ज्ज्देशे चत्वारिंशतो भूमि ४० पिण्डकं मानिका: २० वोतवोरुपप्रदेशे

षष्ठ्येर्भूमि [६०]

४ ········प्रदेशे त्रिशतो भूमि ३० पिण्डकं मानिका: १०८ सीताटीजोलिप्रङ्

प्रदेशे चत्वारिंशतो भूमि ४० पिण्डकं मानिका: २० ५ प्रयिट्रिखा प्रदेशे

त्रिशदुत्तरस्य शतस्य········

५ पिण्डकं मानि ७० २

*This is the only passage in a metre form, which is *Vasanta-tilakā*.

1. Gn [संवत्] 4-माघशुक्ल पक्ष दिव १० ३ ।
2. Gn प्रासादा त्········रू····लर रत्न संघ ।
3. Gn reads प्रङपिङ but DV शतस्य भूमि १०० पिण्डक मानि [का] to fill the gap.
4. Gn त्रिंशत्तार स्य-त ।
5. DV adds a conjecture [भूमि १३०] ।
6. DV omits ङ and reads जोलिप्रङ् प्रदेशे ।

X. Te-Bahal Inscription

(L 3; Gn VII; DV 12; HJ 14) The pedestal of an image of the Sun God. At the present time there is a standing image of Mahākāla over the pedestal, a later replacement over the stone. The pedestal with the image is lying in a corner in the storeroom of a shop to the left side of the entrance to Te-Bahal to the south of the New Road, Kathmandu. The date

is *Samvat 402 Āṣāḍha śukla 15*. The inscribed part is 68 cm
wide and 103 cm long.*

*The metre is *Anuṣṭupa*.

१ [सम्व] त् ४०० २ राज्ञः श्रीमानदेवस्य सम्यक्पालयतो महीम् आषाढ
   शुक्लस्य तिथौ पञ्चदश्यां शुभार्त्थिना

२ वणिजां सार्त्थवाहेन गुहमित्रेण भक्तितः संस्थापितोत्र भगनवानिन्द्रो नाम
   दिवाकरः क्षेत्रं यथा गुम्पद शुम्प्रदेशे¹

३ शतस्य भूमिः पिण्डक मानिकाचु²

1. L गुम्पद प्रदेशे; DV गुम्पद् वृम्प्रदेशे but in S.S.I. 9 he read शु ।
2. चु = ६० ।

XI. The Trident Base Inscription of Jayalaṁbha

(BLI 2; Gn VIII; DV 14; HJ 16)   Round the base
(*Jalahari*) of a *liṅga* opposite to the northern door of the temple
of Paśupatinath on a platform with a tall brass trident. The
inscribed part is about 71 cm wide and 9 cm long. Date:
Samvat 413 (without particulars). The trident is not the part
of the base. Probably it came to be there being installed later.
In the cloth rubbing of BLI the name of the donor appears to
be Jayavarmā, but the ink rubbing shows Jayalaṁbha. The
letter is damaged, but on-the-spot examination confirms DV's
reading *laṁbha*.*

*The metre is *Vasantatilakā*.

१ ॐ सम्वत् ४०० १० ३ श्रीमानदेव नृपते श्चरण प्रसादात् भक्त्या विशुद्ध-
   मतिना जयलम्भनाम्ना ।¹ लिङ्ङ्जयेश्वरमिति प्रथितं नृलोके

२ संस्थापित सनृपतेज्जंगतो हिताय ॥² भगवतोस्य लिङ्गस्य कारणपूजाय³
   स ··········य स्वपुण्याप्यायना र्थन्दत्तमक्षयणीयम्⁴

३ भूमिः ४५० पिण्डकं मा २०० ज्येष्ठशुक्ल दिवा ११⁵

1. Gn and other writers read वर्म्म ।
2. There is a comma like mark here which BLI reads 1.
3. BLI [यै] य नार्थेदत्त etc. Gn reads य-स ।
4. BLI ┄┄मक्षय [नीवि]; Gn┄┄┄स्वप्रण्याप्याय नात्थं दत्तं मक्षय [निवि] ।
5. Gn reads क्र┄┄┄ज्येष्ठशुक्ल । The third line is missing in BLI.

XII. Chabahil Slab of Stone

(DV I; HJ 22) A slab of stone supporting the right pillar (there are two pillars reclining) and the stone has been devised by someone as a support to the pillar to prevent it from falling down. The inscribed part is 12 cm wide and 28 cm long. In the last line the month and lunar days appear, while the year portion is damaged. This mentions also Jupiter's month. DV thinks that this is the first available inscription of ancient Nepal.*

*The metre used here is *Anusṭupa*.

१ दुर्द्धरैरिन्द्रियैः कृत्स्ना वाह्यते यैरियम्प्रजा
दासवत्तानि सन्धार्य कृपयापरिपीड्य ता   दानशील

२ सम्प्राप्यानुत्तरं ज्ञानं प्रजा दुःखात्प्रमोचिता
प्रमोच्य सर्ब्बेदुःखेभ्यो योसौ शान्तम्पदङ्गतः   म┄┄

३ सन्ह्विद्य सुचिरङ्कालम्भवनम्भव विच्छिदः
    ¹ किन्तरीजातकाकीर्णान्निनानाचित्रविराजितम्   श्री┄┄

४ ² चत्वारिंशच्छपञ्चेह यत्र धान्यस्य मानिकाः
    ³ वर्षे वर्षेथ जायन्ते क्षेत्रन्तत्तादृशन्ददौ┄┄┄┄

५ भूयः सङ्घस्य भक्तार्थं पूजार्थञ्च महामुनेः
    ⁴ क्षेत्रन्दत्तन्तया यत्र ह्यष्टाविंशतिमानिकाः

६ विचित्रं देयधर्म्मंम्मे कारयित्वेह यच्छुभम्
   स्त्रीभावं हि विराग्याहं पुरुषत्वमवाप्य च   शोककाममयैवं····

७ ··········माघवर्षे काले आषाढशुदिव १०   अस्यान्दिवसपूर्व्वायाम्भट्टारक
   महाराज श्री·········

1. DV णं ।   2. DV सपञ्चेह ।
3. DV··············   4. ······after मानिका: ।

XIII. Guṇavati's Śivaliṅga at Lazimpat

(DV 15; HJ 18) Around the western part of the base of a
Śivaliṅga placed is a field near the streamlet Tukucha in
Lazimpat. Date: *Samvat 419 Jyeṣṭha śukla 13.* The inscribed
part of the base is 51 cm wide and 7.5 cm long.*

*The metre is *anuṣṭupa.*

१ संवत् ४०० १० ६ ज्येष्ठशुक्ल दिवा १३ अस्यान्दिवस पूर्व्वायाम् भर्त्तु:
   श्रीमानदेवस्य प्रसादोपचितश्रिया

२ भ त्तचा स्थापितं लिग (ङ्गं) ङ गुणवत्या शुभेच्छया शैवन्देवालयस्थस्य
   पितु: किन्नर वर्म्मण: लिङ्गं संस्थाप्य यत्पुण्यधनञ्चाक्षय्यमस्तिवति

XIV. Palanchok Stele

(DV 16; HJ 19). A slab of stone near the temple of
Bhagvati in the village of Palanchok, 15 miles to the east of
Kathmandu outside the valley. The date is *425 Māgha śukla
pūrṇimā.* The two-line inscription covers the space of 5 cm
wide and 6.5 cm long.

१ संवत् ४२५ माघ शुक्ल पौर्ण्णमास्याम् अस्यान्दिवसपूर्व्वायां भट्टारक
   महाराज श्रीमानदेवस्य

२   साग्रं वर्षशतमाज्ञापयतः सम्राड्गृहपते स्वत्न्या विजयस्वामिन्या प्रतिष्ठा
     पिता देवी भगवती विजय इत्री¹*

1. DV reads विजयेश्वरी ।

*The text is also published by M. Naraharinatha in 'Himavat Sanskriti', Pt. I.

XV. Inscription of Kelatol

(DV 17; HJ 8)   The stone was lying in the courtyard of (Takhachhen) within Kelatol near the temple of white Machhendranath in Kathmandu, uptill 1953. It was attached to the wall of the courtyard but is not to be seen now when I went there for re-inspection. Some lines are missing and there is no date. The inscribed part is 42 cm wide and 9 cm long.*

१   ⋯⋯विहिते यो निग्रहे⋯⋯रतः शुद्धात्मा प्रकृते: पितेव दयते श्रीमानदेवो
     [नृपः]
२   ⋯⋯प्राण⋯⋯⋯युक्तात्मना⋯⋯⋯⋯⋯⋯जितवता क्षमा रक्षता सर्व्वंदा
३   ⋯⋯दं श्रुतिधर्म्मंशास्त्र विहितां धर्मंक्रियाङ्कुर्वता लोकानां सुख काम्यया
     सुविमलम्पानीयमानाय्य⋯⋯⋯

*The metre is *Śārdūlavikrīḍita.*

XVI. The Svayambhunath Inscription

(DV 18; HJ I; Rajavamsi AN)

१   ⋯⋯⋯⋯⋯⋯मा⋯⋯⋯रण-ह⋯⋯न्यः
२   ⋯⋯⋯⋯देवसुत⋯⋯⋯रदेवो नरेन्द्र
३   ⋯⋯⋯⋯श्रीमा⋯⋯⋯र शतलक्ष्मी
४   ⋯⋯⋯⋯⋯⋯प्रसादः

५   ·······धार·······वन्य गजेन्द्र मत्त

६   शङ्करइति·······रय·······क[स]ङ्व ज्ञःन[1]

७   ·······दीन·······विनीतभृत्य

८   ·······र्विमान

९   ·······स्पर्ण[2]·······पर·······मर्य्यादिमिति[3]

१०   क्षेत्रञ्चाक्षयं दत्तं·····[श्री] मान विहारे·····[4]

११   ·······मेत्यमन्त्त·······तस्य तनय[5]

१२   ·······महिम्ना धर्म्म·······

१३   ·······लक्ष्मी राजा·····तिर····सर्व्वः

१४   ·······सन्धर्म्म वैभव द्युतिमा नृ-ति·····ईजे[13]

१५   [म] खेरूदारे भूमि परङ्काया[6]

१६   श्रालंबश्रेयः निरूपमः सत्वोवदान्तः[7]

१७   ख्यातः यशोः स्वधर्म्म कर्म्म सुनय[8]

१८   तनयोभिजातः सर्व्वांतिवर्त्तते[9]

१९   गुणै न्र्टंपतीन्यः श्रनुपरत धर्म्म[10]

२०   ·····करुणैकस्त्वम्प्रियः सदा दारणाम्

२१   भव कठिनवांहुः केसरिमत्तेभ विक्रमः[11]

२२   स्थिर धीः याभ्विभ्यति बोधनृपाः[12]

२३   मृगाङ्के सरिणमिवरणेष्व भयः

२४   पितृनिमित्त पतिहितवक्ष सैष्ठव विधान

२५   ·····कर तिमतिमान् रूपवल सत्त्व तेजः श्रु तः कु

२६   शलनिधिकलासु निपुण प्रियवत् शुद्धं·······

२७   साग्रं शतं वर्षाणामाज्ञापयताविचिन्त्य

२८   निपुणाम् श्रेयोर्थिना धृतिमता·····

२९   ···रा वरुणमहेन्द्रवपुषा महता·····

३०   ···········

1. R सङ्ग्ज्ञ, DV वज्र ।
2. R स्पणोपर, DV पर ।

3. R य्यांदिम्, DV य्यांदिम् ।

4. R दत्त, DV दत्तं ।

5. R मेत्यमत DV मत्त ।

6. DV ङ्का य, R ङ्काया ।

7. DV श्रय:, R श्रयं ।

8. DV ख्यात यशा-, R ख्यात यश: ।

9. DV सब्वनिति, R सन्व्वानीति ।

10. DV नृपतीन्य:, R नृपन्तोन्य ।

11. DV मत्तेभ विक्रम:, R मत्तेम विक्रम: ।

12. DV नृपा:, R नमा ।

13. R सन्धर्म्मा एव: मा द्युतिमा—ईंजे, DV सन्धर्मा—द्युतिमा [न्] ईंजे ।

XVII. Effigy-base Inscription of Changu

(Gn IX; DV 19; HJ 21) The base of an effigy (now lost) to
the right of the entrance gate leaning against the outer wall of
the temple precincts of Changu Nārāyaṇa.* The inscribed part
is about 5.5 cm wide and 5 cm long. Date: *Samvat 427 kārtika
śukla diva 13.*

१   सम्वत् ४०० २० ७ कार्त्तिक शुक्ल दिव १० ३ दातर्य्यं तीव विदुषी
    प्रथिन प्रभावे श्रीमानदेव नृपतौ जगती म्भुनत्ति¹

२   तस्यैव शुद्धयशसश्चरण प्रसादात् पित्रो: कृताकृतिरियन्निरपेक्ष
    नाम्ना कृत्वा च तां विधिवदत्र यदस्ति पुण्यम्

३   पुण्येन तेन पितृ दैवत भागिनो मे पित्रो: प्रवास गतयो घ्रुवमस्तु योग:
    ग्रन्यत्र जन्मनि विशुद्ध वतीति कृत्वा

1. DV जगतीं भुनत्ति ।

*The metre is वसन्ततिलका ।

XVIII. Sūryaghāt Śivaliṅga Inscription

(DV 20; HJ 20) Around the base of Śivaliṅga a little above Sūryaghat to the north of Āryaghāt on the hilly bank of the River Bagmati. The inscribed part covers a space of 13 cm in width and 14 cm long. The date is *427 Āṣāḍha śukla diva 1.**

१   यस्मेच्छया जगदिदम्पृथु विश्वरूपम्
                सर्ग स्थिति व्यय जरा व्यसनादियोगै:
        संयुज्यते वत तथा प्रतिमुच्यते च
                        तस्मै नम: सततमस्तु महेश्वराय   १

२   सतत सरल कान्त स्वाङ्ग शोभा समृद्ध:
                            १
                अनुपहृत यशोधी विव्क्रम श्रीप्रभाव:
        सुनय विदनुरक्त स्फीतस [द्] वृत्त लोक:
                        नृपतिरिह हतारि र्म्मानदेवो बभूव   २

३   तस्यानवद्य गुणरत्न निधान भूता
                भूतानुकम्प चतुरा विनयप्रवीणा
        वीणा निनाद मधुरस्वर वल्गु वाक्या
                        श्री भोगिनीति कथितास्य बभूव देवी   ३

४   तस्यां स लिच्छविकुलाम्बर पूर्णचन्द्र:
                चन्द्रप्रभामिव शरन्निशि निर्म्मलायाम्
        स्फीतौजसं दुहितरं जनयाम्बभूव
                        आत्मानुरूप विविधामल सद्गुणाढ्याम्   ४

५   नाम्ना सा विजयवतीति राजपुत्री
                प्रख्याता विविधकला विचक्षणत्वात्
        या पत्यौ हरइव वार्त्तं देव लाभे
                        भक्तत्वात्तदनु नयंक पेशलाभूत्   ५

६   तीव्र प्रसाद जलधौतमन: कलङ्कं
                पुण्यक्रिया परिचयैक रसानुरक्ता
        लिङ्गन्तदत्त्र विजयेश्वरमक्षयाय
                        सातिष्ठिपज्जन मनो नयनाभिरामम्   ६

७   संवत् ४०० २० ७ आषाढ शुह्क दिव१

1. DV read थो probably a misprint.

*The metre up to the 4th verse is śārdūlavikridita but the 5th is Mandakini and thereafter again śārdūlavikridita.

XIX. Chhatra Chaṇḍeśvara

(DV 21; HJ 17) A slab of stone lying to the south of the pedestal of Chaṇḍeśvara facing south. The inscribed part is 78 cm wide and 25.5 cm long.

१ ············त्रैलोक्यनाथ···········

२ ······ ········पूर्वं वात वाहनस्य दक्षिणेन क्षेत्रन्दन्तम्भूमि ३५० पिण्डक
मा २५५···

३ ·······१६ काष्ठमूल्यम्पण मेकैकम्प्रति दिवसं मा२····चैत्रकृष्णपन्चम्याम्
····थन्

४ ·······पुराणा: १५ ज्येष्ठ शुक्ल त्रयोदश्यां राज्यवर्द्धनदेवस्य
स्नपनमङ्कु पूजा ···

५ र्थम्भूते दानवस्तुनि तृष्णाभिभूतमनस पापबुद्धिर्म्मा भूदिति कृत्वा
मया स····

६ मस्य पूर्व्वेण क्षेत्रन्दत्तम्भूमि २३० पिण्डक मा ११० पणका-तैलघट १
राज्ञा राज्यवर्द्धनस्नपनादीनां भूमि—मा ६० इत्थमिह

७ व्यय: मा ५० उभयत्र तैलघट १ भवितारो मद्दइर्ध्वं ये नृपा: कुर्य्युं
रिहान्यथा·······स्तर्हि वयं·······

८ र्मना लेखितोयं क्रियाकार: स्ववंश्या ननुरक्षता

XX. Ādi-Nārāyaṇa Temple Inscription of Thankot

(Gn XII; DV 22; HJ 24) This is inscribed on a slab of stone about 30 cm wide and 76 cm long standing against the outer wall of the quadrangle of the temple of Ādi-Nārāyaṇa in Thankot village, about 6 miles west of Kathmandu. The top is damaged and completely lost. The date is *Samvat 428 Mārga śukla 1.*

The first two lines are missing in the plate. The reading, therefore, is partly conjectural.

१ ॐ स्वस्ति मानगृ [हात्परमदैवतव] प्प भट्टा

२ रक महाराज श्रीपा [दानुद्धयातो श्रुत] नयदया

३ दान दाक्षिण्य पुण्य प्र[ताप विकसित सित]कीर्त्ति

४ भंट्टारक महाराजा श्री [वसन्त देव: कुशली]

५   जय पल्लिका ग्रामे निवा[सोपगता] न् ब्राह्मण पुरस्स

६   रान् व्रह्मा॰ शुल्हंमुंतेपुल॰॰॰॰॰॰॰प्रधानान्ग्राम कुटुम्बिन:

७   साप्टादश प्रकृतीन् कुश [लम्पृ] ष्ट्वा समाज्ञापयति

८   विदितं वोस्तु यथा [स्माभि] रायुष्मन्त्यै प्रियभगिन्यै

९   [ज] य सुन्दर्य्ये स्वसन्तानानुक्रमेण सुस्थित कोट्ट

१०   [म] य्वादि: अचाटाभट प्रवेश्येयं ग्रामो तिसृष्टोस्य

११   [ग्राम] स्यसीमा शीताटी गुल्मकस्य पश्चाद्वा नदी तत: पूर्व्वं

१२   [त:]॰॰॰याव त्पव्वंत चूडिका दक्षिणतो तत एव नद्या

१३   ॰॰॰॰॰॰॰त्य पश्चिमेन दण्ड॰॰॰॰॰पजु यावद्धस्तिमार्गं सम्प्राप्तेति

१४   ततोपि च हस्तिमार्गं॰॰॰॰॰॰[प] श्चिमतो यावन्त्पर्व्वंत चूडिका

१५   पश्चिमत: पर्वताग्रस्य॰॰॰॰॰॰तिप्राग्राप: स्यन्दन्ते पश्चिमोत्तर

१६   णतोपि शिवक देवकुलस्य दक्षिणत: पानीय मार्गाविधि उत्तरेणा

१७   पि थेङ्चोग्रामस्य दक्षिणत: यावन्महापथ: प्रागुत्तरेणापि नव

१८   ग्रामस्य दक्षिणतो मार्ग एवावधिर्य्यावत्पूर्व्वेण नदीम्प्रविष्ट इति

१९   तदे तस्मिन्ग्रामे ये प्रविष्ठा: प्रविविक्षवश्च ब्राह्मण प्रधाना: सा

२०   ष्ठादश प्रकृतयस्तेषामत्र प्रतिवसतान्न केनचिदस्मत्पादोप

२१   जीविना स्वल्पाप्याबाधा कर्त्तव्या यश्चेमामाज्ञां मुल्लङ्घ्यान्यथा कुर्मात्कार

२२   येद्वा तस्याहं दृढन्न मर्षयिष्यामि तदेव विदित्वात्र भवन्द्रि न्निर्वृत विश्व

२३   स्तैरकुतोभयै: स्वकर्म्मविस्थायिभि: परस्परेणा श्वासयन्द्रिश्च समुचि

२४   तभागभोग कर पिण्डक दानादिभिरुपकुर्व्वंद्रि रनया प्रतिपाल्यमाने

२५   राज्ञा श्रवणविधेयै: सुखं प्रतिवस्तव्य इति समाज्ञापना येप्यागामि

२६   नो राजानो समद्वंश्या भविष्यन्ति तेप्येनामसमद्दत्ताम्भूमि मनुमोदितुम

२७   [हं] न्ति यत्कारणम् बहुभिर्वसुधा भुक्ता राजभि: सगरादिभि: यस्ययस्य

२८   यदा भूमि स्तस्य तस्य तदा फलम् स्वदत्तां परदत्तां वा यो हरेत वसुन्ध

२९   राम् स विष्टायां कृमिर्भूत्वा नरकेषु प्रपद्यत इति दूतको याज्ञिक

३०   विरोचन गुप्त: सम्वत् ४०० २० ६ मार्गशीर्ष शुक्ल दिव १

1. DV मयायुष्मत्यै ।
    Gn (स्माभि) रायुष्मत्यै ।

2. Letters are not at all clear but DV reads [तिप] श्चिमे
    while Gn reads [त]॰॰॰॰॰॰   3. Gn थेङ्चे ।

4. Gn पच्यते but DV is right with प्रपद्यत ।

The metre used in the passage is *anuṣṭupa*.

XXI. A Stele of Tistung Village

(DV 23; HJ 26) The village of Tistung on Tribhuvan High-
way, about 20 miles south west of Kathmandu, is approached
after passing through the Khani Khola (rivulet) and then a stiff
climb and descent. The stone lies in a lawn of a primary
school. The date is 434 but the month and day symbols are
worn away. The stone is damaged in the lower portion. The
top shows in relief a discus (chakra) flanked by two conches
(śankhas). The inscribed part is 28.5 cm long and 29 cm wide.
H. Sakya has published the text with a wrong reading (Abhilekha Prakāśa, p. 7), which DV claims to have corrected.

१ [स्व] स्ति नेपालेभ्य: परमदैवंत श्रीबप्प……1

२ [पादानु] ध्यात भट्टारक महाराज श्रीवसन्तदे [व:]

३ [कुशली] [तेष्ठू] ङ्ग ग्रामे निवासोपगतान् प्रधान (पुर)

४ [स्सरान्कुटुम्बि] न: कुशलभिमिधाय समाज्ञापमति

५ [विदि] तमस्तु वो यथा

6 to 9 lines are worn away.

१० ………सर्व्वंदण्डनाय[क]

11 to 14 lines are also missing.

१५ संवत् ४०० ३० ४

1. DV [भट्टारक] ।

XXII. Bahalukhatol (Patan) Inscription

(DV 24; HJ 29) A slab of stone near the temple of
Trilingeśvara in Bahalukha locality, Patan bears this inscription.
The date is *435 Dvitīyā (Second) Pauṣa śukla diva 5*. The ins-
cribed part is 9 cm wide and 33 cm long.

१ ॐ स्वस्ति मानगृहात्………

२ महाराज श्रीपादा [नुध्यात] श्री [वस]

३ न्तदेव: कुशली………

४ धिक्रतान्प्रेषणे………

५   त·····स्त········

६   ························ ···

७   ·················तद····

८   न···············क्षेत्र

९   र्दृत्त ···· ···· ···· शे चत्वारिम्शंतो भूमिः

१०   तत्रे .... प्रदेशे दशानाम्भूमिः ह्रीम्

११   को प्रदेशे विम्शतो भूमिः गुडन्दुलुन्तर प्रदेशे षण्णाम्भू

१२   मिः तदासां पिण्डकं १४२ तदेवं विदिता [त्र्यैन्नक] थं

१३   ञ्चिचचुष्माभिरसमन्पादोपजीविभिरिय माज्ञा विलङ्द्घ

१४   यितव्या यश्चेमामाज्ञामुल्लङ्घ्म स्मरयेत्स्मारयेछा त

१५   स्याहं यथोचितं मर्यादा वन्धमनुष्ठा स्यामीति समाज्ञा

१६   पना इतकोत्र सर्व्वदण्डनायक महाप्रतिहार रवि

१७   गुप्त इति संवत् ४०० ३० ५ द्वितीय पौष शुक्ल दिव ५

XXIII. Jaisideval Stone Inscription

(BLI 3; Gn XIII; DV 25; HJ 27) A slab of stone of which the inscribed part about 42 cm wide and 57 cm long is standing near the sanctuary of Lhugal Devī not far from the Jaisideval in the southern part of the city of Kathmandu, which is known as Lhugaltole. The top of the stone is carved showing a chakra flanked by two śankhas. Date: *Samvat 435 Aśvayuja (Āśvina) śukla diva 1.*

१   ॐ स्वस्ति मानगृहात्परनदेवत बप्प भ

२   ट्टारक महाराज श्रीपादानुध्यातः श्रुतन

३   य दया दान दाक्षिण्य पुण्य प्रताप विकसि

४   तसित कीर्त्ति भट्टारक महाराज श्रीवसन्त

५   देवः कुशली [चतु] र्व्बधिकरणेषु धर्म्म

६   स्था···· ·················णिकाञ्च कुश

७   [ल्म्पृष्ठ्रा समाज्ञापयति] विदितमस्तु वो मया

८   ·····························लिग्वल

९　………………………………………कूथेर

१०　……[मधिक] रणाय[7]

११　………………………………[भ] ट्रारक[8]

१२　………………………………ष्य तेषान्त्र[9]

१३　………………………………दिकार्य्येषु सद्धै[10]

१४　………………………………मयापि तेषाम्

१५　………………………………मोचित………

१६　………………………………

१७　[अस्मत्पा] दोपजीविभिरिय [मा][11] [12]

१८　………यश्चे मामाज्ञा मुल्लङ्घ्य………[13]

१९　………तस्याहं दृढं मर्य्यादा [वन्धमनुष्ठास्या][14] [15]

२०　[मीति] समाज्ञापना संवत् ४०० ३० ५ [ग्रा.श्व][15]

२१　युजि शुल्क दिव १ दूतक: सर्व्वदण्डना

२२　यक महाप्रतिहार रविगुप्त: इति[16]

२३　ब्रह्मुङि च महीशीले व्यवहरतीति

1. BLI सेन: ।
2. This does not occur in BLI.
3. BLI स्था [न] ।
4. BLI णेकाश्च ।
5. Not in BLI.
6. BLI लिखल ।
7. BLI omits.
8. BLI omits भ ।
.9. BLI शष्ये ।
10. BLI दिकार्येषुसद्धि ।
11. Not in BLI.
12. DV [माज्ञा विल] ।
13. BLI तस्याहं ।
14. DV further वन्धुनुष्ठास्या ।

15. DV [मीति] ।
16. DV just गुप्त ।

XXIV. Sitāpaila Stone

(DV 26; HJ 25) A slab of stone in Sitāpaila, a village about 2 miles west of Kathmandu. The inscribed part is 20 cm wide and 36 cm long. The inscription is dated Samvat 435 without a month and day. It is a charter issued by Vasanta-deva.

१ ....
२ ....श्री बप्पभट्टारक पादानुध्यातो.........
३ ....[महाराज] श्री वसन्तदेव: कुशली ....
४ यथा प्रधाना ङ्ग्राम कुटुम्बिन: [कुशल]
५ [मभि] धाय समाज्ञापयति विदितमस्तु
६ ....परमदेवत श्री वप्प भट्टारक पा (दानुध्यात:)
७ ....युष्मदीयग्राम: पूर्वेण तोत्तर
८ ....[पर्व]त शिखरात् दक्षिण पश्चिमदेशे.......
९ ....माग्गत्पश्चिमेन राजभूमे.......
१० ....रमुत्तरेणापि हारागुङ् शिखर.......
११ ....र पूर्व्वमेव यथा ....
१२ ....[त्रायुष्म] त्या प्रिय भगिन्या
१३ ....जयसुन्दर्या.........परमदेव [त].....
१४ ....वप्प भट्टा [रक पादा] नामात्मनश्च श्री
१५ [यसे].........पश्चिम........ प्रणालया: खण्डफुट्ट
१६ ....प्रतिसंस्कार.......डुलुसिञ्जु
१७ ....पञ्च.........दत्तो दूतकश्चात्र
१८ [स] र्वदण्ड नामक महाप्रतिहार रवि [गुप्त:]
१९ ....व्यवहरति संवत ४०० ३० ५¹

----
1. DV omits 5 although the symbol for 5 is clear.

XXV. Kisipidi Inscription

(L 6; Gn XIV; DV 26; HJ 29) A slab of stone with inscribed part, about 38 cm wide and 22 cm long, in the village of Kisipidi near Thankot. Date: *Samvat 449 Prathamāṣāḍha śukla 10.* The first few lines are damaged and except a few all letters are not legible but the last eight lines can be read in toto.

The first few lines are totally worn away. The line numbers are for readable ones.

१ ⋯⋯धिकरणेन पीडा करणीया कूथेर¹

२ ⋯⋯करणमात्र तदुभय मेतद्रू [व] ⋯⋯²

३ प्रतिमुक्ता इत्येवञ्चावेत्य यूयमद्याग्रेण स³

४ मुचितकरं ददन्तः सर्व्वंकृत्येष्वाज्ञा विधे [या:]

५ सन्तो निहद्धिग्न मनसो यथासुखं प्रतिव [स्तव्यमिति]⁴ ⁵

६ इतश्चात्र सर्व्वदण्डनायक महाप्रतिहार

७ रविगुप्तः श्नि संवत् ४०० ४० ६ प्रथमाषा [ढ]

८ शुक्ल दशम्याम्

1. Gn keeps the space vacant upto कुथेर ।
2. The lines 1-2 do not find place in Levi. Gn मेतद्भव ।
3. Gn could not decipher letters before यूयम ।
4. Gn has blank space before मनसो ।
5. DV प्रतिवसतेति ।

XXVI. Khapinchetol Inscription

(DV 28; HJ 31) On a water reservoir of stone attached to the western wall of a large courtyard in Patan known as Khapinche near Chyasaltol to the north east of the old Royal Palace. The inscribed part is 69 cm wide and 7.5 cm long. The date is Samvat 452. The record is devoted to Vaiśampa-

yana (Vyasa's disciple), suggesting that the Harigaon Pillar
inscription might be contemporary.

१ ॐ स्वस्ति महर्षौ वैशम्पायने श्रद्धेये····[संवत्]४०० ५० २ पौषशुक्ल
   तिथौ तृतीयस्याम्भट्टारक महाराज श्रीवसन्तदेवे सम्यग्राज्यम्प्रशासति

२ याज्ञिक विप्रसेनेन वेदकृताम्नाय भगवते का रणपूजात्थम्ब्राह्मण ध्रुवसेनेन
                                           1
   दत्तन्दक्षिण कोलिग्रामे भूशतद्वयम्पिण्डकञ्च त्रिंहिकस्य मानि

३ कया १५० ब्राह्मण वृद्धिषेणेन पिकङ्कूलक प्रदेशे मालात्थं पिण्डक
                         2
   मानि ७ याज्ञिक वेद भट्टेन दत्त्तं दुंलम्ग्रामे भू ४० पिण्डक १२

1.   DV adds [त्री] to correct the mistake.
2.   DV reads 30, which is wrong.

XXVII. Satyanārāyaṇa Pillar Inscription

   (L   4; Gn XI; DV   35; HJ 23) A pillar standing in
front of the western door of the temple of Satya Nārāyaṇa
in a north-west suburb of Kathmandu, called Harigaon. The
inscribed part is about 30 cm wide and 134 cm long. The date
of this inscription is in the damaged portion; therefore is missing, but its characters indicate that 'the inscription belongs to
the reign of Mānadeva or at the latest, of Vasantadeva' as Gnoli
thinks. Gnoli further says: 'The text consists of thirty-four
stanzas. The metre of the stanzas 1-9 seems to be the śloka
(anustupa). The few remaining syllables of stanza 10 did
not enable me to identify its metre. Stanzas 11-20 are in
upajati. The 21 is in rucira. Stanzas 22-25 are in śikhariṇī.
Stanzas 24-25 are in praharṣiṇī. The stanza 26 is in manju-
bhāsinī. Stanzas 27-28 and 32-34 are in mālinī. Stanzas 29-30
are in śragdharā. The stanza 31 is in rucirā.'

१ ·· ···· ···· ·· ···· ··· सयतात्मने

२ ···· ···· ···· ···· ···· ···· धियैष ते नमः

                                                    1
३ ···· ···· ···· ···· ···· ···· त्प्रतिदेह निवृं[तः]

४ .... विकीर्ण्ण भानुना

५ .... सर्व्वमात्मनि

६ .... शिनीवकान्तरा

७ .... म येन तेजसा

८ .... सवितेव ।सते

९ .... पयेनसौगता: [2]

१० .... गिराम्पति र्भीवै:

११ .... स्तर त्रयी त्वया

१२ .... धार्यते

१३ .... न वारणेन

१४ .... त्वया वैरुप्नम्

१५ .... मिद प्रबुद्ध

१६ .... मतिमता म्ब्रजेयु:

१७ .... मातर्ण व [3] ....

१८ .... तये तना मुद्वीक्षया .... मित्थम्

१९ .... करणादृतेन नित्यम्पृथुमतिना [4] ....

२० .... किमिह स्वस्ति वाच्यशेष........कथितन् विद्या

२१ .... परान्नास्तिकताम्प्रपन्नै स्त्रयी भिरोधिर ....मांण [5]

२२ .... धर्म व्यवस्थाप्यत नाद्य लोके धर्म्मो धत्ता त्वमस्यो [6] यदिना भविष्य:

२३ .... वेदं व्यविकीर्ण्ण वाक्त्वादनादिनिष्ठम्............स च [7]

२४ .... कथं वेद इहा भविष्यत्वम्भारतादि यदि ना [र च] ष्य:

२५ (प्र) माण शुद्ध्या विदितार्थं तत्त्व: प्रकम्प्यमानम् [8]........स्वनिष्ठे: [9]

२६ ....[ध] र्म्ममित्थं जगतो हितैषी नप्रातनिष्पद्यति [10]........

२७ ....र्ध्यमात्रा श्रयणादभीक्षणं कुतार्किककैस्त [11]........णम्

२८ ....व्यचैषीन्न पृथक्प्रमाणं कथन्तदस्यातुमिदं........य:

२९ ....प च प्राण वियोगहेतुर्त्त [12] प्रत्यवायो [13]........थैषा

३० ....त्वमेव प्रतिर्वेत्सि सम्पन्न वेदितान्यो भुविकश्चिद [द]स्ति

३१ स्तुति स्यानुव।दतो वा स्तुत्येषु वांचा द्वितय [14]....

३२ [स्तु] निर्गुणानां विधिना न सन्त्वान्न चानुवाद स्त्वयिर····

३३ ····न धर्म्मं सकलं न्यैर्हिंसित्त्व नैवरागादिरयं न्य¹⁵···

३४ ····षिणीं वैधयिकीऊच्च तृष्णां विधूय शुद्धस्त्वमितिप्र····

३५ ····कामाद्य विविक्तरूप यदि व्यवारिष्यते¹⁶·······

३६ ····स्मृतीना।मागते: श्रुतीनां तदेचलोके नियतां व्य¹⁷···

३७ [वि] पाद्य मोहानमृतं व्यसृक्ष त्स्वयङ्च धर्म्मादि जगत्यतिष्ठय¹⁸····

३८ ····यीत्वयागाज्जगति प्रतिष्ठा न्त्वमेव धर्म्मं विविधान तिष्टिप¹⁹

३९ ····रभ बन्दुष्प्रतिपाद मेतत्स्वर्गादि शब्दो पनिबन्ध मात्रम्

४० ····यदस्तीति जनो ग्रहीष्यद्यवानिहेवं यदि न व्यनेक्ष [त्]²⁰

४१ ····ता कुमतिभिरंहसा वृतै: कुतार्किकैः कथमपि सौगतादि भि:²¹

४२ ···त्व यिप्रथतिगिरि प्रभावे यम्पयो निधौ सरिदिव विन्दति स्थितिम्

४३ ····द विनियत पदार्थाद्यनुगमान्तव श्रुत्वा काव्यम् सपदि मनसागम्य·········

          ²²   ²³
४४ ····रत्यत्थर्त्ववाद····परमात्र्थानुसरणेदधात्युच्चैर्म्मोहं सपदिगत विद्येश्व-निय····

४५ ····शास्त्रे मनुयम बृहस्पत्युशनसां विधानं कृत्यानाम सुगम²⁴ पदं लोक····

४६ ····नैवं प्रतिविषयमाधूय निपुणम्फ लेनैवाशेवं त्वमिद मम····

४७ ···न्नृप चरितानुवादि भावात्पादादे: प्रतिनियतन्ततश्च काव्य [म्]²⁵

४८ ····रनुकथनादपीह शास्त्रं त्वं शक्ते रिदमपि भारताद्य कार्षी:

४९ ····स्व भवजलधौ विवर्त्तमाना रागादिप्रपतधिय: प्रगाढ़ मो हा[त्]

५० ···यास्त्विमिति विधाय मुक्तिमार्ग्गं साचीनाम्भुवि पुरुषान्करोषि मन्त्रे

          ²⁶
५१ सु (खिना) विविक्त वचसा त्वया सता कृपया परार्थं विनिवेशि बुद्धिना

५२ ज [ग] तो हिताय सुकृतेह भारते भुवि वाङ्मयं सकलमेव दर्शितम्

५३ विदित विविध धर्म्मो वेदिता वाङ्मयानान्निर वधिक मित्थ्या
    शान्तरागादि दोषम्²⁷

५४ ···रवपरार्त्थंस्तद्ध्वांमोहजाल   न्तिमिरमिव   विवस्वानंशुभि:
    प्रक्षि[णोति]

५५ प्रतिविषय नियोगात्पालकत्वाच्च तासान्निपुण तदव बोधात्द्विवेका
    ददोषा त्

५६ जगति तदुपदेशान्त्वंमिथ स्तद्द्विभागा दुपहित इव मूर्त्तिस्त्व्यात्मना मन्त्र
[28]

वाचाम्
[29]

५७ सौक्ष्मा दूर्ब्बोधधमीशं स्थितमपि सकलं लोकमावृत्य तत्त्वा वाग्बुद्धयो
[30]
रप्यतीत

५८ ···मपि मुनिभिः स्वागमाङ् यातततत्त्वम् विद्यारूपं विशुद्धे
[31]   [32]   [33]
पदमनतिशय

५९ क्षीण संसार बन्धम् स्यादात्मानन्न जातु त्वमिव कथयिता कश्चिदन्यो
द्वितीय:

६० प्रत्याधार स्थितित्वात्पृथगपिन पृथक् तत्स्वरूपा विशेषात् नित्यं
धर्म्मैरयोगा

६१ त्पुनरपि न तथा सर्व्वकालेःप्रतीत : नाशोत्पादाद्ययोगा ट्सिथतमपि

६२ जगत: सर्व्वंगं व्यापि भावात् चैतन्यं रूपपक्ष स्थितमपि कथये

६३ त्को नु लोके त्वदन्य: निरंहसन्दुरितिभिदं विवेकि नंतमोमुषशमि

६४ तभव विपश्चितं गिराम्पति सुधियम झ्री चेतसमयोदि

६५ तं वचनमुपैतु ते सदा शमित भव भयेन क्षायिणा ज्ञानराशे:

६६ स्वयमुपहित धाम्ना वेद्यपारङ्गतेन जगदपरजसेदंतत्त्व

६७ या सर्व्वमारा द्वियदिव तिमिराणां क्षायकेनावभाति

६८ गुण पुरुष विवेक ज्ञान सम्भिन्नजन्मा व्यतियुत विषयाणां त्वं

६९ गिरां संविवेकी जगति धनविरूढ व्यापि सम्मोह भेंदी च्युतजग

७० द निरोध: खे शशीव चका: सि: तदहमिति नुनूषद्द्विन्न संसार

७१ वन्धम् वितमसमरजस्कं त्वाङ्करीयां समाद्यम् कथमपि पर
[34]

७२ लघ्वीं स्वान्तिवध्नामि वाचं तदिह पितरि मे त्वं सम्पदस्संविधत्स्व

७३ भगवतो द्वैपायनस्य स्तोत्रङ्कृत मनुपरमेण
[35]

1. वृ॑ in Gn, DV. 2. L सौगत । 3. DV भवार्णवं···न···वि दा···भञ्जत्
but the letters are quite illegible; Gn मार्त्तण्ड; L omits
the line. 4. L [क]रण···गेन । 5. DV स्त्रथी विरोधेन निवार्यमाण: ।
However the reading is marred by the letters being damaged.
Gn स्त्रयैनिरोधिभिर; L reads स्त्रयैनिरोधिभिर··· । 6. Gn धर्मावर्त्ता-
ढयो; DV स्या । 7. Gn as in our text but DV निषम [वचसा] ।
8. L माणम् । 9. L स्थ । 10. DV यदि । 11. DV द्वि [निवार्यमाणाम्] ।

12. DV यदिनान्य । 13. L छ । 14. DV reads onwards as [म्प्रवृत्तम];
L द्वितया । 15. DV [भान्सी] । 16. L omits व्यवरिष्यत and letters
following. 17. DV न्यस्यत् । 18. L व्यतिष्ठत । 19. DV प । 20. L
व्यतिष्ठत । 21. L सौगतैर । 22. L [नर्तत्वाहन] । 23. Gn धेन्य···
अ. इ. । 24. L नामच···पदाम् । 25. L पाठादे: । 26. Not in L 27. L
श्रमिथ्याचाङ्करादिदोषम् । 29. L व्यात्मनामंत्रवाचम् । 30. L, Gn सौख्या ।
31. DV (कृति) । The letters are damaged but क is clear.
32. DV माद्यात । 33. L विशुद्धे: । 34. L and DV read पर but Gn
परि । 35. The metre as Gnoli says is अनुष्टुप in the beginning
1-6 and उपजाति from 7-20.

XXVIII. The Āryaghāt Mandala Inscription

(DV 29; Gn LXXXVII; HJ 30) The periphery of a raised
Mandala by the side of the temple of Vatsalādevī in the vicinity
of Āryaghāt below the temple of Paśupati. The part inscribed
is about 60 cm wide and 2.5 cm long and is just one line.

१ ॐ संवत् ४०० ५० २········सर्व्वदण्ड नायक पादानुध्यातो (ध्यातेन[1])
ब्राह्मण पुण्यगोमिना स्वपुण्याप्यायनाय पार्थिवशिला स्थापिता धान्य
पिण्डक मा ३०

1. As DV has corrected the grammatical mistake, ध्यातेन
seems to be right, perhaps ध्यात a mistake of the engraver.

XXIX. Chowkitar Inscription

(DV 31; Gn XV; HJ 33) A slab of stone with inscribed
part about 41 cm long and 36 cm wide lying in an open field
called Chowkitar to the right of the so-called Thado Dhungo
in a field below the Dahachok ridge in the Thankot area.
On the top there is a relief of a chakra flanked by two śankhas.
Date: *Samvat 454 Jyeṣṭha śukla 7.*

१ ॐ स्वस्ति मानगृहा त्सम्यक्प्रजा पालन तत्पर

२ भट्टारक महाराज श्रीवसन्तदेव: कुशली‌‌···········

३ पुर: सरान्ग्राम कुटुम्बि [न:] कुशलम्पृष्ट्वा (समाज्ञा) पयति

४ यथा मये·······ञ्च·········ङ्ग···[शोल्ल] कू [थे]

५ राधिकरणाभिलेख्यकैश्च पञ्चापराध ·······सर्व्वदण्डना

६ यक महाप्रतिहार रविगुप्तेन विज्ञापिते [न] चैव सर्व्वदण्डनायक

७ महाप्रतिहार रविगुप्तेन महाराज महा सामन्त श्रीक्रमलीलेन च साकं स

८ मवाप्य तथेति प्रसाद: कृतस्तदित्थम्प्रति यदि कश्चिदसमत्पादोपजी

   [व्य]

९ न्यो बे मामाज्ञा मुत्क्रम्याभिलेख्यं प्रवेशयेद् य इच पञ्चापराधेन स्मरेत्

   स्मार

१० येद्वा तानहं दृढन्त मर्षयिष्याम्येवं विदितार्था यूयं निर्वृत विश्वस्ता

११ सुखं प्रतिवसतेति ततो ग्रामीणैरपि मा भू द्राजकोशस्या पहानिरिति

१२ तत्प्रतिमोचनाय स्वे स्वे ग्रामेधिकरणयो रूभयो: क्षेत्र दत्तम्पश्चि

१३ मोद्दे्णे भूमि ७ पिण्डकम् शोल्लाधिकरणस्य मा २ कू्थेराधिकरणस्य

१४ मा १ दूतकश्चात्र सर्व्वदण्डनायक महाप्रतिहार रविगुप्त: ब्रह्म‌ङ्ङि च

१५ प्रतिहार भवगुप्ते व्यवहरतीति सम्वत् ४०० ५० ४ ज्येष्ठ शुक्ल दिव ७

1   DV   मर्षयिष्यामि एवं ।

XXX. Bhasmeśvara Inscription

(DV 34; HJ 37)   Around the base of a śivaliṅga known
as Bhasmeśvara in a sanctuary just to the south of Paśupati-
natha across the road to Aryaghat. There are more śivaliṅgas
including that of Bhasmeśvara placed close to one another. The
date is 455 Chaitra śukla diva 10.   The inscribed part is 80 cm
wide and 11.5 cm long.

१ ॐ संवत् ४०० ५० ५ चैत्र शुक्ल दिवा ६० भगवत: पशुपते: क्षेत्रे
   स्वयम्प्रतिष्ठापितेभ्यो भद्रेश्वर नाथेश्वर शुभेश्वर

२ स्थितेश्वर रवीश्वरेभ्य: पञ्चभ्य: कारणपूजानिमित्तं खण्डफुट्ट प्रति-
   संस्कार निमित्तञ्च प्रतिहार ध्रुवसङ्घ वार्त्तेन ।

३ स्वपुण्याप्यायनार्थम्मातापित्रो इचनुग्रहार्थञ्च स्वजन गोष्ठिकाधीनां [1]
    कृत्वा यूपग्रामस्य दक्षिणेन सर्वैयेक्षेत्र

४ न्दत्तं भूमि ४०० पिण्डकञ्च मा ४००

1. DV नं ।

XXXI. Narke Mahadeo Base Inscription

(DV 36; HJ 39) Around the base of a śivaliṅga lying in
an open field in a village called Gairigaon, a little north of
Budhanilakantha shrine. The stone is damaged and some
lines are not readable. The date symbols have disappeared.
The inscribed part which is visible is 17 cm long and 105 cm
wide. The name of the king, however, can be traced. But
where to place this inscription in chronological order is a pro-
blem. Our placing here should not be taken as final. Epi-
graphy does help us much in this regard.

१ ···भट्टारक महाराज श्रीमनुदेवे राज्यम्प्रशासति
   ······································

२ ·····································विधिवत्तदस्याश्च कारण पूजाबलि
   भोजन निमित्तन्ते·····················

३ ·······························राज्येविशुद्धमनुजे मनुदेवनाम्न: पादप्र
   बुद्धकमलद्वितय प्रसादात्

४ ·····························संस्थापितात्र विधिवत्प्रतिमा विचित्रा
   शम्भोर्गुणाधिकतया क्षि········आहरन्ती भास्वद्विचित्रमणिरल
   विभूषणाढ्या

५ ···

६ ·····················नाल्पोमि बित्तविभवे मनसापि चार्य्य: [*]

*The metre is Śārdūlavikriḍita.

XXXII. Sankhu Inscription

(DV 37; HJ 38) The pedestal of an image placed in the courtyard of a water conduit called Dhungahiti in Sankhu, a village 7 miles north-east of Kathmandu. Date: *460 Jyeṣṭha śukla aṣṭamī*. The inscribed part is 44 cm wide and 12 cm long.

१ ॐ स्वस्ति संवत् ४०० ६० ज्येष्ठ शुक्ल दिवा अष्टम्याम् भट्टारक
महाराज श्रीवामनदेवस्य (साग्रंवर्षशतं)

२ समाज्ञापयतो भगवतो वामन स्वामिन: क्षेत्रं लेंदुप्रदेशे भूभि १००
पिण्डक मा ५०..............

३ सुब्रंकोप्रदेशे भूमि ४० पिण्डक मा २६ शटस्मि भूमि १० पिण्डक मा ४....

४ गम्मे भूमि १० पिण्डक मा ४ मिङ्क्रोभू ६० पिमा ५० भूमि ५ पिमा ३*

*The underlined represents later addition.

XXXIII. Paśupati Śivaliṅga base of Ābhirī, wife of the son of Paramābhimānī

(Gn XVI; DV 38; HJ 40) The base (*Jalahari*) of Śivaliṅga, with inscribed lines, is about 86 cm wide and 17 cm long, lying near the southern outer gate of Paśupatinātha below the Koṭiliṅga sanctuary. Date: Samvat 402 Jyeṣṭha māsa tithau 2.

१ ॐ आभीरीरुख्यातगुण भार्य्या परमाभिमानिन: सूनो: पुण्यविवृद्धैर्य भर्तु
देवत्वमित: प्रयातस्य पुण्येह निधननिचयें द्विजजनमभिपूज्य दानमानाभ्यां

२ पुत्रेणानुज्ञात (ता) चकार संस्थापनम्शंभो: दत्वा चाक्षयनीबीम्ब
प्रपरिच्छद विभूषादीन् अनुपरमेश्वर संज्ञाञ्च शम्भोर्भुवन सहितस्यास्य

३ भगवते देवदेवायास्मे स्ययम्प्रतिष्ठापितायानुपरमेश्वर संज्ञितायाभ्यङ्ग
स्नपनाच्चन्न गन्धधूप वलि निवेदनादि प्रवर्त्तनार्थं खण्डफुट्ट प्रतिसं

४ संस्कारार्थञ्च पतिदेवप्राणाभीरी गोमिन्या पतये त्रिदिवस्थाय पुण्या-
प्यायनार्थ मायुष्मताञ्चा पत्यानाम्भौमगुप्तादीनाम्भोगारोग्यायुरानन्त्या-
वाप्तये

५   वेम्पाग्रामे स्वयपुपारोपित नदीक्षेत्रं खण्ड द्वयं दत्त मिति । सम्वत् ४००

६० २ ज्येष्ठमासे तिथौ द्वितीयायाम्³

1. DV म ।   2. Gn पुण्याभी री भगिन्यापत्तये ।

3. The metre first आर्या then उपजाति ।

XXXIV. Śivaliṅga base near the Āryaghāt bridge

(Gn XVII; S.S. 2/1.2.3; DV 39) Base of a linga by the
side of the ascent to Mṛgasthali (Deer Park) not far from the
bridge over the Bagmati across Āryaghāt. The inscribed part is
about 44 cm long and 44 cm wide. Date : *Samvat 467 Vaiśākka
śukla 15.*

१   ॐ स्वस्ति सम्वत् ४०० ६७¹ वैशाखे शुक्ल दिव पौर्णमास्याम्भट्टारक
     महाराज

२   श्रीरामदेवस्य साग्रं वर्षशतं समाज्ञापयति महाराज महासामन्त

३   श्रीक्रमलील: कुशली: भगवत: नाथेश्वराय मानमत्या दत्तं दोव

४   ग्रामोद्देशे² शालगम्बिक्षेत्र पिण्डक मा २८ तत्र देशे खुडुस्वामिन:

५   दत्तम् मा २³

1. Gnoli reads 9; DV reads 7.
2. DV ग्रामोद्देशे ।
3. Gn दत्तु ।

XXXV. Lagantole Avalokiteśvara base

(Gn XVIII; S.S.I. 9; DV 40; HJ 42) The pedestal of an
image of Avalokiteśvara in the courtyard of a water conduit
lying half way between Lagantole and Bhimsen Tower. The
inscribed part is about 77 cm wide and 12 cm long. The date
portion is damaged. The inscription belongs to the reign of
Rāmadeva.

१   ॐ स्व [स्ति] ·················· [भट्टारक महारा] ज श्री [राम] देवस्य
     साग्रम् वर्षशतम् समाज्ञा [पयतः]

२   सर्व्वसत्वहित सुखार्थयि भगवत श्रार्या [व] लोकितेश्वरनाथ प्रतिष्ठापितः
     देय धर्म्मोयं परमोपासक मणिगुप्तस्य

३   भार्य्या महेन्द्रमत्या सह यदत्र पुण्य तद्द्रवतु मातापितृपूर्व्वं ङ्गमंकृत्वा
     सर्व्वसत्वाना सर्व्वाकार वरोपेत

४   [तथागत स] व्वंज्ञानावाप्तये

XXXVI. Bharavi's Inscription of Harigaon

(DV 47; HJ 43) A slab of stone originally in Harigaon on
the same spot where Aṃśuvarmā's stones lie.   But now it is in
the collection of National Museum. Date: *Samvat 472 Phalguna
śukla 12.*   The stone was lost to public view for a long time.
But now it has been rescued out of private possession and kept
in the Museum by efforts of Śrī Kaisar Bahadur K.C. The
metre used here is Śārdūlavikridita.

१   संवत्   श्रीमान् प्रभुश्च न च लोकविरुद्धकारी रूपान्वितश्च न
                     च रूपमदम्विभर्ति

२   ४७२   सम्पन्नपौरुषबलश्च बहुक्षमश्च दाता च नाम न च
                     दानविकत्थनश्च

३   फाल्गुन   तेनैवमादिगुणराशिसमन्वितेन श्रीमान्देवनृपतेर्दुहितुस्सुतेन[1]

४   शुक्लदि (व)   सुस्वादुशीतलविशुद्धजलाभिरामा   कीर्तिः   कृतेयमिह
                     भारविना न [वीना]

५   १२

1.   DV reads नृपतेर्द्दुहितु ।

XXXVII. Pharping Kochhutol Inscription

(DV 42; HJ 44) A slab of stone placed in a private garden
leaning on a wall in the village of Pharping by the side of the

main road. The inscription is damaged in the beginning lines
but not wholly. The date symbols reveal 479 Vaiśākha kṛṣṇa
dvādaśyām. The inscribed part is 18 cm wide and 42 cm long.

··········यकारिभिज्ञेय ·······

······तेन महाप्रतिहार सर्व्वंदण्डनायक [भौम]

गुप्तेनविज्ञापितेन मयातामेव······

करणार्थमेवो।·······र्म्संवर्गाीय प्रसाद [शिला]

प ट्रकं शासनमेवं

···केनचिदप्य···

··स्तामाज्ञामप्रमाणीकृत्यान्यथा कुर्वतिकारये [द्वा]

·······तमहमतितरान्न मर्षयाम्यस्मिश्च········

·······राज्ये ये मदूर्ध्वं राजानो भवितारस्तं

रपि·······कृत प्रसादानुवर्त्तिभिरिय·······

·······यत्यस्मिश्च प्रसाद

······[महा] प्रतिहार महासर्व्वंदण्डनायक

[भौ] मगुप्तः संवत् ४०० ७० ६ वैशाख मास कृष्णपक्षे तिथौ

·······द्वादश्याम् ॥   ॥ अर्द्धं

····पन्नदी अर्द्धा भूय वुन्लुनदी [दक्षिण] अर्द्धे·······

····दक्षिणेन मिदिचो भूय खाहिचो भूय·······

भूय······भूय तेग्वङ्गतो दक्षि [ण]

·······पश्चिमेन केखा भूय····

·············भूय······अर्द्धचोभूय त्रेम्गुंचो पश्चि

···········मन्तरेण मोगुं चो भू·······

·······भूय पश्चिमेन·······

·············तिलमकमिति·······

1.   DV omits मेवं ।

XXXVIII. Another Chowkitar Inscription

(Gn XIX; DV 44; HJ 47) A slab of stone with inscribed
space about 35 cm wide and 49 cm long lying in a deserted
village called Chowkitar to the right of the so-called Thado-

dhungo below the Dahachok ridge in the Thankot area. The top of the slab is decorated with a relief showing chakra and two śankhas. Date: *Samvat 482 Āśvina śukla pratipadā*.

१ ॐ स्वस्ति मानगृहाद् बप्पपादानुध्यातो भट्टारक म

२ हाराज श्रीगणदेवः कुशली शीताटिकातले टेग्वल् [ग्रा]

¹

३ मे यथाप्रधान ब्राह्मणपुरस्सरान् सर्व्वनिव कु

४ टुम्बिनः कुशलमृपृष्ट्वा मानयति पूर्व्वराजभिर्य्यु

५ ष्माकं कुथेर शुल्यधिकरणाभ्यान्न प्रवेष्टव्यमित्य

६ नुग्रहः कृतकोधुना मया सर्व्वदण्डनायक

७ महाप्रतिहार श्रीभौमगुप्तानुज्ञापितेन लिङ्ग्वल्

८ माप्चोकाधिकरणाभ्यां एश्चापराधद्वारेण च

९ तुर्भिरप्यधिकरणैर्न्न प्रवेष्टव्यमिति स्थितिपट्ट

१० केन प्रसादः कृतस्त च्यूयमेवं विदित्वा यथै

११ व पूर्व्वमाज्ञा श्रवणविधेयास्तथैवावलगनप

१२ राभूत्वा निर्बृतविश्वस्ताः सुखं प्रतिवत्स्यथ ये चा

१३ स्मद्वंश्या राजानो भविष्यन्तैरपि धर्म्मगुरूभि

१४ र्गुरूकृतप्रसादानुवर्त्तिभिरियमाज्ञा प्रति

१५ पालनीयेति दूतकश्चात्र वभ्रु वर्म्मा ब्रह्म²ङ्

१६ प्रसादगुप्त वार्त्तं व्यवहरतीति संवत्

१७ ४०० ८० २ श्रावणशुक्लप्रतिपदि

1. Here the village is called Tegvala.
2. Gnoli reads the dūtaka's name as Vaṣṭravarmā.

Identical texts recur in 4 other inscriptions found in the same area in the villages of Kisipidi and Balambu with the same date. One lies in the ditch near a *linga* known locally by the name of Luku Mahādeo (hidden Śiva), just outside the village of Balambu. The second was traced in a locality known as Kulachheñtole in the village of Kisipidi across the road west of Balambu. The third which is published by Levi (L 7) is also in the village of Kisipidi. As Gnoli says 'In these last two inscriptions the name of the locality is no longer Sitāṭikā tegvalgrāma but Sitatikatale Kichaprichirgrāma', the latter is applied to Kisipidi, in the Deonani quarter of the village of

Satungal. Gnoli further says 'A comparison of these four
inscriptions, which are in a very poor state of preservation, has
enabled me to re-establish the text with certainty and fill in
Levi's fragmentary reading. The first inscription of this type lies
at Hitigā (a ditch of water conduit) in Balambu by the side of
the temple of Mahālakṣmī.

XXXIX. Luku Mahādeo Stele of Balambu

(Gn pl. XXI; DV 45; HJ 44)   A slab of stone at the site
known as Lukumahādeo, a dith outside the village of Balambu.
The inscribed part is 46 cm wide and 56 cm long.   Date: 482
with the particulars of the preceding record.

१ ॐ स्वस्ति मानगृहाद्वप्पपादानुध्यातो भट्टारक (महाराज)

२ श्रीगणदेव: कुशली शीताटिकातले बु‌·······ङ्‌ग्रामे

३ यथाप्रधान ब्राह्मणपुरस्सरान्सव्वनिव [कुटुम्बिन:]

४ कुशलम्पृष्ट्वा मानयति पूर्व्वराजभिर्यु [ष्माकं कुथेरशुल्या]

५ धिकरणाभ्यां न प्रवेष्टव्यमित्यनुग्रह: [कृताधुनाम]

६ या सर्व्यदण्डनायक महाप्रतिहार श्रीभौमगुप्त विज्ञा

७ पितेन लिङ्ग्वल्माप्चोकाधिकरणाभ्याम्प (उच्चापराधद्वारेण च)

८ तुभिरप्यधिकरणेन्नं प्रवेष्टव्यमिति स्थितिपट्टकेन प्रसाद:

९ कृतस्तद्यूयमेतं विदित्वा यथैव पूर्व्वमाज्ञाश्रवणविधेया

१० स्तथैवावलगनपरा भूत्वा निब्वृ̍तविश्वस्ता: सुखम्प्रतिवत्स्य (थ)

११ ये चास्मद्वंश्या राजानो भवितारस्तैरपि धर्म्मगुरुभिर्गु (रू)

१२ कृतप्रसादानुवर्त्तिभिरियमाज्ञा प्रतिपालनीयेति दूतक

१३ श्चात्र बल्भुवर्म्मा बह्म‌ङ्‌प्रसादगुप्तवार्त्तं ब्यवहरतीति

१४ श्रावण शुक्ल प्रतिपंदि १ संवत् ४०० ८० २

XL. Hiṭigā Stone of Balambu

(DV 46; HJ 48)   A slab of stone in the village of Balambu
in the courtyard of a water conduit called Hiṭigā.   Date: 482 as
in the preceding inscription.

In Newari the word *hiṭi* means a water conduit, and *gā*
means a ditch or a pothole.

१ ॐ स्वस्ति मानगृहाद् वप्पपादानुध्यातो भट्टारक म

२ हाराज श्रीगणदेव: कुशली शीताटिकातले········ग्रा

३ मे यथाप्रधानब्राह्मणपुरस्सरान् सर्व्वनिव कु

४ टुम्बिन: कुशल पृष्टवा मानयति पूर्व्वराजभिर्य्युष्माकं

५ कुथेर शौल्याधिकरणाभ्यां न प्रवेष्ट [व्यमित्य]

६ नुग्रह: कृतकोधुना मया सर्व्वदण्ड [नाय]

७ क महाप्रतिहार श्रीभौमगुप्त विज्ञा [पिते]

८ न लिङ्ग्वल् माप्चोकाधिकरणाम्पञ्चा [पराध]

९ द्वारेण चतुर्भिरप्यधिकरणैर्न्न प्र [वेष्टव्य]

१० मिति स्थितिपट्टकेन प्रसाद: कृत [स्तदयूय]

११ मेवम्विदित्वा यथैव पूर्व्बमाज्ञाश्रवण [विधेया]

१२ स्तथैवावलगनपरा भूवा निर्व्वृतविश्व [स्ता:]

१३ [सुखं] प्रतिवत्स्यथ ये चास्मद्धंश्या राजा (नो भविता)

१४ [रस्तै] रपि धर्म्मगुरुभिर्गुरूकृत प्र [सादा]

१५ [नुव] त्तिभिरियमाज्ञा प्रतिपालनी (येतिदूतक)

१६ [इचा] तत्र बऽभ्रुवर्म्मा ब्रह्म ङ्प्रसाद [गुप्तवार्त्ते]

१७ [व्यवहर] तीति श्रावणशुक्ल प्रतिपदि [सं]वत् ४०० ८० २

In Śrāvaṇa, the 'ṇa' is placed below the line.

XLI. Kisipidi Stone of 482

(L 7; Gn pl. XXIII; DV 47; HJ 50) A slab of stone in
Lhatol in Kisipidi (near Thankot) about 6 miles of Kathmandu
in the west. The length and breadth of the inscribed part are
47 cm and 35 cm respectively and its date is the same as in
the preceding inscription.

१ [ॐ] स्वस्ति मानगृहाद्बप्पपादानु [ध्या]तो भट्टारक

२ महाराज श्रीगणंदेव: कुशली शीताटिका

३ तले किचप्रिचिङ्ग्रामे यथा प्रधानब्राह्मण

४ पुरस्सरान्सर्व्वनिव कुटुम्बिन: कुशलम्पृष्ट्वा

५ मानयति पूर्व्वराजभिर्य्युष्मा कं कुथेरशुल्य धिकर

६ णाभ्यान्न प्रवेष्टव्यमित्यनुग्रह: कृतोधुनामया

७ सर्व्वदण्डनायक महाप्रतिहार श्री भौमगुप्त विज्ञ

८ पितेन लिङ्ग्वलमाप्चोका धिकरणभ्या ञ्चापराधढा

९ रेण चतुर्भिरप्यधिकरणैर्न्नं प्रवेष्टव्यमिति स्थितिप

१० ट्रकेन प्रसाद: कृतस्तद्यूयमेवं विदित्वा यथैव पूर्व्वमाज्ञा

११ श्रवणविधेयास्तथैवावलगन [पराभूत्वा निर्व्व‍‌तविश्वस्ता:]¹

१२ सुखम्प्रतिवत्सयथये चास्मद्‍इश्या [राजानो भवितारस्ते]

१३ रपि धर्म्मगुरूभि र्गुरूकृतप्रसादानुवर्तिभिरियमा

१४ ज्ञा प्रतिपालनीयेति दूतकश्चात्र बभ्रुवर्म्मा ब्रह्मु‍ङ्

१५ प्रसादगुप्तवार्त्तं व्यवहरतीति ॥ संबत् ४०० ५० २

१६ श्रावणशुक्ल प्रतिपदि १

1. Conjectural reading based on a similar expression in other inscriptions. DV adopts the same.

XLII. Kisipidi Inscription of 482

(DV 48; HJ 52) A slab of stone lying in the Kulachhen locality of Kisipidi, a village across the road opposite to Balambu. The measurement of the inscribed part is 55 cm long and 43 cm wide but the date is the same as in the preceding stone.

१ [ॐ स्व] स्ति मानगृहाद्रप्पपादानुध्यातो भट्टारक महाराज

२ [श्रीग] णदेव: कु[शली शीता] टिकातले किचिप्रिचिङ्ग्रामे य

३ [था] प्रधान ब्रा [ह्माणपुर] स्सरान्सर्व्वनिव कुटुम्बिन: कु

४ [श] लम्पृष्ट्वा मानयति पूर्व्वराजभिर्य्युष्माकं कुथेरशुल्य

५ [धिकर] णाभ्यान्न प्रवेष्टव्यमि [त्य] नुग्रह: कृतोधुनाम

६ या सर्व्वदण्डनायक महा प्रतिहार श्रीभौमगुप्त

७ विज्ञापितेन [लिङ्ग्वलमाप्चोका] धिकरणाभ्याम्पञ्चापरा

८ बद्धारेण [चतु] भिरप्यधिकरणैर्ऌं प्रवेष्टव्यमिति .

९ स्थितिपट्टकेन प्रसादः कृतस्तद्यूयमेवम्बिदित्वा

१० यथैव पूर्व्वमाज्ञाश्रवणविधेयास्तथैवावलगन

११ परा भूत्वा निर्वृ॑तविश्वस्ताः सुखम्प्रतिवत्स्यथ ये चा

१२ समद्वंस्या राजानो भवितारस्तैररि धर्म्मगुरूभिर्गु॑

१३ रूकृतप्रसादानु वर्त्तिभिरियमाज्ञा प्रतिपालनी

१४ या दूतकश्चात्र बभ्रुवर्म्मा ब्रह्मा॒ङ्प्रसादगुप्त

१५ वार्त्ते व्यवहरतीति संवत् ४०० ५० २ श्रावणशुक्ल प्रतिपदि

XLIII. Kulāchhetol Stone of Kisipidi

(DV 48; HJ 51; Gn pl. XXII) The stone lies in the
Kulachhetol quarter of the village of Kisipidi across the road
opposite to Balambur. The text with the date is the same as
in the preceding inscriptions. The inscribed part is 55 cm long
and 43 cm wide.

१ स्वस्ति मानगृहाद् वप्पापादा [नुध्यातो भट्टारक]

२ [म]हाराज श्रीगणदेवः कुशली शीताटि [कातले]

३ कादुङ्ग्रामे यथाप्रधान ब्राह्मण [पुरस्सरान्]

४ ⋯⋯ पालक कुटुम्बिनः सर्व्वानिव [कुशल]

५ [स्पृष्ट्वा] मानयति विदितम्वोस्तु यथा [मया सर्व्वं

६ दण्ड] नायक महाप्रतिहार श्रीभौमगुप्त [विज्ञापि]

७ तेन युष्माकं लिङ्ग्वल्माप्चोकादि करणाभ्या

८ ⋯⋯पञ्चापराधद्वारेण न प्रवेष्टव्य [मिति]

९ [स्थितिपट्टकेन] प्रसादः कृतस्तदेवं (विदित्वा)

१० [यथैवपूर्व्वं]माज्ञा श्रवण विधेयास्त (थैवा)

११ [वलगनपरा] भूत्वा निब्वृ॑त विश्वस्ता [सुखं प्रति]

१२ [वत्स्यथ ये चा] समद्वंस्या [राजा] नो भवितार [स्तैरपि]

१३ [धर्म्मगुरूभि] र्गुरूकृत प्रसादानुवर्त्ति[भिरिय

१४ माज्ञा प्रतिपाल] नीयेति दूतकश्चा [त्त्र बभ्रु॒

१५ वर्म्मा ब्रह्मा॒ ङ् प्रसाद गुप्त वार्त्ते व्यवहरतीति संवत् ४०० ५० २]

  ¹
१६ [श्रावण शुक्ल प्रतिपदि]

1. The ण is engraved a little beneath the line.

As it appears the stones are scattered in different villages, which are situated in close proximity to one another in a larger locality called sītāṭikātale (valley). Perhaps the area now covered by the villages of Thankot, Satungal, Kisipidi, Balambu and Chowkitar with the river Balkhu flowing from the northern side below the hills, the river itself forming a bed outskirting the hilly bases, was known as sītaṭīkā and because it was an expansive belt the name *tala* was given to it.

We know that the Chowkitar inscription was addressed to the inhabitants of Tegvalagrāma. But two others are not known fully because of the first letter missing. However, the Kisipidi inscription gives a very meaningful name, Kichaprinchinggrāma. The present and past names look similar and one cannot doubt that the present name is derived from kichaprinchigrama but the names appearing in the *Satungal* and *Balambu* stones do not provide a clue to their past names judged from the nature of the present names.

XLIV. The Inscription of Sheraphat (Valley), Noakot

(DV in JNAS) A slab of stone in a field near the confluence of the Trisuli and Tadi rivers in the valley below the Noakot ridge. The top is adorned by a chakra flanked by śankhas. The inscribed part is 34 cm long and 36 cm wide.

१   स्वस्ति मानगृहाद········

२   ·······भट्टारक महाराज श्रीगण [देव: कुशली]·······

३   ब्राह्मण पुरस्सरान् ग्रामकुदुम्विन: कुशलमाभाष्य

४   समाज्ञापयति विदितमस्तु भवतां यथा सर्व्वदण्डनायक

५   महाप्रतिहार श्रीभौमगुप्त विज्ञापितेन·······

६   ·······लिङ्ग वल्माप्चोक·······घिकरणॆन्नं प्रवे (श)

७   ·······करण·······

८   प्रवेशो नास्तु यदा अत्र म·······

९   वाहा······आनीयन्ते······प्रवेश······

१०   ·······कोट्ट······निमित्यस्य च

११ प्रसादस्य चिरकालस्थितये शिलापट्टकशासनेन प्र

१२ सादः कृतस्तदेवमवगत्य यूयन्निर्वृ ंत विश्वस्ता सुखं

१३ प्रतिवसतेति येपिच मद्वृद्ध्वं राजानो भवितारस्तैरपि

१४ धर्म्मगुरूभि र्ग्गुरूकृत प्रसादानुवर्त्तिभिरियमाज्ञा सम्य

१५ क्प्रतिपालनीयेति दूतकश्चात्र सर्व्वदण्डनायक

१६ महाप्रतिहार श्रीभौमगुप्तो वरीवर्त्ति संवत् ४००

१७ ८० ५ कार्त्तिकमासे शुक्ल दिबा द्वादश्याम् १२

१८ राजपुत्र बन्धुजीवे व्यवहरतीति

XLV. Hari-Hara Pedestal Inscription

(Gn XX; DV 50 Sanskrit Sandeśa 1/8; HJ 53) The pedestal
of an image of Hari-Hara wrongly known as Uma-Maheśvara
in the small garden of a house in Ganchanani near the western
gate of Paśupatināth. The inscribed part is about 68 cm wide
and 30 cm long. Date: Samvat 489 prathamāṣāḍha śukla 2.

१ ॐ पत्योन्नौं पश्य हे श्रीर्य्युगलममिथुनं शूलभृच्छाङ्गं पाण्यो रेकैकस्यात्र
किन्तन्न सुकर मनयोस्तौ यदेकत्र पृक्तौ मूर्ति तय····[1]

२ नूनं सखी मदन रिपोरेव मुक्त्वा भवान्या यो दृष्टो जातु तस्मै सततमिह
नमो स्त्वर्द्धं शौरीश्वराय ॥ सम्वत् ४०० ८० ७[2] प्रधमा षाढ

३ शुक्ल द्वितीयायाम्भट्टारक महाराजा श्रीगणदेव कालमपरिमितं
समाज्ञापयति परमदैवत श्रीभौमगुप्त पादानुध्यातो विदि

४ त विनयः शाश्वतकुशलकर्म्मण्युपहित परमानुग्रहः प्रकृष्टकुलजन्मा
दिवमुपगतयोर्म्मातापित्रो रात्मनश्च पुण्योपचितये

५ स्वामिवार्त्तः सकलभुवनसम्भवस्थितिप्रलयकारणमनादिनिधनं भगवन्त
मिह शङ्करनारायणस्वामिनम्प्रतिष्ठापित वानपि च

६ यो सौ सर्व्वत्रिभुवन गुरूः श्रेयसाञ्चाधिवासो यस्मिन्वद्धा नियमित
फलासम्पद् पुण्यभाजाम् । नानारूपम् भुवनमखिलं

७ धाय्र्यते येन चेदम् तस्मिन्भक्ति नं भवति वृथा शुद्धचित्ताशयानाम् ॥ भिन्ने
पुंसां जगति च तथा देवता भक्तिभावे पक्षग्राह भ्रमित

८ मनसां पक्ष विच्छित्ति हेतोः इत्यर्द्धाभ्यां समुपरचितं यन्मुरारीश्वराभ्या
मेकं रूपं शरदि जघन श्यामगौरं तदव्यात् ॥ पुण्यानि ये

९ प्युभयलोक सुखावहानि कुर्व्वन्ति हि प्रतिदिनं विगताभिभाना: कृत्वापि
चेतन्न विधिवद्विषयोपभोगम् स्वे: कर्म्मंभि: सुकृतिनो दिव

१० मा वसन्ति ॥ पुंसां पापकृतामध: सुकृतिना मुध्वंगतिर्द्धीमता   मित्येवं
प्रविचिन्त्य निश्चितमति: सम्प्रज्ञया प्रज्ञया दृष्टादृष्ट
     3

११ विधिप्रयोग निपुणोबार्त्तं: स्वपुण्याप्तये   मूर्तिङ्कें शवशङ्कराद्धं रचिता
मस्थापयद्यक्तित: ॥
    4   5

1. मूर्तित्य is visible but the next 2 letters are worn off, so Gn's *त्यत्वकें* might be correct as DV's *त्यागेन* ।
2. Gnoli reads 9 but as DV put it the symbol is for 7.
3. Gn निश्चिन्त ।
4. Gn reads स्थापेयद् and thinks that it is a mistake for स्थापयत ।
5. The metres used here are variously स्रग्धरा, मन्दाक्रान्ता, वसन्त-तिलका and शार्दूलविक्रीडिता (Sragdharā, Mandākrāntā, Vasantatilakā and Śārdūlavikriḍitā).

XLVI. Chapaligaon Inscription

(L 8; Gn XXI; DV 51; HJ 54) A slab of stone, about 33 cm wide and 75 cm long, standing on the road in the village of Tsapaligaon, about 3 miles north of Kathmandu on the way to Budhānīlakaṇṭha. Its top is decorated with a chakra and two śankhas. Date: Samvat 489 Śrāvaṇa śukla 12. At the present time the stone is totally damaged. My reading is based on the rubbing taken in 1940. The year symbol is clear.

१ [ॐ स्वस्ति] मानगृहाद् वप्पपादानुध्यातो भट्टा

२ रक महाराज [श्री]गङ्गदेव: [कुशली] ·········
              1

३ ग्रामनिवासिनो···········

४ ·········मनु······· कुशलम्पृष्ट्वा

५ ·······समाज्ञापयति विदितमस्तु भवता

६ म् [सर्बं] दण्डनायक महाप्रतिहार श्री [भौ

७ म]गुप्त विज्ञापितेन मया शिला [पट्ट]

८ के[न] प्रसा[द:] कृत स्त·······

६ ....

१० ....

११ ....[प्र] तिमुच्य

१२ ....

१३ ....करणीयमेवं माभूदेवं........ ..वृत्ति [भुजाँ]

१४ मापहानिरिति ....

१५ ....

१६ ....करण..............................

१७ ....न प्रवि.............................

१८ चिदपि कैश्चित्...............[इ]त्येव म्बिदित्वाद्या

१९ ग्रेन न केनचिदन्यथा करणीयम् यश्चेद

२० मन्यथा कुर्यात् कारयेद्वा तस्याहम् कृत्यका

२१ रिणो वाढन्नमर्षयिष्यामीति भट्टारक

२२ पादीयोप्यत्र दूतको वृषकर्म्मा ।। सम्वत्

२३ ४०० ८० ६ श्रावण शुक्ल दिवा द्वदश्याम्

1. L blank, Gn गणदेव but DV reads as गङ्गादेव. However, the much damaged letter does not allow correct reading.

2. Gn दपि ि ी....; L....

3. L दन्य व्याकरण ।

4. The readings of L and Gn do not vary except that the conjectural reading of Gn is not to be found in L. But they have read in full only 18-23 lines. DV has tried to fill the gap partly by conjectural reading of the first 7 lines as I have done. My reading is based on the rubbing I took in 1940.

XLVII. Mangal Bazar (Patan) Water Conduit Stone

[DV 52; H. Sakya (Abhilekha Prakāśa, p. 5); HJ 55] A stele in the courtyard of a water conduit behind Manimaṇḍapa. The Manimaṇḍapa is an open platform with wooden pillars in front of a temple of Śiva, which stands by the right side of Bhimsena temple in Mangal Bazar, Patan. My reading is based on a rubbing taken in 1940. The date is *492 Vaiśākha śukla 13*.

The inscribed part is 25 cm wide and 20 cm long. The verses are all in Śārdūlavikriḍita metre.

१ ·······प्रलयसम्भव कारणस्य·······कृतेस्तरूपा¹·····

२ स्याति·············भवो दिशतु सन्तत मिष्टमी[श:]

३ नित्यं ख्यात गुणप्रभाव·······वंशेपि लब्धास्पदे·······
<small>2   3</small>

४ जातस्यात्र जनस्य जन्म विफलं कीत्त्या विना जीवित:

५ दृष्टं सौख्यवताम्परत्र च सुखं प्राप्नोति········कीत्त्या मया

६ तां कंतुं न समुत्सुक: प्रयतते को नाम मूढ: स्वय [म्]

७ कीर्त्तें फलं स किल भारविरित्यवेक्ष्य मानुष्यकं क्षणिकमत्थेवताञ्चल
[ग्न:]
<small>4</small>

८ मातापितृस्वकृतपुण्यविवर्द्धनार्थ मेतां भिषग्प्रण्यचकार की[त्तिम्]
<small>5   6</small>

९ अक्षयणीयार्त्थेञ्च यूपग्रामस्य दक्षिण पश्चिमेन
<small>7</small>

१० क्षेत्रं दत्तंयस्य पिण्डकं विशिकया मानिका: पञ्चाशदिति
<small>8</small>

११ संवत ४०० ६० २ वैशाखशुक्लदिवा १० ३

1. DV reads स्तम्भा कृते स्तरूण । 2. DV adds चरिते after प्रभाव ।
3. DV correctly adds स्पदे । 4. DV omits ल[ग्न:] ।
5. DV reads स्वकृत rightly 6. DV भिषग्-प·······चकार ।
   but H· Sakya reads 7. DV's reading is correct·
   सुकृत । 8. DV's reading is correct.

XLVIII. Inscription of Sikubahi

(DV 53; HJ 56) The pedestal of an image of Umā-Maheśvara lying near the confluence of the river Bagmati and Maṇimati (Manoharā) at a site called Sikubahi (but there is no trace of Bahi, i.e. vihāra, here). Date 495 without particulars. The inscribed part is 76 cm wide and 28 cm long.

१ ऊँ बर्हिदेशाद्दशिणस्यां राजपुत्र वज्ररथनाम्नो·············

२ आसीत्तद्गोत्रजेनैकेन याश्च वाग्वत्या मणिमत्याश्च सन्निधिदेशे·············

३ मातर: स्थापिता आसन् मृन्मयास्ता: कालक्रमेण चिरन्तनतयाति विशीर्णं

भग्नपतित पाणिपादा जाता इत्थम्भूताश्च तामवलोक्य·············
<small>1</small>

४ नेन च पश्चातपरम धार्म्मिकेन ब॰भ्रु वर्म्मनाम्नासामेव मातृणाम्प्रति
संस्कार क्रिया चिन्तिनतमासीदसम्भाव्यैव ताङ्क्रियां स काल धर्म्मवंशं····

५ फलोपभुक्तयेदिवन्नीतवां² तदधुना तद् भ्रातृष्पुत्रस्य नित्य धर्म्माभिरत
चेतस्कस्य परम भागवतस्य देशवर्म्मनाम्नो मात्रा पतिव्रतया

६ धर्म्मिष्ठया देशभट्टारिकया तस्यैव कालगतस्य ब॰भ्रुवर्म्मेण: स्वर्गानन्त्याय
मातापित्रोर्भंत्तु̄³ श्चात्मनश्च पुण्याभिवृद्धये पुनरन्यथा

७ देव्यो मातर: शैल्या: कारिता इति संवत्वर्षशत⁴ ४०० ६० ५

1. DV ता अवलोक्य ।
2. स is not there, but DV puts (स) after तवां ।
3. DV रा in place of श्चा ।
4. DV संवत् वर्ष ।

XLIX. Viṣṇupāduka Stele

(DV 54; HJ 57) A stele at the foot hill near Budhanilakantha in the upper reach of the Visnumati river as it
touches the slightly raised ground above the even ground level
of the Valley. The stele is in the same spot as the Śivalinga
inscription. The initial few lines and the top are lost. The
inscribed part covers a space of 25 cm wide and 64 cm long.
The date is 512 Jyeṣṭha śukla 10. This is the first inscription
of Śivadeva I's reign without Amśuvarmā's presence in it
but with Bhaumagupta who seems to have continued as
Chief Minister. The passage in verse is in Sragdharā
metre.

१ ···
२ ··············लाकुलाङ्ग··········
३ श्री जम्मीजनिकर·········ल··········· ····
४ ···लर्ा···व्जाजिविलासैरलसमृदुगति र्व्वसुदेव: स पातु
५ विद्यात्मरूपम्भवभयशमनङ्कोटिसंसर्गमाद्य [म्]
६ [स] व्व्किारं दृढन्तम्पुन रणुमनयं सर्व्वकल्पव्यतीतम्
७ दुर्भी क्षेण·········दमित रजसो वेधस: संश्रयी[य:]

1

८   ····वासन्तेनै स जयति सततं विश्वधामा स्मरारि:

९   [स्वस्ति मा] नगृहाद्वप्पपादानुध्यातस्सततमुपचीयमान

१० [शशाङ्क] किरणामलयश: प्रतानो लिच्छविकुलकेतु

११ [भट्टारक महा] राज श्रीशिवदेव: कुशली थंतुरीद्रङ्ग

१२ [प्रधानपुर] स्सरान्ग्राम कुटुम्बिन: कुशलमाभाष्य समा

१३ [ज्ञापयति] विदितमस्तु वो यदे तत्पूर्वराजैरस्य द्रङ्ग

१४ ····[उ] प कर्म्मपरितुष्टेन मल्लकर करणीयङ्कार्षा

१५ [पणा] दूर्ध्वंन ग्रहीनव्यमिति प्रसाद: कृत····देयं²

१६ प्रसादस्य दृढीकरणार्थे सर्व्वदण्डनायक महाप्रतीहार³

१७ श्री भौमगुप्त विज्ञापितेन मया शिलापट्टकेन प्रसाद:⁴

१८ कृत: इति समाज्ञापना दूतकश्चात्र महाबलाध्यक्ष

१९ कुल प्रवीर: इति।। संवत् ५०० १० २ ज्येष्टशुक्ल दशम्याम्

1. DV adds [य:] hereafter.
2. DV omits देय ।
3. DV reads र in the next line.
4. DV omits श्री and thinks that Bhaumagupta enjoyed a less important status than earlier. But श्री is there, which goes to refute DV's theory.

L. Inscription of Chapagaon

(Gn XXXII; DV 55; HJ 58) A slab of stone standing on the main road in the village of Chapagaon near the temple of Vajra Vārāhī, south of Patan, on the way to Lele. The stone goes without the top as it is broken. The date is effaced. The inscribed part is 48 cm wide and 86 cm long. A few lines in the mid portion are also damaged.

१ स्वस्ति मानगृहादपरिमितयशा:[बप्पपादानुध्यातो लिच्छविकु]ल

२ लकेतुर्भट्टारक महाराज श्रीशिवदेव: [कुशली····नि]

३ वासिना: प्रधान पुरस्सरा न्कुटुम्बिन: कुशलमा [भाष्य] समाज्ञाप

४ यति विदितम्भवतु भवताम् यथेह [स्थरु] द्रङ्ग¹······

५ मत्स्योपक्रयङ्कृत्वा प्रतिनिवर्त्तमानानामेकस्य पु······

६ शुल्कापहासेन काष्ठिकामत्स्यभारक एकस्मिंश्च त····[ताम्रि]

७ कपणत्रयञ्च भुक्कुण्डिका मत्स्य भारके दशभुक्कुण्डिका······

८ त्रिपणा: राजग्रीवके दशराज ग्रीव मत्स्या: पणात्र (य)

९ रीमत्स्य भारके······त्रिपणा: मुक्ता मत्स्यभारके

१० यम्····पञ्चाशत्तम शुल्क न्तदस्य²····

११ केतु········कल्य प्राङ्नृपतिभि····

१२ ········व्यापियश····

१३ ········म स्मि न्प्रसादे

१४ ········कोवेकै···प········

१५ ········[चिरकाल] स्थितये चारस्य प्र[सा]

१६ दस्य······[शिलापट्टन] शासनमि दम् दत्तम्

१७ ········र भविविभिश्चायम्

१८ प्रसाद:········[भूप] तिभिर्द्धर्म्मंगु

१९ रूभिर्गुरू [कृतप्रसादनुवर्त्तिभि रियमाज्ञा सम्यक्पालनीये] ति समाज्ञापना

२० दूतकाश्चात्र········वैशाख शुक्ल पञ्चम्याम्

1. DV स्थरुद्रङ्गे, but letters are damaged. Gn ········द········

2. DV [प]ञ्चाशत्तमशुल्क ·· etc, but Gn त्वमशुल्कन्तदस्य ।

LI. The Chyasaltol (Patan) Stele

(Gn XXII; DV 56; HJ 59) A slab of stone with inscribed part about 48 cm wide standing in the quadrangle of a water conduit in Chyasaltol locality in Patan. The top of the stone is broken and about a dozen lines are not readable. The lower portion is partially readable. The date is *Samvat 515 Phālguṇa śukla 5.*

12-13 lines are missing. The readable lines are numbered thus.

१ ········चा स्मत्कृत प्रसादो¹

२ ········न्यथा कुर्या त्कारये द्वा········

३   ·······य·····धर्मगुरूभि²·······

४   ·······प्रतिपालनीया

५   सुकृतिराद·······मति····एवंश्रूयते·····³

६   ···············भूसम्प्रदान फलभाग सन्नित दान्तदा⁴·······

७   ···············स्वर्गे निरास्थो निवसेन्मनस्वी⁵·······

८   ···············तावच्च चिरक दुःख भाक् स्यात्···

९   ···············म् महीम्भुजाम् ह्यपहरे च्छलाद्वा·······

१०   ···············पश्य सोज्ञो । जायेत पश्चान्निरयेषु स्थि·······

११   ···············न गोमीति सम्वत् ५०० १० ५ फालुन शुक्ल दिवात्रयोद⁶
      [श्याम्]

1. The letters cannot be deciphered. DV reads as above
    but Gnoli all blank.
2. Gn·······यहस्तिन·······
3. DV omits सुकृतिराद and puts मती·······
4. DV reads फलभाक् स तदा तदा स्या(त्)
    Gn·······सम्प्रसाद-रिषत् तदा तदा·······
5. ······ स्स्वर्गनिरास्थो नि- स- सन्मनस्वी·······
6. DV reads त्र[योदश्याम्] ।

LII. Bhadgaon (Kumhaletol) Stone

(DV 57; HJ 60) A stone inside a small temple near the
public platform (dabali) of the Kumhale (Potters) tol (quarter)
of Bhadgaon or Bhaktapur. The letters are much damaged and
many are worn away including the date. The inscribed part is
35 cm wide and 48 cm long.

१   ································ ·······

२   ·······भट्टारक महाराज लिच्छवि कुलकेतु·······

३   ···············[कु]शली माखोदुलुं·······

४ ···················णोत्तरतरं फुथुल्व··········

५ ···············मार्गस्य हेली तिलं·········

६ ···············उत्तरत: बि यरवोट्टु सूल्पमार्ग········

७ ···········सङ्क्लोसन्जरासम्पात नद्या: प्रणालीश्चर·······

८ ············वृह [त्] पथस्य दट्टृणदल्प सपूर्वोत्तर···लमस्य···

९ लदेवी मार्गे·····················सीमापरिक्षि·········

१० (प्रधान पुरस्सरान्)·········कुशलमाभाष्य·······

११ ·················भवतु[भ]······

१२ [व]यथा············तय······

१३ व·····················

१४ ···························

१५ ••••···························

१६ ···························

१७ प्रसाद········प्रवे······ले

१८ रव्यदान···············तिप्रसा·······

१९ त दे[वं वेदिभि]·············चास्मत्पादो पजीविभि:·······

२० त···दे

All the lines are not in the plate. The first line is totally
lost, out of the eight lines preserved two are damaged, one a
little and another (the first to be seen) ninety per cent.

LIII. Inscription in front of the Changu Nārāyaṇa Temple

(Gn XXXIV; DV 58; HJ 61) A slab of stone in front
of the western gate of the temple of Changu Nārāyaṇa near the
victory pillar of Mānadeva and behind the image of Garuḍa.
The top of the stone shows a vessel bearing a bunch of flowers
at the centre and on two sides a decorative design of flowers in
full bloom, all in relief. Date illegible because of the last line
being damaged. The inscribed part is 46 cm wide and 62 cm
long. The inscription belongs to the reign of Śivadeva I.

१ स्वस्ति मानगृहात्प्रशस्तानेकगुणगणाधारो लिच्छवि कुलकेनु भंट्टारक महा

२ राज श्रीशिवदेव: कुशली गुङ्ग्दीमक ग्राम निवासित:प्रधान पुरस्सरान्ग्राम कु

३ दुम्विन: कुशल परिप्रश्रन पूर्व्वं समाज्ञापयति विदितम्भवतु भवतां यथाने

४ न स्वयशो मरिचिविस्तारव्याप्ताशेष दिङ्मण्डलेन प्रणत सामन्त शिरोमणि

५ मयूरव विक्षुरित चरणारविन्द द्युतिना श्रीसामन्ताम्शु वर्म्मणा विज्ञापितेन

६ मयैतद् बहुमानाद् युष्मदनुकम्पया चानेनैव साकं समवाय्यपूर्व्वं एव

७ [क्] त्यवमान……दाहतैर्य्यथाज्ञामनुतिष्ठ द्यिर्य्युष्म त्पूर्व्वकं राराधितं
रस्भ दगुरु

८ भि: कृतसीम निर्णयो योयं सर्व्वकोट्टमर्यादोपपन्नत्वाद चाटभटा प्रवेश्यो

९ वसतये कृषिकम्भर्णे च कोट्टो त: प्रतिपादित आसीद स्योत्तर पूर्व्वतो
घस्त्ताद् दक्षिण

१० राजकुल पुण्ड्रि राजकुलयो भूमि क्षेत्रै: परिवर्त्त्य प्रीतसनसा मयापि
पूर्व्वलब्धेन सहैकीकृत्य शि

११ लापट्टक शासनमिदं वो दत्त मङ्क्षारञ्च चक्क सरल काष्ठमेवं
चान्यत्प्रसादश्च इदं

१२ प्रागाद्घि क्षिप्तस्त्वद ग्रे रस्ति……श्रो भो परिखा मोङ्खा……वाग्वत्या
त्य……ग्राम……महानु

१३ व्द……परनद्या: पुरो युष्मद्……सैंश्च कैश्चिद विक्रेयताशिलकं च कश्चिद
प्यशेष

१४ मविक्रेयं यथा प्रतिषिद्धवस्तु द्वयमज्ञाना धर्मं दद्धिञ्चस्तु

१५ कृताङ्क्षारञ्च लका क्षेपोसौ भवद्भ्यो मुच्येत स्ववनादाहृत्य……गृह
निवर्त……

१६ चत्वारिंशद् सरल काष्ठं विक्रीणानां वो वस्कराधिकृतं……

१७ स्मद् गौत्रजा ये कोट्टाद् वहिरन्यत्रनिवसेयुस्तेषा ङ्कार्य्यं प्रयोजने
स्वकोट्टा……

१८ -व द्वारङ्कोट्टसीमा च ग्रामस्य पश्चिमतो दक्षिणत्श्च दोलाशिखराट
वी पप्य्यं

१९ न्तश्च तदुदल्भलकसेतु शातुन्ती दुल्छिला गृह्खिल भूमि बुर्द्रु
म्वादुल्नदीसङ्गम……

२० ……श उत्तरतो मणिमतीम्पुरीनु सृत्य भारवी श्रमण स्थानस्य पूर्व्वतो……
……र……ठ……

२१ पानीयस्रोतस्ततो रिप्शङ्क्षोसेतु म्प्रोंझम्बु प्रोङ्नि प्रङ्प्रोङ् प्रोबाङ्
संक्रमेण तत:

२२ पर्व्वतमूलन्ततो नदी पूर्व्वतो विह्लङ्खोस्रोत: पर्व्वतस्योपरि विह्लङ्
मार्गदक्षिणेव

२३ पानीयपातस्ततो मार्गे शिलां सेतु सरल वृक्ष प्लक्ष मूलानि यथाक्रमन्तदे

२४ तत्सीम परिक्षिप्तेस्मिन् कोट्टे न कैश्चिदस्मत्पाद प्रसादोपजी
भिरन्यैर्व्वा सूक्ष्मा

२५ पि पीडा काय्र्याः यस्त्विमाज्ञां विलँध्यान्यथा कुय्र्यात्कारयेद् वा तमहं न
मर्षयि

२६ ष्यामि येपि मद्वृद्धव भ्भुजो भवितारस्त्तैरपि धर्म्मगुरुभिर्गुरुकृत प्रसादा

२७ नु वर्त्तिभिरीयमाज्ञा सम्यक्प्रतिपालनीया यत्कारणं बहुभिर्व्वसुधा दत्ता
राजभि

२८ स्सगरा दिभिः यस्य यस्य यदा भूमि स्तस्थ तस्य तदा फलम् षष्ठि
वर्ष सहस्त्राणि

२९ स्वर्गे मोदति भूमिदः आक्षेप्ता चानुमन्ता च तावन्ति नरके बसेत्
स्वदत्ताम् परद

३० त्ताम् वा [यो हरेत वसुन्धराम् स विष्टयां क्रिमिर्भूत्वा पितृभिः सह
पच्यते] सम्वत्

३१ ·············वार्तइति

LIV. Bhimsena Temple (Patan) Inscription

(Gn XXIII; DV 60; HJ 63) A slab of stone about 44 cm
wide and 64 cm long lying in upturned position and being used
as a bridge over a conduit in front of the temple of Bhimsena,
Mangal Bazar, Patan. Now it is deposited in the National
Museum. Date: *Samvat 516 Vaiśākha śukla 10.*

१ [ॐ स्वस्ति मानगृहात्] उपचीयभान कल्याणो निरुपमगुण

२ [भ] ट्टारक महाराज श्रीशिवदेवः कुशली

३ ······[निवासि] नः प्रधान पुरस्सरा न्ग्रामकुटुम्बिनः कू

४ [शलमाभाष्य समाज्ञा] पयति विदितम्भवतु भवताम्यथाने

५ [न]······प्रणत······चरण युगलेन प्रख्याता

६ [मल विपुलयशसा] श्रीसामान्तांशुवर्म्मणा विज्ञापितेन मयैतद्गौगारवा
च्युष्म

७ [दनुकम्पया च] कुथेवृं त्यधिकृतानां समुचित स्त्रिकरमात्रसाधना [यै]

५ [व प्रवेशो] स्मिन्द्रङ्कं प्रवेशेन[1] लिङ्‌वल्‌शुल्लिपञ्चापराधादि निमित्त
   न्त्व प्र [वे]

६ [श इति] प्रसादो व: कृतो लशुन [प] लाण्डुकराभ्याम् प्रतिमुक्ता
   श्चिर स्थितये चास्य

१० [प्र] सादस्य शिलापट्टक शासनमिदन्दत्तन्त देवं वेदिभि रस्मत्पा[2]

११ दोपजीविभिरन्यैर्व्वा न कैश्चिदयम्प्रसादोन्यथा करणीयो यस्त्वे

१२ तामाज्ञां विलङ्ध्यान्यथा कुर्य्यात्कारयेडा तमह मतिनरान्न मर्षयिष्या[3]

१३ मि भाविभिरपि भूपतिभि धर्म्भं गुरुभि गुरूकृत प्रसादानु

१४ वर्त्तिभि रियमाज्ञा सम्य क्पालनीयेति समाज्ञापना दूतक श्चात्व

१५ रामशील वार्त्त: सम्वत् ५०० १० ६ वैशाख मासे शुक्ल दिवा दशम्याम्[4]

1. DV प्रवेशेन.
2. Gn, DV put त्पा in the next line.
3. Gn, DV put ष्या in the next line.
4. Gnoli reads 7 while DV reads 6.

LV. Banepa Stele

(Gn XXXIII; DV 59; HJ; 62) A slab of stone in the village of Banepa. The inscribed part is about 35 cm wide and 67 cm long. The top is decorated by a relief of a chakra flanked by two śaṅkhas. The date portion is damaged.

१ [स्व] स्ति मानगृहादनवगीत·········

२ ····ताहितप्रतापधन्या········[वप्पपादानुध्यातो लिच्छविकुलकेनु भट्टारक]

३ [म] हाराज श्रीशिवदेव: कु [शली] ······[कु]

४ टुम्बिङ्कं शलमाभाष्य [समाज्ञापयति विदितम्भवतु भवतां यथानेनना]

५ नेक विद्यामय परिज्ञाना दचिर:···कले शाप हारि[1]

८ ···विशेष वादेन दिगन्तंर विसारि यश: सामन्त समूह शिरोमणि[2][3]

  प्रणताशेष   सामन्तमण्डलेन   महा[राजा]धिराज   श्रीसामन्तां
  शुवर्म्मं[णा]····

८ ना़ङ्कु...सम्प्रधाय्यंतदनु मतेन......क्लेशाप हारि......

९ दोला शिखर स्वामिन [ना]...[चाटभ]टा प्रवेश्यकोट्टमर्यादि[दोपपन्न]

१० ग्रामः कृतोस्यचोत्तर......[मा] ग्गंस्तमनुसृत्य

११ [देव] कुलम् ततः पूर्वं दक्षिणेन...[नु] सृत्य स्मशान बृहत्......

१२ ...पूर्वेण तेखुं दुल्श्रोतस्त......मार्गंगोटान क्षेत्रः......

१३ ...पर्व्वंतमूलं दक्षिणेन......ततः पच्छिमेन......

१४ ततो दक्षिणेन घेलन्ती नदी स......पश्चिम् चन्द्रेश्वरस्य......

१५ ...ङ ग्रामस्त तदुत्तरेण दक्षिणेश्वर स्ततः पूर्व्वंतमूलम् पूर्व्वं......

१६ ...पानीयमार्गः श्त्येतत्सीम परिक्षिप्तस्तस्यात्र चिरका [लस्थितये]

१७ [शि] लापट्टक शासनन्तेभ्यो दत्तामिति क्रैश्चिदसत्पाद प्रसादोपजीवि

१८ [भि] रन्यैर्व्वा नात्र सूक्ष्मा पि पीडा काय्यां[ये] इ मामाज्ञामुत्क्र[म्या]

१९ [न्य] था कुर्य्युः कारयेयुर्व्वा......

२० ......लिच्छवि वङ्शक्रमागतो य्यंरक्षिणीय......[धर्म्मगु]

२१ [रुभि] ग्गंरुक्कृत प्रसादानु वर्त्तिभिरियमा [ज्ञा सम्यक्प्रतिपालनी]

२२ [येति] समाज्ञापना दूतक श्चात्र......गोमी [सम्वत्]५००...

२३ श्रावण मासे शुक्ल पक्षे......

1. DV ज्ञान ।
2. Gnoli सामन्त ...श्राशा but DV is correct.
3. DV misses this expression.
4. Gnoli's reading is correct but this is not full.
5. While correcting Gnoli's ना DV puts : (visarga) which does not exist.
6. DV ल ।
7. Gnoli शुशान-ह......but DV has corrected.
8. DV ट । Gn......मार्ग गोट नक्षेत्र......

LVI. Golmadhitole (Bhaktapur) Inscription

(Gn XXIV; DV 61; HJ 64; Ben I) A slab of stone at Golmadhitole, Bhaktapur. The inscribed part is about 50 cm

wide and 62 cm long. Its top is decorated with a chakra flanked
by two śankhas. Date: *Samvat 516 Jyeṣṭha śukla divā daśamyām*.
Bendall read the date symbol as Samvat 316 or 318. But he was
wrong. The symbol for 500 is clear. Gnoli and writers following
Levi have read it as 500, which is correct.

१ स्वस्ति मानगृहादपरिमितगुण समुदयोद् भासितयशा ब

२ प्पपादानुद्धयातो लिच्छवि कुलकेनु भंट्टारक महाराज श्रीशिवदे

३ व: कुशली माखोपृ॑ सतल द्रङ्ग निवासिन: प्रधान पुरस्सरा

४ न्ग्राम कुटुम्बिन: कुशल परिप्रश्नपूर्ब्ब समाज्ञापयति विदि

५ तम्भवतु भवतां यथानेन प्रख्यातामल विपुलयशसा स्वप

६ राक्रमोपशमितामित्रपक्ष प्रभावेन श्रीमहासामतांशु वर्म्म

७ णा विज्ञापितेन मर्यैतद् गौरवा द्युष्मदनुकम्पया च कुथेव्बृ॑

८ त्याधिकृता नामत्र समुचित स्त्रिकरसात्र साधनायेव प्रवे

९ शो लेख्यदान पञ्चापराधादात्थर्न्त्च प्रवेश इति प्रसादो व:

१० कृतस्तदेवं वेदिभिरस्मत्पाद प्रसादोपजीविभिरन्यैव्ब्वा न

११ कैश्चिदयमन्यथा करणीयो यस्त्वेतामाज्ञां विलङ्घ्यान्यथा कु

१२ र्वांतिकार येद्वा तमहमति तरान्न मर्षयिष्यामि येपि मदू

१३ द्धम्भूभुजो भवितार स्तैरपि धर्मगुरूभि ग्र्गुरूकृत प्रसा

१४ दानुवर्त्तिभिरियमाज्ञा सम्यक्प्रतिपालनीयेति समाज्ञापना

१५ दूनकश्चात्रभोगवर्म्मंगोमी संवत् ५०० १० ६ ज्येष्ठशुक्ल दिवा
  दशम्याम्

1. Ben पृ॑ सत्सर.   2. Ben विपुल······प.
3. Bendall read 300 10 6; Gnoli read 517, and DV 516.

LVII. Tulachhentole (Bhaktapur) Inscription

(L 9; Gn XXV; DV 62; HJ 62) A slab of stone at
Tulachhentole, Bhaktapur. The inscribed part is about 40 cm
wide and 75 cm long now deposited in the Bhaktapur Old Palace

Museum. The top of the stone has a relief with a chakra
flanked by two śankhas. It also shows flowery designs outside
the space covered by the śankhas and chakra. Date: Samvat 517
as read by Gnoli but DV read as 516, and DV is correct.

१ स्वस्ति मानगृहाद परिमित गुणा समुदयो द्यासि

२ तयशा वप्पपादानुध्यातो लिच्छविकुलकेतु भ

३ ट्टा रक महाराज श्रीशिवदेव: कुशली खृपुङ्ग्राम

४ आसूर्य विध्वद्याग्रान्निवासिन: प्रधान पुरस्सरान्ग्राम

५ कुटुम्बिन: कुशलपरि प्रश्नपूर्व्वं समाज्ञापयति विदि

६ तम्भवतु भवतां [यथा] नेन प्रख्यातामल विपुलयशसा

७ स्वपराक्र [मोपशमि] तामित्रपक्षप्रभावेन श्रीमहा

८ सामन्तांशु [वर्म्मणा] विज्ञापितेन मर्यैतद्गौरवाद्घ्षम

९ दनुकम्प या च कुथे वृ त्यधि [कृता]नामत्र समुचितस्त्रिक

१० रमात्र साधनायैव प्रवेशो लेख्यदान पञ्चापराधा

११ द्वार्थन्त्व प्रबेश इति प्रसादो व: कृतस्तदेवं वेदिभि

१२ रस्मत्पादप्रसादोपजीविभि रन्यैर्व्वा न कैश्चिदयमन्य

१३ था करणीयो यस्त्वेतामाज्ञां विलङ्घ्यान्यथा कुय्र्यात्कारये

१४ द्वा: तमहमतितरान्न मर्षयिष्यामि येपि महद्दूर्द्धम्भूभू

१५ भुजो भवितारस्तैरपि धर्म्मगुरुभि [ग्र्रूक्क] तप्रसादा

१६ नुवर्त्तिभिरियमाज्ञा स (म्यक्प) रिपालनीयेति समाज्ञा

१७ पना [दूतक इचात्र भो] गवर्म्मंगोमी संवत् ५०० १०

१८ ६···शुक्ल दिवा पञ्चम्याम्

1. L प्रतिवद ग्राम नू ।

2. L ··· कम्प ···[कू] ठ···मू···

3. DV, Gn put ज्ञा in the next line.

4. L 500 10···क्ल···म्यामू; DV १० ६ [शु]क्ल दिवा
[प]ञ्चम्याम । He places 10 in the 18th line whereas in
the stone it is in the 17th.

LVIII. Dharamsthali Inscription

(Gn XXVI; DV 63: HJ 66) A slab of stone standing in
the village of Dharamsthali on the way to Jitpur. The top of
the stone is of a chakra with śankhas on two sides. The
inscribed part is about 44 cm wide and 54 cm long. Date:
Samvat 518 as read by Gnoli but it should be read as 7 as read
by DV. Other particulars of the date are *prathamāṣāḍha śukla
diva dvādaśyām*. The year has an intercalary month.

१   स्वस्ति मानगृहात्प्रथितामल विपुलयशा निरुपम गुण गणो

२   [लि] च्छविकुलुकेतु भंट्टारक महाराज श्रीशिवदेव: कुशली दु

३   ········ग्राम निवासिन: प्रधान पुरस्तरा न्ग्राम कुटुम्बिन········

४   [प] रिप्रश्नपूर्छं समाज्ञापयति विदितम्भवतु भवतां यथानेन····

५   ····पनमितानेक क्षितिपति शिरो विभूषण मणि रूचा·······चर¹···

६   ण युगलेन सम्यक्प्रजापालन परिश्रमो पार्जित दिगन्तब्याप्त प

७   [रा] क्रम श्रीमहा सामन्तांशु वर्म्भंणा युष्मदनुग्रहाय········

८   कुथेर वृत्त्यधिकृतानामिह समुचित स्त्रिकर मात्र साधनायैव [प्रवे]

९   शो लेख्य दानंपञ्चापराधादि निमित्त न्त्व प्रवेश: इति प्रसादो व:
      कृतस्त [दे]

१०   वं वेदिभि रस्मच्चरणोपजीविविभि रन्यैर्व्वा न कैश्चिदयं प्रसादो
      न्यथा (क)

११   रणीयो यस्त्वेतामाज्ञा मुल्लङ्घ्यान्यथा कुर्य्यात्कारयेद्वा तमहमति

१२   तरान्न सर्वयिष्यामि येपि मदूर्ध्वंभूभूजो भवितारस्तेनं रपि धर्म्मंगु

१३   रूभिर्गुरू कृतप्रसादानु वर्त्तिभि रियमाज्ञा सम्यक्प्रतिपालनीया

१४   दूतकश्चात्र विप्रवर्म्मंगोमी संवत् ५०० १० ७ प्रथमाषा²

१५   ढ शुक्ल दिवा द्वादश्याम्

1. The 5 lines in the beginning are damaged. Much of the
reading here is based on conjectures as here and there stray
letters come to notice. DV's reading also is conjectural.
Gnoli reads the initial 5 lines as follows: 1. [स्वस्तिमानगृहाइ]
अमल·········· 2. ······श्रीशिवदेवकुशली···· 3. ·······कु······
4. ···क्षिपिपति··· 5. ······लन······

2. DV's reading 7 is correct.

LIX. Būḍhānīlakaṇṭha Stone Inscription

(Gn XXVII; DV 64; HJ 67) A slab of stone standing
near the gate of the walled tank of Śeṣaśāyī Viṣṇu called
Būḍhānīlakaṇṭha near the foot of the Śivapuri hill, 4 miles due
north of Kathmandu. The top of the stone has a design of
flowers. The stone is broken into two pieces. The piece giving
the text up to 10 lines as published by BLI still exists. Another
piece is missing. But there is a rubbing of this fragment from
which the rest of the inscription is available. The inscribed space
is 40 cm wide and 60 cm long. Date: Samvat 518 according to
Gnoli, but following the preceding inscription it is safe to read
it as 7. Probably both were issued on the same day.*

१ ॐ स्वस्ति मानगृहाच्छूतनयविनयगाम्भीर्य्यं धैर्य्यवीचार्द्धि शेष

२ सद्गुणगणाधारो लिच्छविकुलकेतु भंट्टारक महाराज श्रीशि

३ वदेव: कुशली श्राङ्लावक सपितानर्सिंहोभय पाञ्चाली[1]

४ निवासिनो यथाप्रधानाङ्ग्राम कुटुम्बिन: कुशलमाभाष्य

५ समाज्ञापयति दिदितम्भवतु भवतां यथानेन पृथुस

६ मर सम्पातनिर्जयाधिगत शौर्य्यप्रतापोपहत सक[2]

७ लशत्रुपक्ष प्रभावेन सम्यक्प्रजापालन परिश्रमोपार्जि

८ तशुभ्रयशोभिव्याप्त दिङ्मण्डलेन श्रीमहासामन्तांशुवर्म्मं[3]

९ णा युष्मद्धितविधानाय विज्ञापितेन मयेतद्गौरवा

१० [युष्मदनुकम्प] या च कूथेवृत्याधिकृतानां समुचित स्त्री[4]

११ करमात्र साधनायैव प्रवेशो लेख्यदान

१२ पञ्चापराधादि निमित्तस्त्वप्रवेश इति प्रसादो व: कृ

१३ तस्तदेवं वेदिभि रसमच्चरण तलोपजीविभि रन्यैर्व्वा

१४ न कैश्चिदयम्प्रसादोन्यथा करणीयो यस्त्वेतामाज्ञां विलङ्घ्या

१५ न्यथा कुर्य्यात्कारयेद्वा तमहमतितरा [न्न] मर्षयिष्या

१६ मि भाविभिरपि भूपतिभि धर्म्मंगुरूभिर्गुरूकृत प्रसा

१७ दानुवर्त्तिभिरियमाज्ञा सम्यप्रतिपालनीया दूतकञ्श्चात्र

१८ विप्रवर्म्मं गोमी सम्वत् ५०० १० ७ प्रथमाषाढ शुक्ल द्वादश्याम्[5]

*Gnoli gives only the half portion of the stone in his
photograph.

1. BLI वदेव: कुशली······पिता नरसिंहहोभय······
2. BLI : प्रतापापेहृत ।
3. म is engraved beneath the line.
4. This line in BLI reads······न्यधिकृता नासमुचित. The dirgha
   स्त्री is a mistake for स्त्रि.
5. Gnoli reads 518 but DV's reading is correct.

LX. Inscription of Satungal

(Gn XXVIII; DV 65; HJ 68) A slab of stone on the
outskirt of the village of Satungal near Balambu across the
main road. Its top is adorned with chakra flanked by śankhas.
Date: *Samvat 519 prathama pauṣa śukla.*

The inscribed part is about 34 cm wide and 66 cm long.

१ [ॐ स्वास्ति मान गृहा] न्निरतिशय गुणसमुद यो [द्वासित्तयशा वप्प]¹

२ [पादानुध्यातो]² [लि]च्छवि कुलकेतु भंट्टारक महाराज[श्री]

३ [शिव]देव: कुशली कादुङ्ग्राम निवासिन: प्रधान पु[रस्स]

४ [रान्ग्रामकुटुम्बि] न: कुशलमाभाष्य समाज्ञापय [ति वि]

५ [दितम् भवतु भव] तां यथानेन शरदघनशशाङ्क्षमु [खेन]

६ [शत्रु] संख्याप्रमितवल पराक्रमेण श्रीमहासा [म]

७ [न्तांशु] वर्म्मणा विज्ञापितेन सता मर्यैतदगौरवाद्बु

८ ष्म [दनु] कम्पया च शिलापट्टकशासनेभिलिख्य

९ प्र[सादो] यं व: कृतो युष्मद्ग्राम निवासिना मित:

१० काष्ठ [घा] स पत्राहरणाय सर्व्वंत्रवनभूमि³

११ ङ्च्छतान्तदादायागच्छताञ्चाध्वनि फेरङ्कोट्टिनि

१२ वासिभिरन्यैश्च न कैश्चिद्रात्रकट्टारक कुठार

१३ काष्ठाद्याक्षेपो विधारणा वा कार्य्या यस्त्वेत्वामा

१४ ज्ञामविगणयान्यथा कुर्य्यात्कारये द्वा स नि

१५ [य] तन्नृपाज्ञातिक्रमनियमनमवाप्स्यति भ⁴

१६ [वि] ष्यद्भिरपि भूपतिभिर्घर्म्मंगुरूभिर्गुरूकृत

१७ [प्रसा] दानुवर्त्तिभिरयम्प्रसादो नुपालनीय

१८ [इति] समाज्ञापना दूतकञ्श्चात्र वार्तपुत्त्र गुणचन्द्रः

१६ [संवत्] ५०० १० ६ प्रथम पौषशुक्ल दिवा द्वादश्याम्

1. Gn समुद but DV सम्पद ।
2. DV keeps the space vacant. The integration by Gnoli as also incorporated here is based on a parallel expression of other inscriptions of the time, e.g. the two inscriptions of Bhadgaon.
3. Gn तो[र]ण सुपत्रहरणाय, DV as in the above text and is correct with काष्टघास etc.
4. य does not exist but as DV thinks, the engraver probably has omitted it by mistake.

LXI. Inscription of Tokha

(L 10; Gn XXIX; DV 66; HJ 69) A slab of stone standing in the village of Tokha, about 6 miles north west of Kathmandu. The inscribed part is 39 cm wide and 68 cm long. On the top of the stone is a chakra flanked by śankhas. Date: Samvat 519...śukla 12, probably prathama pauṣa as in the preceding one. The right side of the stone is considerably eroded and letters have worn away.

Lines 1 to 6 are illegible.

७ ······ त्ययथे ··परभोग परापर······ [1]

८ ·········गुल्म दक्षिण पश्चिमेन······ [2]

६ ········ संगमस्ततस्तमेवति [लमकम्] [3]

१० ········नुसारेण···सेतु······ ङ्ग····· [3]

११ ······ परि······ स् ततो मार्गं मनुसृत्य····· [4]

१२ ·········शालवृक्षस्तस्य चाधस्ति लमक··· [5]

१३ ⋯⋯तदेव[मनु] सूत्यवासे⋯तस्मादुत्तर⋯⋯ ⁶

१४ ⋯⋯⋯रे उदक्पानीय पात्र स्तस्मादुत्त [र] ⁷

१५ ⋯⋯⋯पञ्चकश्च ततो दक्षिणानुसारतो⋯⋯ ⁸

१६ ⋯⋯⋯तो तस्येव नासिका मनुसृत्यरिन्⋯⋯ ⁹

१७ ⋯⋯⋯स्य दक्षिणतो ज्ञातिखुन्नदीतस्या⋯⋯ ¹⁰

१८ ⋯⋯⋯स्तदेव⋯⋯⋯परिक्षिप्त⋯ ¹¹

१९ ⋯[न कैश्चिद समत्पाद प्रसादोप जीविविभि] रन्यैर्व्वा सूक्ष्मापिपीडा काय्यो ¹²

२० [यस्त्वेतामाज्ञां विलङ्घ्यान्यथा कुय्योत्किार] येद्वा तमहं न मर्वयिष्यामिये [पि] ¹³

२१ [मद्धर्वम्भू भुजो भविता रस्तैरपि धर्म्म] गुरुभिर्गुरु कृत प्रसादा नुव [त्ति] ¹⁴

२२ [भि रियमाज्ञा सम्यवप्रतिपालनीया]⋯श्रूयते भूपालैर्व्बहु भि ¹⁵

२३ ⋯⋯⋯⋯⋯⋯ण्ड⋯त विक्रमार्ज्जित धनैदान⋯

२४ ⋯⋯सत्तोयावलीयं खला ये

२५ ⋯⋯तदा तस्य फलम् दत्तम्⋯आज्ञा⋯प्यानानि

२६ ⋯⋯रे⋯इ⋯दाता⋯चान्यग्वजति नरके दत्तामुपहरन्

२७ ⋯⋯नन्त⋯घ्नन्न कर्त्तव्यम्भू⋯दत्तामुपहरन्

२८ ⋯⋯दूतकश्चात्र विप्रवर्म्मं गोमी सम्वत् ५०० १० ६

२९ ⋯शुक्ल दिवा दशम्याम्

1. Gn यथे⋯ but DV reads upto पर भोग । 2. DV गुल्म दक्षिण पश्चिमेन । 3. Gn reads upto सङ्गमस्ततस्त while DV adds मेवतिलमकम् though letters are much damaged. 4. Gn⋯⋯ सेतु-ङ्ग । 5. L and Gn omit शा । 6. Not in L. 7. DV [तीरे] । 8. Levi reads (line 15) as ⋯ततो दक्षिणानुसार । 9. L (line 16)⋯ मनुसत्य⋯ 10. L (line 17) ⋯स्थदक्षिणतोजतिखिन्नदी⋯ 11. L (line 18) ⋯परिक्षिप्त⋯ 12. L (line 19) ⋯न्यैर्व्वा⋯ 13. L (line 20) ⋯मर्षयिष्या⋯ 14. L (line 21) ⋯⋯प्रसादुनुव⋯ 15. Gn ⋯यतो, DV's assumed reading is like ours.

LXII. Dharampur Inscription

(L 11; Gn XXX; DV 67; HJ 70) A slab of stone standing in the village of Dharampur near a small temple. Letters in the upper part of the stone are eroded and not legible. But the date figure along with the last 8 lines are preserved. The date is 520 Māgha śukla 12. Gnoli could not trace the inscription as he says. But Levi has published the rubbing. The inscription is still there near a water pipe and a small shrine. The inscribed part is about 25 cm wide and 66 cm long.

About 13 lines are totally damaged. The following numbers start from the readable word.

१ ... ...प्रसाद¹

२ ... ...

३ ... ...निवासितः

४ [प्र] धानपुरस्सरान् ग्रामकुटुम्बिनः कुश [ल]

५ [प्र] इनपूर्व्वं समाज्ञापयति विदितम्भवतु भ[वतां]

६ [यथा] यङ्ग्रामः पूर्व्वराजकृतप्रसादा नुगृहित ...

७ [चा] र्ब्भटा प्रवेश्यः सर्व्वकोट्टमर्य्यादोपपन्न ......

८ ... ...सी... ... ...

९ ... ...सि... ... ...

१० ... ...

११ ... ...

१२ ... ...

१३ ... ...

१४ ... ...तेभ्यश्च मल्लकर... ... ...

१५ [स] मुचितताम्रपण चतुष्टयादूद्धर्वं [न्ग्रा]

१६ ह्यमिति प्रसादद्वयं समधिकन्दत्तंतदे²

१७ वभ्वेदिभिर्न्नं कैश्चिदिदमप्रमाणङ्का र्यं

१८ येप्यस्मदूद्धंम्भूभुजो भवितारस्तेर

१९ पि धर्म्मंगुरूभिर्ग्लरू कृत प्रसादानु

२० रोधिभिरेव भाव्यमिति समाज्ञापना

२१ दूतकश्चात्र वार्त्तं भोगचन्द्रः सम्वत्

२२ ५०० २० माघशुक्ल द्वादश्याम्

1. The upper portion is totally damaged but some letters and words can be read from an old rubbing and I have reconstructed the lines 4-7 that way. I think DV also has done the same thing in reading the record. Actually the undamaged portion starts from the 14th line and the text is clear upto the end. Levi and Gnoli cover lines 14-22. DV's conjectural reading is reasonable.

2. Gn, DV समधिकन्दत्तं ।

LXIII. Inscription of Khopasi

(L 12; Gn XXXI; DV 68; HJ 71)   A slab of stone standing on a thoroughfare in a place called Khopasi, which lies in the south-east outside the Nepal valley about 4 miles to the south-east of Bhatgaon.   The inscribed part is 34 cm wide and 54 cm long. Date: 520 Māgha kṛṣṇapakṣa 5.

Gnoli says 'It was not possible for me to examine this inscription on the spot. The characters of this inscription are very clearly engraved. The rubbing of the Bibliotheque Nationale of Paris, which I have compared, confirms in full Levi's reading.' But the stone was there standing on the main thoroughfare in 1953 when I visited the area and took the impression.

१   स्वस्ति मानगृहादपरिमित गुण सम्पद लिच्छवि कुलानन्द करो

२   [भ] ट्टारक महाराज श्रीशिवदेव: कुशली कुप्पासी ग्रामनिवा

३   सिन: प्रधानपुरस्सरान्कुटुम्बिन: कुशल मभिधाय समाज्ञा

४   पयति विदितमस्तुवो यथानेन स्वगुणमणिमयूखालोक

५   ध्वस्ताज्ञानंतिमिरेण भगवद्द्वयपाद पङ्कज प्रणामा नुष्ठा

६   न तात्पर्यो यात्तायति हित श्रेयसा स्वभुजयुगवलोत्खाता

७   खिलवैरिवर्ग्गेण श्रीमहासामन्तांशु वर्म्मणा मां विज्ञात्प्य मदनु

८   [ज्ञा] तेन सता युस्माकं सर्व्वाधिकरण प्रवेशेन प्रसाद: कृत:

६   स मुपस्थित विचारणीय कार्य्येषु स्वतलस्वामिनैव यूयं विचा

१०   रणीया: सर्व्वकार्य्येषु चैकमेव वो द्वारं द्वारोद्घाटन कैलास

११ [कूट] यात्रा योश्च भर्वन्द्रि: प्रत्येकं पञ्चाशज्जाति शुक्ल मृत्तिका देया

१२ शिचर स्थितये चास्य प्रासादस्य शिलापट्टकेन प्रसाद: कृतस्त

१३ देवं वेदिभि रस्मत्पाद प्रसादोपजीविभिरन्यैर्व्वां नायं प्रासादो

१४ न्यथा करणीयो यत्त्वेतामाज्ञा मुत्क्रम्यान्यथा कूर्य्यात्कारयेद्वा त

१५ महं मर्य्यादा भङ्ककारिण मतितरान्न मर्षयिष्यामि भाविभिर

१६ पि भूपतिभिर्द्धर्म्मगुरूभि गर्रू कृत प्रसादान्वर्त्तिभिरिय

१७ माज्ञा सम्यगनुपालनीयेति समाज्ञापना ॥ दूतकश्चात्र

१८ देशवर्म्मं गोमी सम्वत् ५०० २० चैत्र कृष्णपक्षे तिथौ पञ्चम्याम्

1. All writers up till now have read कुर्प्पासी ।

LXIV. Inscription of Dhāpāsi

(DV 69; HJ 72) A slab of stone lying near a large banyan tree in the village of Dhāpāsi, a village on the western extension of the raised level of Bansbari, a suburb of the capital in the northern sector. Dhāpāsi lies about 2 miles north west of the town of Kathmandu. Dhāpāsi is approached through a small route west of the Indian Embassy along the river Viṣṇumati for some distance and then an ascent to the right. The stone is now damaged but my reading is based on the rubbing I took in 1940. The top of the stone is adorned with a chakra flanked by śankhas. The inscribed part is 34 cm wide and 46 cm long. The date is 526 Vaiśākha śukla 5 as also read by DV.

१ [स्वस्ति] मानगृहाद खण्डमण्डलेन्दु किरणावदातयशोवितानस्थगिता

२ [खि] लदिङ्मण्डलो लिच्छवि कुलकेतुभ्रंट्टारक महाराज श्रीशिवदे[व:कु]

३ [श] ली प्रणाली दिमकग्रामनिवासिन: प्रधानपुरस्सरान्कुटु [म्बिन:]

४ कुशलमाभाष्य समाज्ञापयति विदितं भवतु भवतां यथाने [न]

५ पृथुसमरसम्पात निर्जयाधिगत पराक्रमोपनमितोन्य [क्षि]

६ तिपतिशिरोमणिप्रभाभासितचरणारविन्दयुगलेनाशेष [सा]

७ मन्तावगाहनिकृत···न्दच्चक्षुषा श्रीमहासामन्तांशुवर्म्मणा

८ मां विज्ञाप्य मदनुज्ञातेन सता कुर्थेलिङ्वल्पञ्चापराधमात्राप्रवे

९ शेन: व: प्रसाद: कृत: समुचितत्रिकरमात्रसाधनाय तु तद

१० धिकृतैं: प्रवेष्टव्यमेव चिरस्थितये चास्य शिलापट्टक शासन

११ मिदन्दत्तं तदेवंवेदिदिभिरस्म त्पादप्रसादोपजीविभिरन्यें

१२ र्व्वा न कैश्चिदिदमप्रमाणङ्कार्यं यस्त्वेतामाज्ञां विलङ्घ्यान्यथा

१३ कुर्य्यात्कारयेद्वा तमहमन्यायकारिणन्न मर्षयिष्यामि भा [वि]

१४ भिरपि भूपतिभिर्द्धर्म्मगुरूकृतप्रसादानु र्वत्तिभिरि

१५ यमाज्ञा सम्यक्प्रतिपालनीयेति समाज्ञापना दूतकश्चात्र

१६ लच्छागोमी संवत् ५०० २० ६ वैशाखशुक्ल दिवा पञ्चम्यापाम्

1. DV मितान्य ।
2. DV puts वे in the next line.

LXV. Lele Stele

(DV 70; HJ 73) A slab of stone in the village of Lele about 8 miles south of Kathmandu in the district of Patan. Lele is situated on the outskirt of the valley outside the inner mountain range. The date is 526 Āśvayuja (Asvina) śukla divā (no actual tithi). The inscribed part is 61 cm wide and 62.5 cm long.

The top is decorated in relief by a chakra just at the centre and linear designs around it as in Balambu Vihar stone.

१ स्वस्ति मानगृहादपरिमितगुणसमुदयोद्द्रासित यशा बप्पपादा नुदध्यातो लिच्छवि कुलकेतु

२ भंट्टारक महाराज श्रीशिवदेव: कुशली लेम्बटीद्रङ्ग निवासिन: प्रधानपुर-स्सरान्कुन्दम्विन: कुश

३ ल प्रश्नपूर्व्वं समाज्ञापयति विदितम्भवनु भवतां यथैतस्यां युष्मद्ग्राम सीमाभ्यन्तरभू

४ मौ पूर्व्वराजभिरन्यैश्च साधुभि: श्रेयोभिवृद्धये क्षेत्राण्यतिसृष्टकान्यासं-स्तेषामेव कैश्चि

५ दप्र्यनाक्षेपाय चिरस्थितिनिमित्तमनुपरतपुण्य सन्तानोपचीयमान विशदकीर्त्ति मालामो

६ दित दिगन्तर: श्रीमहासामन्तांशुवर्म्मस्मिदनुमोदनया शिलापट्टशासन मिदन्दत्तवान् क्षेत्र

७ परिमाणं सिंहमण्डपे भगवद्वासुदेव ब्राह्मण गौष्ठिकानाम्मा २० आरोग्य-शालाया: मा २००

८ माद्ध्यवशालाया: मा ७५ प्रदीपगौष्ठिकानाम्मा ६० पश्चिमशालाया: मा
  ६० पानीयं गौष्ठिकानाम्

९ मा ४० विश्वेश्वरस्य मा १० ब्राह्मण गौष्ठिकानाम्मा १० प्रदीप-[1]
  गौष्ठिकानाम्मा १० दौलम्पानीय गौष्ठिका[2]

१० नाम्मा १० मल्लयुद्ध गौष्ठिकानाम्मा ६८ धूपगौष्ठिकानाम्मा २ इन्द्र-
  गौष्ठिका नाम्मा ४ उत्तरशाला

११ या: मा १२ वादित्र गौष्ठिका नाम्मा १०···रस्य मा ४० प्रदीप-
  गौष्ठिका नाम्मा ८ अर्च्चा गौष्ठिकानाम्

१२ मा २ ध्वज गौष्ठिकानाम्मा १७ प्र···गौष्ठिकानाम्मा २० प्रणाली
  गौष्ठिकानाम्मा ८ ब्राह्मण सा

१३ नाथ्यगौष्ठिकानाम्मा १० हिद्दिमशालाया मा···प्रदीप गौष्टिका
  नाम्मा प्रवहण गौ

१४ ष्ठिकानाम्मा २० उत्तरशालाया: मा २०···ध्वजगौष्ठिकानाम्मा ११[3]
  भूयोध्वजगौ

१५ ष्ठिकानाम्मा १० मल्लयुद्धगौष्ठिकानाम्मा ३ अर्च्चनीयगौष्ठिका
  नाम्मा ४ इन्द्रगौष्ठिका नाम्मा ६

१६ पूर्व्वशालाया: मा १० भगवत इच्चूडिके श्वरस्य पाञ्चालिकं···मानङ्ग्रा-
  मस्य पूर्व्वत: मा ४० पश्चिमनश्च

१७ मा ४० तदेतेषां क्षेत्त्राणान्न केनचिदाक्षेप:पीडा वा कार्य्यो यस्त्वेनामाज्ञा-
  मतिक्रम्यान्यथा प्रवर्त्ति

१८ ष्यते तमहन्न मर्षयितास्मि दूतकश्चात्र प्रतिहार लच्छागोभी संवत्
  ५०० २० ६ आश्वयुज शुक्ल दिवा

1· DV puts it within brackets but the letters are readable.
2· DV reads पौलम्पानीय ।
3· DV पूर्व्वशालाया: मा १० but the letters are not at all legible.

LXVI. Inscription on the main road between Lagantol and Jaisideval

(BLI 4; Gn XL; DV 80; HJ 83)   A slab of stone standing
on the road to Lagan in front of a house near Jyabahal to the

east of Jaisideval in Kathmandu. The inscribed part is 38 cm
wide and 58 cm long. The top of the stone is broken and lost.
Date: Samvat 535 Śrāvaṇa śukla 7. The inscription is generally
attributed to Śivadeva in view of the era used herein. But it
seems to me that through the Na-bahil inscription was made
a grant of land by Amsuvarmā functioning as the main ruler.
The word *deva* in our first line refers to a divinity and not to
any king on the throne.

१   ······देव······

२   ······न पुण्यो······
           1

३   ······यं व: प्रसादी कृ [त:]······
              2

४   ······नुझ: पृथूल्क्षेत्रं पूर्व······
           3

५   ······मङ्गलस्य क्षेत्रम् ततो भरतश्रम···
                4   5

६   ······तुलक्षेत्रम् ततस्तेग्वल् प्रा···
           6

७   आदित्यगुप्तस्य क्षेत्रम् पूर्वदक्षि [णे] न···

८   ···भट्टाक्षेत्रम् तत स्त्रेग्वल नारायण स्वामी···
                              7

९   -क्षिप्तम्····प्रदीप गौष्ठिकानाम् तस्या भूमेर्दक्षिण···
        8

१०   ···दक्षिण राजकुलस्य दक्षिण पाश्चिमेन···

११   पाञ्चलिकानाम् पश्चिमेन पूर्वत···

१२   ···पश्चिमोत्तरेण पर्वत दक्षिणम्
                            9

१३   ···परिक्षिप्तेयम्भूमि रित्यवगम्य न कैश्चिदस्म

१४   त्पादोपजीविभि रयम्प्रसादोन्यथा करणीयो य [स्त्वेता]
        10   11

१५   माज्ञा मनादृत्या न्यथा कुर्यात्किारयेद्वा तमह मुत्पथ [गा]

१६   मिनं नियतमनुशासितास्मि भविष्यद्धिरपिभूप तिभि [र्गु]

१७   रुक्तप्रसादानुवर्तिभिरेव भवितव्यमिति दूतकाश्चा
           12   13

१८   च राजपुत्र विक्रमसेन: सम्बत् ५०० ३० ५ श्रा [व]

१९   ण शुक्ल दिवा सप्तम्याम्

1. BLI omits ण I 2. BLI राया I 3. BL omits नु I 4. BLI
omits मङ्ग I 5. Gn, BLI भरताश्रा I 6. BLI reads तुला I

7. BLI नारायण; DV omits स्वामी । 8. DV reads -स्तेग्वल ।
9. BLI भूमे दंक्षिण····; DV omits दक्षिणम् । 10. BLI स्मत्पादो, स्म
should have been placed in the upper line but he reads at
the end of that line the letters दप्य । 11. BLI करणीयोय···
12. BLI omits रू । 13. BLI दूतको ।

LXVII. Nabahil Stele

(DV 81; HJ 82; Ballinger 92 no text but just a photo) A
slab of stone originally belonging to Nabahil, Patan is now
deposited in the National Museum. Date symbols are missing
except the symbol for 500. The inscribed part is 37 cm long and
30 cm wide.

१   स्वस्ति [कैलाशकूट भवना] ·द्भुवत्पशुपतिभट्टारकपादा

२   नु [ध्यातो] वप्प [पादानुगृहीत] श्री महासामान्तांशुवर्मा कु [श]

३   ली····ग्राम निवासोपगता न्कुटुम्बि

४   [नो यथा] कु[शलयाभाष्य] समा [ज्ञाप] यति [विदितम्भवतु]

५   भवताम्मिर्मं लीतिशङ्करनारायणस्य····

६   स सम्यक्प्रतिपालनात्पश्चिमा धि [क रण]····

७   तक स्प्रतिमुच्य····मधिकरण····

८   श्यङ्कृत्वा प्रति संस्कृत्य मया व: स···

९   प्रसाद: कृतस्तदेव मधिगतार्थं नं [कैश्चिद्]

१०   पीडा विधेया यस्त्वेत्तामाज्ञा [मुम्मुल्लध्य]····[ता]

११   न्न मर्षयिष्यामि भविष्यद्भिरपि [भूपतिभिपूर्वराज]

१२   कृत धर्माधिकार पालनावृते [दूतकोत्र]

१३   महासामन्त भोगवर्मा ॥ संवत् ५००·······

1. After पादानु DV adds ध्यात and वप्पपादानुध्यात a conjectural
reading. 2. Hereafter follows the name of the king followed
by कुशली । The record undoubtedly belongs to the reign of
Amśuvarmā. 3. The symbol 500 is distinct. At the initial
stage of his independent career Amśuvarmā used the old era.

The inscription bears a date of the old era but the charter is issued by Amśuvarmā. Śivadeva's name disappears. The inscription should be placed before the Bungmati charter in chronological order.

The witness is Mahāsāmanta Bhogavarmā. One Bhoga-varmā Gomi figures as witness in the two Bhadgaon charters of Śivadeva. Could they be identified as one person? Perhaps Bhogavarmā Gomi was a follower of Amśuvarmā and was promoted to the rank of Mahāsāmanta at the date of the Na-bahil inscription.

LXVIII. Bungmati Inscription of Amśuvarmā

(BLI 6; Gn XXXIX; DV 71; HJ 74) A slab of stone buried in the ground in the neighbourhood of the village of Bungmati, 6 miles to the south of Kathmandu in the district of Patan. The stone is now lost. According to BLI 'The stone is taken out every 12th year on the occasion of the 12 yearly festival of Machhendranath when his car is drawn from Bung-mati to Patan and back.' The stone at the top has Buddhist symbols, viz. the wheel of the law flanked by two deer. Date: Samvat 29 Jyeṣṭha śukla 10 as rightly read by DV. Gnoli and many others wrongly read it as 34. As Gnoli says 'The rubbing published by BLI is the only rubbing for the decipher-ment of this inscription.' The inscribed part of the stone is 36 cm wide and 48 cm long.

१   स्वस्ति कैलाशकूटभवनाड्रुगवतपशुपत्तिभट्टारकपादा

२   नुगृहीतो बप्पपादानुध्यातः श्रीमहा सामन्तांशुवर्मा कुशली

३   वूगायूमी ग्राम निवासोपगता कुटुम्बिनो यथाप्रधानङ्कुश

४   लमाभाष्य समाज्ञापयति विदितम्भवतु भवताङ्कुक्कुटसू

५   करणाँ मल्लपोता नां मत्स्यानाञ्चावाधनेनपरितुष्टैरस्माभि

६   भंट्टा धिकरणा प्रवेशेन वः प्रसादः कृतो युष्माभिरप्ये

७   त···य···नीयंयदा च पुनर्धर्मसङ्करराणि

८   [कार्याणि] समुत्पन्ने तदा राजकुलं स्वयम्प्रविचार[6]   [7]

९   [णीयम्] तदेवमधिगतार्थे न कैश्चिदयं प्रसादोस्मत्प्र[8]

१० [सादोप जीविमि]भिरन्यैर्वान्यथा कार्यौ यस्त्वेता माज्ञां विलङ्घ्यान्यथा[9]

११ [कुर्यात्कारयेद्वा]⋯⋯वर्तिनो नियतम्पुष्कला मर्यादाव

१२ ⋯⋯⋯⋯भूपतिभिः पूर्वराजकृतप्रसादा

१३ नुर्वर्ति [भिरेवभाव्य मिति] स्वयमाज्ञा दूतक श्चात्रत्र महासर्वं

१४ [दण्ड] नायक विक्र [मसेन] संवत् २० ९ ज्येष्ठशुक्ल दशम्याम्[10]

1. DV fills the gap. 2. DV [न्] । 3. Gn कराणा⋯नां । 4. Gn
वधानेन । 5. Gnoli⋯यदा etc. 6. त्प is there but द्य is wrong as
made out by DV. There is no place for 3 letters. 7. DV
puts...after विचार but there is no letter after र । 8. Upto this
Gnoli's line is blank. 9. Upto this Gnoli's line is blank.
10. Gnoli and others read 34. 1 also followed the usual
reading. But DV is correct to read 29. The symbols for 20
and 9 are clear.

LXIX. Harigaon Inscription of Amśuvarmā

(L 13; Gn XXXV; DV 72; HJ 75) A slab of stone
standing near the platform of Dathutol in Harigaon, a suburb
of Kathmandu, to the north east. The top of the stone has in
a relief a water vessel with a śankha on the right and a chakra
on the left. Date: Samvat 30 Jyeṣṭha śukla ṣaṣṭyām. The
inscribed part is 36 cm wide and 62 cm long.

१   स्वस्ति कैलासकूट भवनात्परहितनिरत प्रवृत्तितया कृतयुग

२   ⋯कारानुकारी भगवत्पशुपति भट्टारक पादानुध्यातो[1]

३   वप्पपादपरिगृहीतः श्रीमहासामन्तांशुवर्मा कुशली करिष्यमा

४   ण प्रसादां स्तन्मर्यादापण ग्रहणाधिकृतांश्च वर्तमानान्भवि

५   ष्यतश्च समाज्ञापयति विदितम्भवतु भवतां सर्वत्र राज प्रासा[2]

६   देषु कृतप्रसादें मर्यादा निमित्तं यावन्तः पणा देयाभूतेषां[3]

७　यथोचित दानेन माभूदुभयेषाम् [पी]डेति मया पूर्वराजानुवृ[4]

८　त्या यथोचितप्रदानाय शासनोपनिवन्ध[5]···लिखितो यत्र[6]

९　श्रीदेव्या पु ३ प १ अग्नेः पु[7] ३ प १ श्रीकुलदेवस्य···[पु][8] ३ प १ षष्ठीदे

१०　वकुलस्य पु ३ प १ श्रीभट्टारकपादानाम् प्रत्येकम् पु २० ४[9] महाबलाद्ध्यक्ष

११　स्य पु २० प्रसादाधिकृतस्य पु २० अभिषेक हस्ति [नः] पु ३ प
　　१ अभिषे

१२　काश्वस्य पु ३ प १ धावके गेच्छिज्जाकस्य पु[10] ३ प १ भाण्ड ना
　　[यक][11] स्य पु २ प १

१३　चामरधारस्य पु २ प २ ध्वजमनुष्यस्य पु २ प २ देवकुलानाम्[12] पु २

१४　प २ पानीयकर्मान्तिकस्य पु २ प २ पीठाध्यक्षस्य पु २···पणां[13] पु २

१५　प २ पुष्पभुवाक वाहस्य पु २ प २ नन्दीशङ्खवादयोः[14] पु २५ भट[15]

१६　नायकस्य पु ६ प २ अश्वस्यार्घे[16] पु ६ प २ दक्षिणद्वारस्य पु ३ प···

१७　भट स्य पु १ प ४ प्रतोल्याः पु १ प ४ पश्चिमद्वारस्य पु १ प ४
　　आ. स्य. पु.

१८　प ४ मानगृह्द्वारस्य पु १ प ४ मध्यमद्वारस्य पु १ प ४ उत्तर द्वारस्य
　　पु १ प १

१९　सम्माार्जयिन्याः पु १ प ४ यदि यात्रायाम् विश्वसिकनायकयोः पु २०

२०　प ५ तदेव वेदिभिरस्मत्पादप्रसाद प्रतिवद्धा जीवनैरन्येर्वा न कैश्चि

२१　दयम्प्रसादो न्यथा करणीयः भविष्यद्भिरपि गुरूकृत

२२　प्रसादानुवर्त्तिभिरेव भाव्यमिति स्वयमाज्ञा सम्वत् ३० ज्येष्ठशुक्ल
　　षष्ठयाम्

1. L परिकारान् etc. 2. Gn प्रसा; L राजाप्रसा। 3. L येनस्त for यावना etc. 4. DV पी[डे]ति; Gn सा····ई; L दुन्कुयसा for दुभयेषाम् as above. 5. Gn omits this word. 6. L योत्र। 7. Gn अग्रो:; DV अग्ने: । 8. L omits these words. 9. L पु-प। 10. Gn ढा for जा and both missing in L. 11. L omits this word but Gn reads भारकस्य। 12. Gn देत्ना। 13. L रण-श्रां for पणां। 14. ····भट। 15. L प्र-टाना। 16. L omits.

LXX. Inscription of Bhatuwal

(DV 73; HS in AS, p. 13; HJ 77)   Not far from the village
of Tistung lies the village of Bhatuwal in the north east.   The
stone is standing in an open cultivated field.   The inscribed
part is 42 cm long and 34 cm wide.   The top is decorated with
a chakra flanked by śankhas amidst floral designs.   The date is
Samvat 31 *prathama* (month missing) *pañchamyām*. The stone
is not well preserved, and many letters here and there are
damaged.

१ स्वस्ति नैपालेभ्य: सकल जगद्विसारिकीर्त्ति रनतिवृत्ताय्यंमय्यां

२ दा सेतुभगतपशुपति भट्टारक पादानुगृहीतो बप्पपादानु

३ [ध्यात:] श्रीमहासामन्तांशुवर्म्मा कुशली कुण्डशुल्क तापनाधिकृता

४ न्पुरत:कृत्वा पश्चिमद्वार प्रतिवद्धं विषयपतितदायुक्तक शौल्किक

५ गौल्मिकादीङ्क शल माभाष्य समाज्ञापयति विदितम्भवतु भव

६ तां यथास्माभिरेषां···नग्रामीणानां लोहचामर मृगरो

७ मकस्तुरिकाकृत ताम्रभाण्डान्यनिहर्ाय्य्राण्य वास्य तदन्यद्रव्य ाण्या

८ दायोपक्रयार्थंमितोनिर्गच्छताम्प्रसाधोपक्रयञ्चान्त: [प्रविश

९ तां शुल्कतापनादि] यथादेयम्प्रतिमुक्तमेवं वेदिभिरस्मत्प्र

१० तिबद्ध जीवनैरन्य॑वर्ा न कैश्चिदप्ययम्प्रसादोन्यथा कार्यो

११ यस्त्वेतामाज्ञामतिवत्त्यान्यथा प्रवर्तिष्यते तमहन्नरपतिकृत

१२ मर्चादाभेदिनन्न मर्षयिष्यामि भविष्यद्भिरपि भूपतिभि:

१३ सुकृत विपाकोपनत···मिच्छद्भिग्गर्ुकृतप्रसादा

१४ नुयायिभिरेव भवितव्यमिति [समाज्ञापना] दूतकोत्र महाराज

१५ विप्रवर्म्मा संवत् ३१ प्रथम [पौष]···पञ्चम्याम्

1.   Hereafter letters are totally damaged but DV reads
रनतिवृत्ताय॑मर्या and obviously he follows the line 1 of the
following inscription.

2.   DV adds तापनाधिकृता and in the 4th line न्पुरत: कृत्वापश्चिम
द्वारप्रतिवद्ध but the passage cannot easily be read. However,
this occurs in the next inscription. So this must be
correct.

3. DV लोह् चामर मृगरोम । I am, however, unable to read the letters but the guess-work can be correct in view of another inscription·

4. But it must be a month of Pauṣa as the Inayatol (Bhadgaon) inscription shows·

LXXI. Another Stele of Tistung

(DV 74; HJ 76) One of the two stones lying in the lawn of the primary school, east of the row of the bazar houses, in the village of Tistung. Together with that of Bhatuwal the two stones of Tistung form a class by themselves of which the contents are more or less similar. As the last line is completely damaged, the date symbols are missing. The same chakra flanked by śankhas adorns the top. The inscribed part is 54 cm long and 35 cm wide.

१   स्वस्ति नैपालेभ्यः सकलजगद्विसारिकीर्त्तिरन

२   निवृत्ताचर्म्मचर्दिा सेतु भंगवत्पशुपति भट्टा

३   रक पादानुगृहीतो बप्पपादानुध्यातः श्रीमहासा

४   मन्तांशुवर्म्मा कुशली कुण्डशुल्कतापनाधिकृता

५   न्पुरतः कृत्वा पश्चिमद्वारप्रतिबद्धविषय प

६   तितदायुक्तकशौल्किक गौल्मिकादिङ्कुशलमाभाष्य

७   समाज्ञापयति विदितम्भवतु भवतां यथास्मा

८   भिरेषां तेस्तुङ्ग ग्राम्क्षीणानाम् लोह्चामरमृग

९   रोमकस्तूरिका कृत ताम्रभाण्डान्य निह्र्चाण्यवास्य

१० तदन्य द्रव्याण्यादायोपक्रययार्थमितो निर्गंच्छता

११ म्प्रसाध्योपक्र ञ्चान्तः प्रविशतां शुल्कतापनादि यथा

१२ देयम्प्रतिमुक्त मेवं वेदिभिरस्मत्पतिबद्धजीवन

१३ रन्यैर्व्वा न कैश्चिदप्ययम्प्रसादोन्यथा कार्योयस्त्वे

१४ तिमाज्ञा मतिवत्त्यन्यथा प्रवर्त्तिष्यते तमहन्नरप

१५ [ति] कृत मर्य्यादाभेदिनं न मर्षयिव्यस्यामि भविष्यद्भि

१६ [रपि भू] पतिभिः सुकृत विपाकोपनत···

१७ ··················

1. There should be no doubt about या which is superfluous.
2. DV adds (य) but there is no such letter. However it means क्रय । The omission was the error of the engraver.

LXXII. Inscription of Inayatol, Bhadgaon

(DV 75) A slab of stone placed near the temple of Māheśvarī at Inayatol in Bhadgaon. The upper portion of the stone is completely damaged. The inscribed part is 32 cm wide and 16 cm long. Date: *Samvat 31 dvitiyā pauṣa śukla aṣṭamyām.*

१ ···यस्त्वेतामाज्ञां विलङ्ध्यान्यथा प्रवतिष्यते···

२ मर्यादाज्ञाव्यतिक्रमकारिणो व्यधिति भाविभि

३ रपि भूपतिभि र्धर्मगुरूतया गुरूकृतप्रसादान् [व]

४ [त्ति] भिरेव भवितव्यमिति स्वयमाज्ञा दूतकोत्र राजपु

५ त्र स्थितिवर्मा संवत् ३१ द्वितीय पौष शुक्लाष्टम्याम्

1. DV omits this word.

LXXIII. Chāṅgunārāyaṇa Image Inscription of Aṃśuvarmā

(DV 76; HJ 78; DR in Ancient Nepal, p. 166 docc) Inscribed on a gold leaf attached to the golden coat of arms of the image of Narayana at Changu. The date is Ekatrimsāt Māgha śukla 13 in words and not in symbols. The inscribed part is 15 cm wide and 25 cm long. This is the only occasion when no symbols are used for the year in date particulars. For the first time we get a weekday and nakṣatra together here.

१ ॐ एकत्रिशत्तमे वर्षे वर्त्तमाने स्वसंस्थया माघशुक्ल त्रयोदश्या म्पुष्येण सवितुर्दिने

२ कालेन शीर्णमवलोक्य समस्तमाद्यं हैमं हरेर्भगवतः कवचं सताक्ष्यम्

३ तस्मान्निदर्शनमवाप्य जगद्धितार्थं सञ्चस्कृतवान्नरपतिः पुनरंशुवर्मा

LXXIV. Another Inscription of Amśuvarmā at Harigaon

(L 14; Gn XXXV; DV 77; HJ 79)   A slab of stone standing
attached to a platform in the village of Harigaon. The
inscribed part is 38 cm wide and 70 cm long. The top
presents a chakra flanked by śankhas in relief.   Date: *Samvat*
32 *Āṣāḍha śukla.*

१   स्वस्ति कैलासकूट भवनाद् ··········
२   नो भगवत्पशुपति भट्टारक पादान् [गृहीतोवप्पपादानुध्या]
३   तः श्रीमहासामन्ताँशुवर्मा कु [शली]········
४   गृहिक्षेत्रिकादि कुटुम्बिनोय [थार्हम्प्रतिमान्यानु दर्शयति वि]
५   दितम्भवतु भवताङ्गृह क्षेत्रादि श्रावणिकादान········
६   भिरयम्मर्यादाबन्धः कृतएत्तेन भवद्भिर्व्यवहर्तव्यं यत्र········
७   तः पशुपतेः पु ६ प २ दोला शिखरस्वामिनः पु ६ प २····
८   गुंविहारस्य पु ६ प २ श्रीमानविहारस्य पु ६ प २ श्री [रा] ज
९   ज विहारस्य पु ६ प २ खर्जूरिका विहारस्य पु ६ प २ म [ध्य]
१० म विहारस्य पु ६ प २ सामान्य विहाराणां पु ३ प १ रामेश्व
११ रस्य पु ३ प १ हंस गृहदेवस्य पु ३ प १ मानेश्वरस्य पु ३
१२ प १ साम्ब्वपुरस्य पु ३ प १ वाग्वतीपारदेवस्य पु ३ प १ धारा
१३ मानेश्वरस्य पु ३ प १ पर्वतेश्वरदेवस्य पु ३ प १ नर्सिंह
१४ देवस्य पु ३ प १ कैलासेश्वरस्य पु ३ प १ भुम्भुक्किकाजलश
१५ यनस्य पु ३ प १ तदन्यदेवकुलानाम् पु २ प २ श्रीभट्टारक
१६ पादानां पु ६ प २ सपेलापाञ्चाल्याः पु ६ प २ सामान्य
१७ पाञ्चाल्याः पु ३ प १ राजकुलवस्तुना नियुक्त मनुष्यस्य
१८ पु २ प २ गौष्ठिकाणां पु २ प २ कृतप्रसादस्य पु १ ब्राह्मणा [नाम्]
१९ पु १ सामान्य मनुष्याणाम् पु ४········रयं व्यवहार···
२० न चायम्मर्यादाबन्धः कैश्चिद [प्यन्य] थार क [रणी] यो यतः
२१ प्रजाहितार्थोद्यत शुद्धचेतसां [शुवर्मणा श्री] कलहाभिमानिना
२२ कथम्प्रजा मे सुखिता भवेदिति [प्रि] य व्यवस्थेय कारि धीमता
२३ संवत् ३० २ आषाढ शुक्ल त्रयोदश्याम्

1. L in a note य (था प्रधानाना) भाष्या (नुदिचति) विदितं ।

2. L दानानि········
3. Levi and Gnoli read 7, DV reads 6. The latter is correct·
4. L श्रीर ।
5. L खर्जूरिक ।
6. L भूम् ।

LXXV. Sanga Inscription of Amśuvarmā

(L 15; Gn XXXVII; DV 78; HJ 80) A slab of stone about 38 cm wide and 68 cm long in a locality on a hill called Sanga near the village of the same name due east of Bhadgaon forming the outskirt of the valley. The stone lies standing a little east of the village in a field. The top stone has two chakras in relief. The date Samvat 32 *Bhādrapada śukla divā*. The inscribed part is about 38 cm wide and 68 cm long.

१ कर्णालङ्कार रौद्र श्वसदहि पवन व्यस्त पर्यस्त (के) शं
२ प्रत्यग्रच्छेच तापा [निव] तरुधिर शिरोमालभारी····
३ उच्चैमुॅक्ता ट्रहासम्परिविगल दसृङ् नाग चर्मोत्तरी यं
४ पायात्तद्रूपमैशं हिमगिरि तनया भीत भीतेक्षितं व:
५ स्वस्ति क्षितितल तिलक भूतात्कुतूहलि जनता निमेष
६ नयनावलोक्य माना तकैलास कूट भवना त्प्रजाहित
७ समाधान तत्परो भगवत्पशुपति भट्टारक पादा
८ नुगृहीतो वप्पपादानुध्यात: श्रीमहासामन्तांशुवर्मा
९ कुशली शङ्गाग्राम निवासिन: कुटुम्बिन: प्रधान पु
१० रस्सरा न्कुशल माभाष्य समाज्ञापयति विदितम्भव
११ तु भवता मस्माभि: हाम्हुंवस्तु द्वादश तैलघटा: कूम्हुं
१२ वस्तु च पञ्च भवताम्पीडाकर मित्यवगम्य युस्मत्पी
१३ डापनोदार्थं मद्याग्रेण प्रतिमुक्तास्तदेव मवसाय
१४ नात: परेणैतद्वस्तु तैलङ्कस्यचिद्देयं भविष्यद्धिरपि
१५ भूपतिभि पूर्वराजकृतप्रसादानुवर्त्तिभिरेव भवि

१६   तव्यमिति स्वयमाज्ञा दूतकश्चात्र सर्वदण्ड नायको

१७   राजपुत्र विक्रमसेनः सम्वत् ३० २ भाद्रपद शुक्ल दिवा ६

१८   तैल्यशालासु करणीयं इदस्तमधिकरण विवर्जि
         ¹¹   ¹²   ¹³

१६   तानि ॥
         ¹⁴

1. Gn रौद्रेश्वर····; L क-लंकार । 2. Gn पवनव्य····; L···· 3. DV
दतापा; Gn reads प्रत्याश्रम for प्रत्यग्र··· रुचिर etc but after भा
which L reads as परिविगल····प्रत्यय··· 4. L मुक्ताङ्ह्हा···· 5. Gn
omits. 6. Gn reads onwards····तिते; L reads····तिता । 8. Gn
ढह्मु[वस्तु] । 9. L कुह्मम् । 10. L चे । 11. Gn omits. 12. DV
omitted इदस्तम । 13. Gn विभाजितानि; L reads (18 line)
तस्यगण्डश्च करणीयमिह चङ्गाधिकरणविगिरावतानि । 14. स्रग्धरा metre.

LXXVI. The Sundhara (literally a gold water conduit) Inscription of Aṁśuvarmā

(BJN 2, Appendix 1, pp. 74-76; Gn XXXVIII; DV
79; HJ 81) A slab of stone in a place called Sundhara, Patan
(now in the National Museum). The top of stone is decorated
with a chakra flanked by two śankhas in relief. Date: *Samvat
34 prathama pauṣa śukla.* The inscribed part is 37 cm wide and
60 cm long.

१   स्वस्ति कैलासकूट भवनाद्भगव त्पशुपति [भट्टारकपादा]

२   नुगृ [हीतो] वप्पपादानुध्यातः श्री [महासामन्तांशुवर्म्मा]

३   कुशली वर्तमान भविष्यतो मा टिङ्ग्रामस्य········कुटुम्बिनो [कु]
              ¹   ²

४   शलमाभाष्य समाज्ञापयति विदितम्भवतु भवतां [यथास्माभि]
         ³   ⁴

५   मांटिन्देवकुलमर्घविनिपतितेष्टका पङ्क्ति विवर प्रविष्ट
                      ⁵

६   नकुलकुलाकुलितमूषिका सार्थंदूर विघटित निरव
                           ⁶

७   शेषद्वारकपाट वातायनादि जीर्णदारूसंघातं यत्नतः
              ⁷

८   प्रतिसंस्कार्य तस्य दी [र्घं] तर पश्चात्काल सौस्थित्य निर्मित्तं

९ तदक्षयनीविप्रतिवद्ध मेवं माटिङ्ग्रामस्य दक्षिणतो राज

१० भोग्यता मापन्नं विंशतिकया चतुः षष्टिमानिका पिण्डकं क्षेत्र

११ न्दक्षिण पश्चिमतश्च पण्मानिका पिण्डकम्माटिङ्ग्राम पा

१२ ञ्चालिकेभ्यः प्रतिपादित मेवं वेदिमिर्नं कश्चिदस्मत्पाद

१३ प्रतिवद्ध जीवनैरन्यैर्वाप्यन्धर्माधिकारो न्यथा करणीयो

१४ यस्त्वेता माज्ञामुलङ्घ्यान्यथा कुर्यात्कारयेद्वा तं वयन्न म

१५ षयिष्यामो भविष्यद्भिरपि भूपतिभिः र्धर्मगुरुभि धर्माधि

१६ कार प्रतिपालनादृतैं भंवितव्यम् सम्वत् ३ ० ४ प्रथमपौष

१७ शुक्ल द्वितीयायाम् दूतकोत्र महावला ढ्यक्ष विन्दुस्वामी

1. Ben omits कुशली । 2. Ben omits मा but as Gnoli says,
this can be restored as माटिङ्ग्रामकुटुम्विनो यथार्थम् । 3. Ben
omits शलमाभाष्य । 4. Ben omits the conjectural reading.
5. Ben मा·····नृपकुलमथ and the other portion of the line as
above. 6. Ben ·····पुर । 7. Gn & Ben कवाट । 8. Ben omits
चतुः । 9. Ben text पिण्डकां but in the footnote पिण्डकम् ।
10. Ben यः । Generally Ben makes many mistakes while Gn is
correct.

LXXVII. Inscription of Taukhel (near Tistung)

(DV 82; HJ 84)   A slab of stone lying in the village of
Tistung about 3 miles south east of Tistung. The stone at the
top bears in relief a chakra flanked by śankhas. The inscribed
part is 36 cm wide and 48 cm long. The date is 37 *Phalguṇa*
śukla 5. The stone is well preserved.

१ ॐ स्वस्ति कैलासकूट भवनाद निशम शेष सत्वसुखस

२ मुदयोपपादनोदितचित्तसन्तति भंगवत्पशुपति भट्टा

३ रक पादानुगृहीतो बप्पपादानुध्यातः श्रीमहासामन्ताशुवर्मा

४ कुशली चुस्तु ङ्ग्राम कुटुम्बिनः प्रधानपुरस्सरान्कुशलमाभा

५ ष्य समाज्ञापयति विदितम्भवतु भवतां युष्मदीय ग्राम भू

६ मौ महती महिषीपीडेत्यतस्तत्पीडा परिजिहीर्षया परिब

७ र्तनिमित्तमस्माभि रियम्भूमिः पूर्वेण चुस्तुन्नदी दक्षिणेन

८ खातक: पश्चिमेन पर्वतचूडामुत्तरेण चुप्रिङ्नदीन्येतत्सीम

९ मध्योप निपातिनी भवताङ्ग्राम सन्निवेशार्थम्प्रसादीकृता भ

१० वद्द्रिरपि तेस्तुशु ल्म्हुंङ्ब्रह्मङ्य्यङ्ङ्करणीयञ्ङ्ङशतत्त्रयन्देय

११ न्तदेवं विदितार्थैरस्मत्पादप्रसादोपजीविविभिरन्यैर्वा न कैंश्चि

१२ दयम्प्रसादोन्यथा करणीयो यस्त्वेतामज्ञां विलङ्ध्यान्यथा

१३ कुर्यात्कारयेद्वा तं वयन्न मर्षयिष्यामो भविष्यद्द्रिरपि भूप

१४ तिभिधर्मंगुरूतयापूर्वराजकृतप्रसादानुपालनावहितमा

१५ नसैर्भवितव्यमिति स्वयमाज्ञापना दूतकश्चात्र युवरा

१६ जोदयदेव: संवत् ३७ फाल्गुनशुक्ल दिवा पञ्चम्याम् ।।

LXXVIII. Otutol Inscription of Kathmandu

(Gn XLIII; DV 83; Sans. Sandesh 1.8; HJ 87) A slab of
stone standing in the open ground before an image of Mṛtyun-
jaya in a locality known as Guchchatol, Otu, Kathmandu. The
stone is not well preserved. The top is damaged, and the
symbols are missing. The inscribed part is 42 cm wide and
60 cm long. The record belongs to the reign of Aṃśuvarmā.
The date can be read with difficulty as 38.

१ ॐ स्वस्ति कैलाशकूट भवनात्·······

२ ·····दिङ्मण्डले भगवत्पशुपति भट्टारकपादा नु [ध्यातो]

३ [वप्प] पादपरिगृहीत: श्रीमहासामन्तांशुवर्मा कु [शली]

४ [पा] ञ्चालिकान्यथा प्रधानाङ्कुशलमाभाष्य समाज्ञापयति·····

५ ···शालाप्रणाली कर्मपरितोषिते रस्माभि·········

६ ····वासिन:···ब्रम्शामल्लपोतसूकर कराणां····

७ ···चाक···डम्मुक्त्वापञ्चापराधेनास्य

८ ····पण्यानि मृन्द्राण्डानि तथैव कतु···

९ ···क···म्वहिरनति वाह्यवि····

१० [व]: कु [तस्तदे] वम्वेदिभि [रस्म] त्पादप्रतिबद्ध जीवनैर्
[न्यैर्व्वान्]

११ [कैंश्चिदयम्प्र] सादोन्यथा कर [णीयो] यस्वेत्तामाज्ञा मुल्लङ्ध्या
[न्यथा]

१२ कुर्यात्कार्ये [द्वा]····नियतं पुक्कला म····

१३ ····भविष्य [द्धि रपि भूप] तिमिर्गुरूकृत प्रसादा [नुव]

१४ [तिभिरे] व [भ] वितव्यमिति स्वयमाज्ञा दूतकश्चात्र युवरा [ज]

१५ [उदयदेव सं]वत् ३३० ६ आषाढ शुक्ल दिवा पञ्चम्याम्

1. Gn····ला····म् । 2. Gn omits मृद्धाण्डा तथैव कर्तु····but DV is correct. 3. Earlier in S.S.I. 8.42 ff. DV tried to fill up the gap and this was followed by a conjectural parallel [तम्वयमुनमर्षयिष्यामि]. 4. Here DV read म only but [यर्दादेयम्····] in S.S.I. 8.42 ff. 5. DV read in S.S. भाविभिर पि etc. but as he kept the place vacant against his reading in S.S. in the f.n. signs 3 and 4, he substituted भविष्यद्धि for भाविमि । 6. Also see DV. The year of the date was not read so far.

LXXIX. Gairidhārā Inscription of Kathmandu

(Gn XLII; DV 84; HJ 88) A slab of stone on the road just above the courtyard of a water conduit known as Bhansa hiti or Gairidhara in Kathmandu in its north eastern suburb. It has also the image of reclining bull on the top. The date is missing as the particular portion is in damaged condition. The inscribed space is 40 cm wide and 52 cm long.

१ ॐ स्वस्ति कैलासकूट भवना दनन्य नरपति सुकरानति प

२ र पुण्याधिकार स्थिति निबन्धनोन्नीयमान मनस्समाधानो [भ]

३ गवत्पशुपति भट्टारक पादानुगृहीतो बप्पपादानुध्यातः

४ श्री महासामन्तांशु वर्मा कुशली जोञ्जोन्दिङ्ग्राम निवासिनः प्रधा

५ न पुरस्सरा न्कुटुम्बिनः कुशलमाभाष्य समाज्ञापयति विदि

६ तम्भवतु भवतान्नीलीशाला प्रणाली कर्म परितोषितैं रस्माभिः

७ लिङ्गवल् षण्ढाश्विक वाहिकागन्त्रीबलीवर्दानाम प्रवेशेन वः प्रसा

८ दः कृतस्तदेव मधिगतार्थैं नं कैश्चिदेष प्रसादोन्यथा कर

६ णीयो यस्त्वेनामाज्ञां विलङ्घ्यान्यथा कुर्यात्किारयेद्वा तं वयन्न

१० मर्षयिष्यामो भविष्यद्द्भि [रपि भूपतिभिः पूर्वेरा] ज कृत प्रसा

११ दा नुर्वतिभि [रेव भवितव्यम् चिरस्थितये चास्य प्र] सादस्य

१२ शिलापट्रक शासने [न प्रसादः कृत इति स्वयमाज्ञा दू] तकश्चात्र

१३ युवराजोदयदेवः [सम्वत्]·······अष्टस्याम्

1. DV reads स; Gn [स] ।

LXXX. Inscription on the cross road near the western gate of Paśupati

(BLI 7; Gn XLI; DV 85; HJ 89)   A slab of stone by the
side of the open temple of Ganeśa on the cross road not
far away from the western gate of the temple of Paśupati. The
inscribed part is 34 cm wide and 68 cm long. On the top of the
stone is a reclining bull supposed to be the carrier of Śiva. Gnoli
says: 'I was unable to take a rubbing of the last part of this
inscription (lines 19-22), which is deeply buried in the ground.'
The rubbing published by BLI confirms his reading.   But in
1953 when I took the rubbing and up till now (1977) it is
exposed to its full length.   The inscription is well preserved.
The date is *Samvat* 39 *Vaiśākha śukla* 10.

१ ॐ स्वस्ति कैलासकूट भवनाद् निशि निशि चानेकशा

२ स्त्रार्थ विमर्शा वसादिता सदृर्शनतया धर्माधिका

३ रस्थितिकारण मेवोत्सव मनतिशयम्मान्यमा

४ नो भगवत्पशुपति भट्टारक पादानुगृहीतो बप्प

५ पादानुध्यातः श्र्यंशु वर्मा कुशली पश्चिमाधिक

६ रणवृत्तिभुजो वर्त्तमाना न्भविष्यतश्च यथार्ह

७ ङ्कुशलमाभाष्य समाज्ञापयति विदितम्भव

८ तु भवताम्पशुपतौ भगवाञ्छर भोगेश्वरोसमङ्कु

९ गिन्या श्रीभोगवर्मे जनन्या भोगदेव्या स्वभर्तूराज

१० पुत्र शूरसेनस्य पुण्योपचयाय प्रतिष्ठापितो

११ यश्च तद्दुहित्रास्मद्द्वागिनेय्या भाग्यदेव्या प्रतिष्ठा

१२ पितो लडितमहेश्वरो यश्चैतत्पूर्वंजैः प्रतिष्ठापि

१३ तो दक्षिणेश्वर स्तेषामध: शाला पाञ्चालिकेभ्य: प्रतिपा

१४ लनायातिसृष्टानामस्माभि: पश्चिमाधिकरणस्याप्र

१५ वेशेन प्रसाद: कृतो यदा च पाञ्चालिकानां यतिकञ्चन

१६ कार्यं मेतद्गत मुत्पत्स्यते यथाकालं च नियमितं व

१७ स्तु परिह्रापयिष्यन्ते तदा स्वयमेव राजभिरन्तरा

१८ सनेन विचार: करणीयो यस्त्वेतामाज्ञामतिक्रम्यान्यथा

१९ प्रवर्त्तिष्यते तं वयन्न मर्षयिष्यामो भाविभिरपि भूप

२० तिभि र्धर्मगुरूतया पूर्वराजकृत प्रसादानु वर्तिभि

२१ रेवं भवितव्यमिति स्वयमाज्ञा दूतका श्चान्त्र युवरा

२२ जोदयदेव: सम्वत् ३ ० ९ वैशाखशुक्ल दिवा दशभ्याम्

1. च is omitted by DV and Gnoli's plate omits the last 4 lines.

LXXXI. Inscription of Kisipidi

(Gn XLIV; DV 86; HJ 90) A slab of stone at Lachhitol, Kisipidi. The top of the stone has a reclining bull occupying the centre. The inscribed part is 43 cm wide and 58 cm long. The date portion is worn away.

१ [स्व] स्ति……………

२ ……यानुग्राह्या भिराधि [न]……भगवत्प शुपति भट्टारक पादानु [गृही]

३ तो वप्प पादानुध्यात: [श्र्यं] शुवर्मा कुशली भिगरि……प्रतिवद्ध……

४ ……निवासिन: कुटुम्बि [नो यथा] प्रधानङ्कुशलमाभाष्य समाज्ञापयति

५ विदि [तम्भवतुभ] वतां या……युष्मद्ग्राम सीमा……द……

६ ……अस्माभिर्युष्मद्ग्रामेत्र प्र [साद]……म……तदेवं वेदिभिर [स्म]

७ त्पादोपजीविभिरन्यैर्वा न कैश्चिदयम्प्रसादो [न्यथा] कर [णी] यो यस्त्वामा

८ ज्ञा मुल्लङ्घ्यान्यथा कुर्यात्कारयेद्वा मर्षयितव्यो भविष्यद्भ्रि रपि भूप

९ तिभि: पूर्व्व [राजकृत प्रसादानुव] र्त्तिभिरेव भाव्यञ्चि [र] स्थि [तये] चास्य [प्र]

१० सादस्य शि [लापट्टक शासन] मिदन्दत्तमि [ति स्व] यमा [ज्ञा दूतक श्चा]

११ त्र युवरा] ज्ञ्री [उदयदेव:]………

LXXXII. Bankali Pedestal Inscription near Pasupatinatha

(Gn XLVI; DV 87; HJ 91) On the pedestal of the image of Goddess Ban Kali at Gausala (cowshed) near the temple of Pasupati. The inscribed part is about 58 cm wide and 6 cm long. The two lines are long from right to left. It is not wholly readable. The date is missing.*

१ ······ प्रासाद पिण्डं स्थलं सद्भित्यामृत वर्मणा·· प·····शिलापट्टकम् ।

२ [भर्तुः पुण्यं] विवृद्धये भवगति क्लेश क्षयायात्मनः भार्य्या श्रीकल
हाभिमानि नृपते लंब्ध्वा प्रसादोदय [म्]

*Metre: Śārdūlavikriḍita.

LXXXIII. Fragmentary stone of Pharping

(DV 88; HJ 88) Lying in a field near the village of Pharping, situated 4-1/2 miles to the south west of Kathmandu on a ridge skirting the valley was an inscribed stone when I explored the region in 1952-53. Later it was traced in Gunkhel by the side of the road near the Nakhu village. The stone wholly readable even though fragmentary is now in the Government Museum in Patan. There is no date because of damage. The inscribed part is 36-1/4 cm wide and 21 cm long.

१ ॐ स्वतनु वसुशिरः करादिदानैं रूपकृत मर्थिजनस्य येन सकल····

२ सन्तप्तस्य कलीश्वरेैं रतिशठैं नित्यङ्गुण द्वेषिभि लोकेस्यास्य सुखावहो
म···

३ स श्रीमान्कलहाभिमानि नृपतिः सर्वज्ञता प्राप्तुयात् ।। येनैंकेन कला-
वपिस्थिरधिया····

४ तेनेयं स्वयशोमरीचि विमल स्फीताम्भुवि स्यन्दिनीं राज्ञा श्री कलहा-
भिमानि····

५ प्रविष्ठा पातालम्पुनरपि परावृत्य तरसा द्रवीभूता कीर्तिः प्र चुरय

६ आर्यावासस्य भूषा प्रणिधि विरहिता नित्यमन्यार्थवृत्ति····

७ कुर्वाणे वोपमान ङ् क्षितितल शशिनस्तस्य राज्ञः कृपाया [ः]····

८ सकल जगदुदन्याशान्तये शीततोयामिहयति वरवासे पातयित्वा प्रणालीम्

LXXXIV. Another fragment of a stone in Pharping

(DV 90; HJ 93) We do not know whether these two fragments form one stone. This gives the date figure 43. The characters are not dissimilar and there is no doubt that both belong to Aṃśuvarmā's regnal years. The inscribed part is 78 cm wide and 18 cm long.

१ ⋯⋯⋯⋯⋯

२ (मा) त्त्रा जयवार्तिकया मान २ सुगृहीतनामा⋯⋯⋯दायतनं शासितुश्च
   कुमारविजयिनः⋯⋯लय⋯⋯⋯

३ २० मानिका प्रयच्छे च्छत्त्राच्छादनपुष्पसिन्दूर दीपवादित्त्राद्युपयोगाय
   द्वादश १२ मानिकाः यच्च दीप⋯⋯⋯

४ यथा भिलिखितमासदिवसविपर्य्यये चासति⋯⋯प⋯⋯प्रत्यायेन कथञ्चन
   करणीयं इति व्यजिज्ञपत् संवत् ४३ ज्येष्ठ कृष्ण⋯⋯⋯

LXXXV. Degutale platform slab

(DV 91) A slab of stone forming a part of the platform in the temple of Degutale in the Hanumandhoka Palace complex.

१ विविधशकुन्तप⋯ङ्कृतयुद्धरूह⋯⋯तक किरानवर्षधर⋯करः यः⋯

२ चिरन्तनं लिच्छविराजकारितं [पुरा] तनै वृ॑त्तिभ टॐ॑प्रूपे[क्षितम]

३ ⋯⋯⋯रूहः

४ ⋯⋯⋯क्षेत्त्रस्मभग्नक

५ ⋯⋯⋯⋯पुनः पुनर्व्वसुः ॥

1. DV वृ॑त्तिभटॐ रूपेक्षित ।

LXXXVI. Inscription of Gokarṇa

(M. Khanal; DV 89; HJ 92) Gokarṇa known after the Sivalinga Gokarneśvara is a village about 3 miles to the north east of Kathmandu. The stone lies inside a small temple adjacent to the Temple of Gokarneśvara, a little further northwest. The inscription is much damaged but letters here and there can be read. No dates are visible. But the characters belong to post-Aṃśuvarmā period.

१   यानु^१·········

२   ·········ज्रयानं

३   ·········पादानुगृहीत

४   ·········श्र्यंशुवर्मा

५   ·········नाङ्कुशल

६   ·········तिबुद्धिभि

७   ·········सम्पदा

८   ·········भूचैत्यभट्टा

९   [र क]·········गुज टुग्रामा^२

१० ·········दिवम

११ भू··ननं···साद···

१२ ·········रपि प्रतिवर्ष······

१३ ·········शुक्लपञ्चम्याम्प्रातरेव स्नातानु

१४ ·········गृहालङ्कार [भू तो]

१५ ·········

1. DV misses यानु ।
2. DV misses गुजटु ।

LXXXVII. Inscription of Dumjā

(M. Khanal· DV 92; HJ 96)   The stone lies by the side of the temple of Kumbheśvara near the confluence of the river Sunkosi, where it is joined by the stream Rosi in the village of Dumja. The inscription belongs to the regime of Aṃśuvarmā but is considerably damaged. As I found totally damaged the stone in my exploration in 1953, I have relied on M. Khanal's reading.*

१   ·········कीर्त्तिमाला में दिगदिगन्तर······

२ ·········
३ ········श्रीकलहाभिमानी नृपती······
४ ········क्षेत्रे पिण्डक मा ४०······
५ ········श्वरस्य··मा १०
६ [द्रु|तकोन्न······[सं]वत······

*Published by M. Khanal in his book 'Abhilekha Sankalan', pp. 1-3.

LXXXVIII. Ancient Water Tank Inscription of the year 45 'Amśuvarmā'

(BLI 8; Gn XLVIII; DV 93; HJ 97) The stone water tank (*jaladroṇī*) of an ancient sprout, which lay on the road from Kathmandu to the British Residency near the Ranipokhari tank. Date: *Samvat* 45 *Jyeṣṭha śukla*. The inscription is now missing. The reading is based on the photograph published by Bhagwanlal Indraji.

१ सम्वत् ४० ५ ज्येष्ठ शुक्ल······
२ श्र्यंशु वर्म्मा प्रसादेन पितुः पुण्य विवृद्धये
३ कारिता सत्प्रणालीयं वार्त्तेन विभुवर्म्मणा

LXXXIX. Harigaon Brick Inscription

On a rectangular brick found amidst the ruins of a dilapidated palace in the Harigaon quarter of Kathmandu in the north east near Dhumvārāhī where similar inscribed bricks were abundantly discovered.*

महासामन्तां शुवर्म्मणः

*Published by Thakurlal Manandhar, Journal of the Nepal Research Centre, Vol. I, p. 83 ff.

XC. Chapatol (Ilananhi) Inscription

(DV 95; HJ 34) The pedestal of an image of Buddha Sakyamuni flanked by two Bodhisattvas at Chapatol in the Ilananhi quarter of Patan. There is no date but the characters seem to belong to the period of Amśuvarma-Jisnugupta period. The inscribed part is 20 cm long and 80 cm wide.

१   ....

२   देय घम्मोयम्परमोपासिकायाः विशिष्ट धम्मंपाल भोगिन्या मृगिन्याः यदत्र पुण्यं तद्ध्रुवतु समाता पितृ भतृ पूर्व्वंङ्गमानां सर्व्वंसत्वानां

३   निश्शेष दुःख विनिवत्तंये स्वात्मनश्चाग्र प्रवरतरामृतकाय प्रतिलाभाय भूयात् गन्धकुटी प्रतिसंस्करणाय तद्प्रयोजने च चातुर्व्विंश

४   महायान प्रतिपन्नार्य्यं भिक्षुणी सङ्घ्वपरिभोगायाक्षयणीवी प्रतिपादिता पनप्फुनाम पश्चिमप्रदे [शे] भूमिशत १०० पिण्डमान्या पञ्चाश ५०

५   भूय ग्राम दक्षिण प्रदेशे भूमि षष्टि ६० पिण्डमान्या षट्त्रिङ्श ३६ गृह प्रस्थषष्ठ शताय

1. DV व ।
2. There is no श । The engraver seems to have committed an error in omitting it.   3. DV श्शताय ।

XCI. Inscription on a Chaitya

(DV 98; HJ 86) On all four sides of the Chaitya in the courtyard of a Vahi in Tyagaltol, Eastern Patan. There are two lines on a slab placed one above the other where letters are engraved. The photograph will show the exact placing. The inscribed portion on each side is 15 cm in breadth and 7.5 cm in length.

North[1]

१   ॐ अक्षोभ्यमक्षोभ्य शिताग्र मूर्ति न्तथागतं स्तौम्यमितोभिरम्यम्

२   समन्तभद्रम्भुवि भद्रकारिण न्तथैव सन्निर्मलकीर्तिमालिनम्

West

३ यावत्‌·········म्भक्त्याद्य तन्नमत शाक्यमुनिम्मु····

४ मैत्य्याद्धें········ङ्गुह्याधिपं बिमलवज्रधरं सहाब्जम्‌

South

५ सद्धमँरत्न कुसुमस्तवकाचिताङ्गम्बुद्धं समन्तकुसुमन्नमताब्जवत्याम्‌

६ मज्जुश्रियम्परमधर्मविदङ्कुमार न्नित्यञ्च सुस्थितमतिकरुणेंकतानम्‌

East

७ महाप्रज्ञालोकक्षतभवमहामोहतिमिरं सुखावत्यां वन्दे सततममिता-
भज्जिनरविम्‌

८ सलोकेशं लोकोद्भवभयहरम्पङ्कुजधरम्महास्थामप्रा [प्तं²] ····पास्नि-
ग्धमन [सम्‌]

1. In the plate the arrangement is a little disturbed. The
   eastern face has followed the southern, whereas it should
   have preceded.
2. Also see DV for conjectural reading which seems to be
   correct.

XCII. Bhimsena Temple Inscription of Patan

(Gn XLV; DV 99; HJ 94) A slab of stone was lying in
the quadrangle in front of the temple of Bhimsena, Mangal
Bazar, Patan until some years back but is now deposited in the
National Museum. The inscribed part is about 30 cm wide and
48 cm long. The central part of the stone has Buddhist symbols
with the Buddha sitting and two deer and there are also two
kneeling men in devotion. The date is not available. Gnoli
rightly says that 'The characters seem to me to belong to the
time of Aṃśuvarmā.' The stone is much damaged and many
letters are mutilated.

१ त्वोत्रसङ्‌घाय········

२ अनादि निबन्धनम् संसारस्य········

········यो: पूजार्थंमाश्वयुज: कृष्ण········

········तपु····रपदं य निमित्त········

३ ⋯⋯⋯डिविचमिहइे¹⋯⋯स्था⋯⋯²

४ ⋯⋯⋯⋯⋯ज⋯क्षेत्रवसा स्था⋯⋯

⋯⋯⋯⋯⋯⋯⋯⋯

⋯⋯ना⋯ति⋯⋯राजानं⋯⋯

⋯⋯⋯⋯⋯⋯खितस्य

५ ⋯⋯⋯⋯⋯⋯⋯खितस्य⋯⋯

६ ⋯⋯⋯⋯⋯⋯

७ कूप⋯⋯त्वा खाद्यते

भि⋯⋯⋯⋯⋯

८ ⋯⋯⋯⋯⋯श ज³

दशमानिका⋯⋯⋯⋯माद्यतो

९ ⋯⋯⋯⋯⋯व त तो मानेभ्या

⋯⋯⋯⋯हारस⋯⋯⋯

१० ⋯⋯⋯⋯⋯प्रदेशेक्षेत्र⋯चतुर्विंशतिकया १०

⋯⋯⋯⋯खूङ्प्रदेशे क्षेत्र⋯⋯⋯

११ ⋯⋯⋯⋯प्रदेशेक्षेत्र⋯विंशतया दशमानि [का]

1. DV मित्र । 2. DV has no स्था । 3. DV omits माद्यतो ।

XCIII. Inscription of Bhwaginanitol in Patan

(DV 100; Gn XLVII; HJ 95) A damaged water tank of stone attached on a wall at Bhwaginanitol, Patan. The date is not available. Gnoli rightly says that the characters seem to belong to the time of Aṃśuvarmā. The inscribed part is 30 cm wide and 8 cm long.

१ कोत्र⋯⋯पूर्व⋯वा यथा¹

२ मुङ्ग दिशां काम्बरमा⋯न⋯⋯ ⋯

३ एतां स्थिति यो विगणय्यभिना²⋯⋯⋯

४ स्फटिकमिव विलीनंच³⋯⋯⋯⋯⋯

५ ⋯⋯⋯⋯⋯⋯⋯हं⋯⋯

1. DV has not given this line. 2. DV एता । 3. Gn सन्झिक ।

XCIV. Inscription of Thimi

(L 5; Gn XLIX; DV 101; HJ 98) There were two inscriptions on the southern outskirts of Thimi, a village situated between Kathmandu and Bhadgaon, about 4 miles from Kathmandu. Gnoli says that he was unable to find L 5 inscription but this was very much in evidence in 1952. The characters here as Gnoli says might belong to the time of Amśuvarmā (cf., moreover, the expression svayamājñā, instead of the more ancient samājñāpanā). Gnoli says 'Levi assumes from the doubling of the consonants after the *repha*—which is however doubtful—that this inscription dates back to the time of Vasantadeva.' I agree with Gnoli that a reading of the rubbing taken by Levi confirms his transcription, excepting that of line 6. The inscription is missing at the moment. But my rubbing is similar to that of Levi.

. . . .

१ यना . . . .

२ मशेषनैं . . . .

३ गुरो ब्वसुदेवस्य . . . . . .

४ र्थे भूयादित्यस्मा [भि] : . . . . . .

५ णानुस्मरणमि . . . . . .

६ ्द्रू सर्वैरनुसमम ए . . . . . .¹

७ सतावदा क्रष्टव्योयम् . . . . . .

८ वासौ न सम्पन्नातिक

९ तिक . . . धान्यमानि

Some lines here cannot be read and the right margin is effaced.

१० ्द्रूर पि . . .

११ स्वयमाज्ञा दू [तकाश्र्वा] त्र देवप . . . . . .

1. L रङ्ग सममसने ।

XCV. Naksāl Viṣṇu Pedestal

(DV 102; HJ 110) On the pedestal of the image of Visnu over the ancient water conduit in Naksal but now deposited in the National Museum. Out of the 4 lines only one line (the last) is preserved. The inscribed part is 55 cm wide and 10 cm long.

१   ....

२   ....

···सदृशमुच्छ्वास वातोद्भवात् मध्ये तोयनिधे: प्रचण्ड पवनेना प्रोद्धृत चैलाग्रतो द···

XCVI. Chitlang Stone[1]

(DV 104; HJ 101)   On a slab of stone lying inside a small temple of Ganeśa not far from Chitlang, a village at the foot of the Chandragiri hill (7000 ft high) from the southern and western side. The inscription belongs to the reign of Udayadeva and is the only extant indigenous record in his name. The date symbol and letters in some lines are damaged. The inscribed part is 34 cm wide and 56 cm long. The date 40 is marked but another symbol can only be conjectural between 5 and 8.

१   ....

२   ···भगवत्पशुपति भट्टारक पादानुगृहीतो ब

३   [प्पपादा] नुध्यातो भट्टारक महाराजाधिराज श्रीउदयदेव: कु

४   [शली]···निवासिनः कुटुम्बिनो यथाप्रधानङ्कुशलमाभाष्य

५   [समा] ज्ञापयति विदितमस्तु वो यो युष्मदीयतल प्रतिबद्ध···

६   ···भट्टारक महाराजाधिराज श्र्यंशुवर्मंपादै पतीप पाञ्चा

७   लिकानामग्रहारोयं प्रसादीकृतोभूत्तद रस्माभिरेष···पाञ्चा

८   लिकानां यथासुखम्परिभोगार्थमग्रहारत्वेन प्रसादीकृत [शिचर]

९   स्थितये चाभिलेख्य···शासनमिदन्दत्तं सीमा चास्य ···

१०   ······तत्र···खातकः म वन्य गुँशिखिरा

११   न्यैर्बा न कैंश्चि [दल्पापि] पीडा विधेया य

१३   स्त्वेतामाज्ञामतिक्रम्यान्यथा कुर्या [त्कारयेद्वा···]

१४   ···[र्षयिद्विरमो] भविष्यस्यापि भूपतिभिरस्मत्कृत प्रसादोन्य

१५ [थान] करणीय इति······दूतक श्वात्त्र सर्व

१६ ···संवत् ४०···[श्रा]² षाढकृष्ण द्वादश्याम्

1. Abhilekhaprakasa by H.R. Sakya talks of this inscription more specially.
2. The 3 lines at the end are damaged specially the last portion. The symbol for 5 is hardly marked as made out by DV.

XCVII. Tavajhyā (large window) Inscription

(Gn L; BLI 9; DV 105; HJ 102) A slab of stone standing near the temple of Mummuro or Chinnamastikā Devī in the Tavajhya (large window) quarter of Patan. The inscribed part is 43 cm wide and 64 cm long. At the top of the stone is a relief representing a fish. Date: *Samvat* 48 *Kārtika śukla* 2. This is the first inscription of Jiṣṇugupta issued with Dhruvadeva as sovereign.

There is a verse in upajāti of upendravajrā and Indravajrā in the second and third line.

१ ॐ स्वस्ति [मानगृहाद्]···दितचित्त सन्तति लिच्छविकुलकेतुर्भंट्टारक¹ महाराज

२ श्रीध्रुवदेवः² सहितेन निरस्तमात्सर्यं विशुद्धवुद्धिः प्रजाहितैषी निर-वृद्यवृत्तः

३ पुण्यान्वयादागतराज्यसम्प त्समस्तपौरार्चित शाशनो यः कैलासकुट भ

४ वनाद् भगवत्पश्रुपति भट्टारक पादानुगृहीतो बप्पपादानुध्यातः श्रीजिष्णु-गुप्तः

५ [कु]³ शली थम्बूगाङ्शुल्मूलवाटिकाग्रामेषु निवासमुपगता न्कुटुम्बिनः कुशल

६ साभाष्य समाज्ञापयति विदितमस्तु भवताम्भट्टारक महाराजाधिराज श्र्यंशु

७ वर्म्मंपादैं र्युष्मदीय ग्रामाणा मुपकाराय योसौ तिलमक श्रानीतोभूत्प

८ तिसंस्काराभावाद्विनष्टमुद्रीक्ष सामन्त चन्द्रवर्मं विज्ञप्तैरस्माभिस्तस्यै

६ व प्रसादी कृतस्तेन चास्मदनुज्ञातेन युष्मद्ग्रामाणा मेवोपकाराय प्र

१० तिसंस्कृततोस्य चोपकारस्य पारम्पर्या विच्छेदेन चिरतरकालोद्वहना⁴

११ य युष्माकं वाटिका अपि प्रसादीकृता स्तदेताभ्यो यथाकालम्पिण्ड

१२ कमुपसंहृत्य भवद्भिरेव तिलमक प्रति संस्कार: करणीय एतद्ग्राम

१३ त्रयव्यतिरेकेण चान्यग्राम निवासिनान्न केषाञ्चि न्नेतुं लभ्यतेस्य च

१४ प्रसादस्य चिरस्थितये शिलापट्टक शासन मिदन्दत्त मेवं वेदिभिर्नं

१५ कैश्चिदय म्प्रसादोन्यथा करणीयो यस्त्वेतामाज्ञामतिक्रम्यान्यथा तिलम

१६ [क] न्नयेत्तस्यावश्यन्दण्ड: पातयितव्यो भविष्यद्भिरपि भूपतिभि:
     पूर्वरा

१७ ज कृत प्रसादा नुवर्तिभिरेव भवितव्यमिति अपि चात्र वाटिकानामुद्देश्य

१८ ····ग्रामस्य दक्षिणोद्देशे पूर्वेणारामं विमा रितिलमकस्य पश्चिमप्रदेशे मा⁵

१९ [दे] व कुलं पूर्वेण मा ४ सूलवाटिका ग्रामस्योत्तरत: अशिङ्क्रोप्रदेशे
     मा ६

२० ···प्रदेशे मा १ गाङ्शुल्ग्रामं⁶ पश्चिमेन कडम्प्रिङ्प्रदेशे मा ४कङ्कू लं प्रदेशे

२१ मा ४ स्वयमाज्ञा सम्वत् ४० ८ कार्त्तिक शुक्ल २ दूतको युवराज
     श्रीविष्णुगुप्त:

1. DV दितचित्तसन्तति । This expression occurs in 3 inscriptions of Dhruvadeva. The expression might be correct if we had not deciphered otherwise. But this is not a conjectural reading. Letters are readable.

2. DV सहितोनिरत्समात्सर्यं विशुद्धबुद्धि:; BLI श्रीध्रुवदेव[स्य]···
The expression सहित after ध्रुवदेव was used only once by Jiṣṇugupta while he ruled. पुरस्सर has been the common expression.

3. BLI गाङ्गुल ।

4. DV uses only भिर ।

5. BLI सर्वि ।

6. BLI गाङुल ।

XCVIII. Malitar Inscription

(BLI 9; Gn LI; DV 106; HJ 103) A slab of stone in Malitar, a village about 2 miles to the west of the village of Balambu, in the vicinity of Thankot. The top is damaged not to reveal any symbol. Date: *Samvat* 49 *Māgha kṛṣṇa* 12. The inscription is not well preserved. The inscribed part is 42 cm wide and 43 cm long.

१ स्वस्ति मानगृहाद् ⋯⋯⋯⋯लिच्छवि [कु]

२ [ल] केतु भंट्टारक महाराज श्रीध्रुवदेव⋯या सन्निवेश वि

३ ⋯यितसु⋯सदनुवि⋯[कैलासकूटभ] वनाद् विशुद्धपुण्यो

४ दितचित्तसन्नतिः पराक्रृतापाय⋯⋯धर्मस्थितिभूतशासनः

५ समस्त⋯⋯[भगवत्पशुपति भट्टार]क पादानु गृहीतो ब⋯

६ प्पपादानुध्यातः [श्रीजिष्णुगुप्त कुशली]⋯वृत्तिभुज स्तदाधिकृतांश्च

७ ⋯कुशल [माभाष्य] ⋯[विदितम्भवतु] भवतां माग्वलग्रामकुट्

८ [म्बि]नः ⋯प्रभुज्यमान मस्माभिः

९ ⋯⋯⋯न राय पातितां प्रणालीं

१० ⋯⋯⋯तः ख⋯क्षि⋯प्रवेशेन माग्गोल ग्रामपाञ्चा

११ [लिकानां] प्रसाद⋯विदित⋯वान कैश्चिदस्मप्रसा

१२ [द]⋯यो⋯स्मदा (ज्ञां) विलङध्यान्यथात्वमापादयेत्तद

१३ ⋯⋯भवितारस्तेरपि पूर्व्वं

१४ ⋯⋯गुरू⋯नुमोदनानुपालनीय

१५ ⋯⋯मवश्यं⋯न⋯य संवत् ४० ९

१६ [मा] घकृष्ण द्वादश्यां दूतक⋯युवराज श्रीविष्णुगुप्त इति

XCIX. Bhairavdhokā (southern gate) Inscription in Kathmandu

(BLI 10; Gn LII; DV 107; HJ 104) A slab of stone standing by the side of the road near the southern gate of Kathmandu opposite to the temple of Viṣṇu called Mīna-Nārāyaṇa. The stone is partially damaged. The top represents the relief of a chakra flanked by śankhas. The lines giving date symbols are missing. The inscribed part is 45 cm wide and 82 cm long.

The first 3 lines are in verse rendered in Sragdharā metre.

१   ॐ देहा᳴······व-यावञ्चितो दूरमात्मा पौरस्त्यमु पन्न

२   ······भिमुख हुंसित मिति सौङ्ङे रादिमे तञ्चान्य त्रिरत्न स्तवयि
      परवश······

३   न्दन या स्व सन्ध्या जलैर्वंः स्वकर मप हरन्त्य [बिघ] जासेश्वरा [श्रीः]

४   स्वस्ति मानगृ [हा]द्··· दितचित्त सन्तति लिच्छवी कुलकेतु भट्टारक
      [महा]

५   राज श्री   ध्रुवदेव पुरस्सरः सकल जननिरूपद्रवोपायसन्विधानार्पित
      [मा]
      नसः कैलासकूट भवनाद् भगवत्पशुपति भट्टारक पादानुगृहीतो वप्प

७   पादानुध्यातः श्रीजिष्णुगुप्तः कुशली दक्षिणकोलीग्रामे गीटा पाञ्चालिका

८   ······गान्कुशलमाभाष्य समनुदर्शयति विदितम्भवतु भवताम्···

९   ······समधिगतनय विधिज्ञाना दुपात्तायती रूपेणानुपमो गुणी*

१०   ···मृश म्पूजितः इत्येवम्प्रथितोपि यः प्रियहितम्प्र त्याद

११   ······न्वि···क्षिति भ्योशिन वलवन्तः शत्रुन्वभञ्ज स्वयमिच्छम्भू

१२   [ते]ना स्मदनुमोदितेन तदात्वायति

१३   ···ष्ठानं व्याप्रियमाणे [न]लो का नुग्रह प्रवृत्त चेतसा महासा [मन्त]

१४   श्रीजीवदेवेन यथायन्तिलमको भवताम्न्येषाञ्चोपकारायमा

१५   ······पिण्डक दशभागम्प्रत्याकलय्य भवन्द्विरे वोप संहर्तव्यः···

१६   ···श्वरस्वामिनः पूजा पाञ्चाली भोजनञ्च दिवस नियमेन य

१७   था तिलमक प्रतिसंस्कारश्च कालानन्तिक्रमणेव कार्य इत्येषो

१८   स्य पुण्याधिकारो व्यवस्था चास्मत्प्रसादोपजीविभि रन्यैर्वा न केश्चिद

१९   न्यथा करणीया यः कश्चिदेतामाज्ञामतिलङ्घ्यान्यथा कुर्यत्किारयेद्वा

२०   त···ज्ञातिक्रमकृतो वश्यमेव दण्डो विधातव्यो येप्यस्म द्कृत प्र[साद]**

२१   ······संभविष्यन्ति तेरप्यात्मीयः स्वपुण्याधिकारो स्मत्कृत प्रसाद

२२   ······स्य रक्षाया मनुपालने च···हितंभवित [व्यम्]

२३   ······स्यदेव······

२४   दत्तातः इति······

1. BLI, Gn देवा । 2. Gn omits वण्या and L reads वन्याइरत्त,
BLI reads यावस्थिति in place of वञ्चितो । 3. BLI यन्न । 4. Gn
भुख । 5. DV न्दनीयास्य सन्ध्या । 6. DV भृशम्पूजित; Gn has
blank space after भृ । 7. Gn ‥‥‥; DV ‥‥न्वितेत‥‥क्षितौवलवत:
but वलवन्त is distinct. 8. Gn omits जीव । 9. Not legible.
10. Legible. 11. DV तस्या[स्मदा] ज्ञाति but the letters are
totally destroyed. 12. BLI has just क्रम । 13. Gn स्य‥‥; DV
[दूध्वं] but letters are not readable. 14. DV [सतत]मवहि ।
15. DV त्र इति ।

*DV omits गुणी ।
**DV omits साद ।

C. Ādeśvara Śivaliṅga Inscription

(Gn LIII; DV 108; HJ 106) A slab of stone in the temple
of Ādeśvara (Sk. Ādīśvara) near Kathmandu. On the top of the
stone is a reclining bull in relief. The inscribed part is 50 cm
wide and 48 cm long. The date figures are damaged. The letters
are slightly damaged here and there in lines after 8.

१ स्वस्ति मानगृहादनेक दिगन्तर प्रथित पृथु पराक्रमो लिच्छवि कुला-
लङ्कार भूतो भट्टार

२ क महाराज श्रीध्रुवदेवस्तत्पुर: सर: कैलासकूट भवनाद् सुलभ नृपति
गुणावभासि

३ त सकल महीमण्डलो भगवत्पशुपति भट्टारक पादानुगृहीतो बप्पपादानु-
ध्यात:

४ श्रीजिष्णुगुप्त: कुशली छोगुंयुवीसामातलञ्जु ग्रामेषु निवासमुपगता
न्कुटुम्बिन: प्रधान पु

५ रस्सरान्कुशलमाभाष्य समाज्ञापयति विदितम्भवतु भवतां राजपुत्र
नन्दवर्मणा

६ स्वपितु:राजपुत्र जिष्णुवर्म्मणो मातुर्वत्सदेव्या भ्रातृणाञ्च श्रीभीमवर्म
प्रभृतीनां स्व

७ र्लोक सुखोपभोग परंपराविच्छेदहेतो भंगवतो नाथेश्वरस्य प्रतिष्ठानं
यत्तदस्यै

८   व प्रतिपादनाय   विज्ञप्तैरस्माभि स्तलञ्जुगामेषु···दक्षिणपश्चिमोत्तरा

९   णामद्रि श्रृङ्गाणाम्पानीय···स···रवस्···को

१० टृङ् कृत्वा प्रति [पादि] तमेव [म्बेदि] भि···परिपालनीय

११ ······प्यत्रपा···त्र·····

१२ प्रत···प्रतिप······ञ्च· क्षपयैरति······

१३ ····· विपाक······तदनुष्ठा···ह···ति नियमोस्य

१४ ······[दूतक] श्चात्र युवराज श्री विष्णुगुप्तः इति

1. Gn सलञ्जु but DV correctly reads तलञ्जु ।

2. DV reads correctly, but Gn reads नामति [सृष्टेन] ।

3. DV after नुस्ष्ठान adds महंन्तीति नियमोस्य ।
   Gn तदनु-हूं-ति-नियमोस्य ।

CI. Kevalpur Inscription

(Gn LIV; DV 109; Itihāsa Prakāśa I.i by Mahanta
Naraharinath; HJ 107) A slab of stone lying in a field in the
village of Kevalpur in west no. 1 district of Dhading on its
southern part. The top shows a relief of a reclining bull. The
date is lost as the last two lines are damaged. The inscribed part
is 43 cm wide and 75 cm long. The stone is well preserved.

१   ॐ स्वस्ति मानगृहात्सकलसत्वानुग्रहाहितमनोनिरभिमानर

२   मणीयचरित लिच्छविकुलकेतु भट्टारक महाराज श्रीध्रुव

३   देव पुरस्सरः प्रजाहितोद्युक्त विशुद्धमानसः प्रभाव [शौर्य] प्र

४   नतारि मण्डलः गुणैरूपेतो नृपमैरिहात्मवान् प्रिय···

५   मपि चन्द्रमाइव सोयमित्थम्भतः कैलाशकूट भवनाङ्गव

६   त्पशुपति भट्टारक पादानुगृहीतो बप्पपादानुध्यातः श्रीजिष्णु

७   गुप्तः कुशली नृप्पुन्न द्रङ्गनिवासिनः प्रधान पुरस्सरा न्कुटुम्बिनः

८   कुशलाग्रेसरं समाज्ञापयति विदितमस्तु वो भट्टारक महारा

९   ज श्रीवसुराज श्रीमहीदेव श्रीमानदेव श्रीगणदेवास्मत्पिताम

१० ह श्रीभूमगुप्त इत्येतैः पूर्व्वराजभि रस्मद्गुरुभिः परानुग्रह प्र

११ वृत्तितया शिलापट्टकशा [सन] तयेन वो यः प्रसादविशे [षै]

१२ रनुग्रह कृतोभूद्वान्ध·····निच द्वादश भाग वस्तुतो या

१३ नि प्रसादीकृतानि कैं [शिच]·····तया राजभोग्यतामापादितान्य

१४ स्माभिर्भवत्साहाय्यादि कर्म परितुष्टैः शतद्वय न्नुष्पुन्ने भगव

१५ न्नारायणास्वामिनो भवद्भिरेव कारणपूजादि प्रवर्तनार्थम्प्रतिपा

१६ दितन्दशशतानि भवतामेव पूर्वराजकृत व्यवस्थया प्रतिमुच्य

१७ दङ्खुट्टार्थादिकरणीय प्रतिमोचनार्थ लिङ्ग्वल्शोल्लादीनाम प्रवे

१८ शाय पूर्वराज शासनेषु ये प्रसादा स्तेषाम् सर्वेषामेव [युष्म]

१९ दतिसृष्टाना मनुमति शासन मिद मस्माभिरपि प्रसादी [कृत]

२० मेवंवेदिभिं भंवद्भि रस्मत्प्रसादप्रतिबद्धजीवनैरन्यैर्वा [न कैशिच]

२१ दियमाज्ञान्यथा करणीया यस्त्वेतामाज्ञामुत्क्र [म्यान्यथा करि]

२२ ष्यते कारयिष्यते वा तस्योत्पथ [गासिनः][1]······

२३ ······दण्ड[2]···वि···ये····

1. DV व [तिनः] ।   2. DV दण्ड,ᶠGn ण् ।

CII. Balambu (Dhakasitol) Inscription

(Gn LV; DV 110; HJ 108) A slab of stone standing on a deserted place outside the village of Balambu near the dilapidated temple of Mahalakṣmī. The top is too much damaged to reveal any symbol. The inscribed part is 43 cm wide and 112 cm long. The date is Samvat 55 Āśvayuja (Āśvina) śukla 5.

१ [ॐ स्वस्ति मानगृहाद्]··········नो नयनाभिरामो

२ [लिच्छवि] कुलकेतु भट्टारक महाराज श्रीभीमार्जुन

३ [देवस्त] त्पुरस्सरः कैलासकूट भवनादतिमहापुण्य[1]

४ ·······पदाप लक्ष्मीपरिष्वङ्को भगवत्पशुप

५ ति भट्टारक पादानुगृहीतो बप्पपादानुध्यातः श्रीजि

६ ण्णगुप्तः कुशली गीनुङ् वृत्तिभुजो दिग्वार वृत्ति भुजश्च य

७ थार्हम्प्रतिमान्यानुदर्शयति विदितम्भवतु भवता

८ मस्साभिर्जोल्प्रिङ्ग्रामे स्वादु शुचिशीतल सलिलाम्भो[2]

९ ····हृजनि कीम्पातयित्वा प्रणालीमस्या एवानुपालन हेतोः गीनु[3] [ङ्]

१० भूमौसरलाराम ङ्वारयित्वा स॰॰॰ण्डुदेव कुलदिग्ब्वार वस्तु स

११ हि [तं] जोल्प्रिङ्ग्राम पाञ्चालिकानां चैलकरं प्रतिमुच्य प्रसादीकृतं

१२ तस्याइच गीनुड्वृत्ते सीमा पश्चिमेन ह्वागुं मार्ग खातकः उत्तरे

१३ ण तैडोस्थल दक्षिण खातकः पूर्वेण नतिदुल् दक्षिणेन कंशम

१४ सान खातकः ततः॰॰॰॰॰॰मार्गं खातकः इत्येतर्सीम परिरिक्षि

१५ प्तायाम्भूमावसमतप्रसादोप[जीविभिरन्यै] र्वनि कैश्चिदप्यल्पापि पी [डा]

१६ करणीया ये त्वेता मा [ज्ञामुलङ्] ध्यान्यथा कुर्युः कारयेयु

१७ र्वां तानत्यर्थमेव वयन्न मर्षयिष्यामो भविष्यद्भिरपि भूपतिभिः

१८ पूर्वं भूपति धर्माधिकारानुपालनादृतै र्भवितव्यं चिरकालस्थित

१९ ये चास्य धर्माधिकारस्य शिलापट्रकशासन मिदन्दत्तमिति स्वयमाज्ञा

२० दूतक श्चात्रत्र युवराज श्रीविष्णु गुप्तः संवत् ५० ५ आश्वयुज शुक्ल
      पञ्चम्याम्

1. DV दति॰॰॰॰; Gn दभिमत [पुण्य]॰॰॰॰ 2. Gn स्त्रावजनिकीम, which also goes to the next line· 3. Not at all clear· 4. Gn तैलकर। 5. Gn न्ह्वाकं। 6. Gn शुंशुशान। 7. DV इत्येतर्सीम; Gn ततः स॰॰॰कइत्यैव etc·

CIII. Yengahiti (Kathmandu) Inscription

(Gn LVIII, DV; HJ III) A slab of stone standing in the courtyard of a water conduit called Yengahiti, Kathmandu. The inscribed part is 36 cm wide and 75 cm long. The top of the stone shows in relief a chakra flanked by two śankhas. The date is lost as the last lines are eroded. Some five lines are mutilated.

१ ॐ स्वस्ति मातगृहादभिनवोदित दिवस करकराधिकतर

२ दीप्त यशोम्शुमाली लिच्छविकुलतिलको भट्टारक महाराज

३ श्रीभीमार्जुनदेव स्तत्सहितश्च नरपतिगुण सम्पद् भूषितो

४ भूरि जागत॰॰॰॰शशि शुभान्ङ्कीर्त्ति मुच्चैर्दधानः मुदितजन

५ ॰॰॰॰न मान्य॰॰॰रायप्रमथित रिपुपक्षो देशसौर्ख्यैक

६ चित्तो भगवत्पशुपति भट्टारक पादानुगृहीतो वप्पपादानु

७ ध्यातः श्रीजिष्णुगुप्तः कुशली दक्षिण कोलीग्राम निवासनो

८ ब्राह्मण प्रधान पुरः सरान् सर्वं पाञ्चाली कुटुम्बिनः कुशलमभि

९ धाय समाज्ञापयति विदितम्भवतु भवतां यो युष्माकम्म

१० ल्लकरः पूर्वं···· ··इचतुभिस्तान्त्रिकपणैः प्रतिमु

११ क्तो भूदस्माभि···········[प] णाः प्रतिमुक्ता मल्लपोतकानाम

१२ पि मर्यादा·······समलङ्कृत्य यन्निष्क्रमणन्तदपि प्रतिमुक्त

१३ म्भट्टाबिक [रण]·······बस्तु ना च यूयन्नानुस्मर

१४ णीया इत्य·······प्रसादीकृतं शक्त वाट करणीय

१५ स्तु [चतु] भि [स्तान्त्रिक] पणैः प्रतिमुक्तो····तपन नदी देवकुल प्रासाद

१६ स्य··· त्य··पुरुष····कृ····जातीव्य

१७ कालघर····यज्यते स···न्द्रूर···कृता···दे

१८ धनीय······सादाशी····य इ-प···

१९ वः प्र [सादः] कृ [त]·······[द]

२० क्षिणकोली [ग्रामे]······

२१ ष्यते··········

२२ त्रिभि···········

२३ नीय·········

२४ ति इ···········

1. Gn जाजीत्य ।

CIV. Chaṇḍeśvara Pillar Inscription

(BLI II; Gn LIX; DV 112; HJ 112) A pillar of stone supporting a parasol against which leans a naked image of Chaṇḍeśvara standing a little to the south of the southern gate of the temple of Paśupati. The date is missing in the lines damaged. The inscribed part is 21 cm wide and 75 cm long.

The metre used is Sragdharā.

१ सम्यग्ज्ञानादि युक्तः सक

२ [ल] गुणगणं क्षोभयित्वा प्र

३ धानम् ब्रह्मादिस्थावरान्त

४ ज्जगदिदम खिलं यो सृज

५   द्विशचरूपम् श्राजीव्यं सर्व्व

६   पुं'साञ्झिरितरु गहनं यः करो¹

७   त्येक रूपम् पायात्सोड्ड प्रस

८   न्नः स्मरतदनु वहन इछत्रन्न च

९   ण्डेश्वरो वः स्वस्ति श्री जिष्णुगुप्त²

१०   स्य प्रवर्द्धन मान विजयराज्ये श्रा

११   चार्य भगवत्प्रनर्द्दन प्राणकौ

१२   शिकेन भगवतः इछत्रचण्डेश्वरस्य

१३   ताकू ग्रामेप्रणाल्नीकाया इच ख³

१४   [ण्ड] स्फुटित समाधानार्थंमुद्दि

१५   [श्य] मुण्डश्रृह्वलिकपाशुपता चा

१६   यं पर्षदि वाराहस्वामि धर्म⁴

१७   सोम⁵ छत्रसोमखड्डुका⁶ नाञ्च अशी

१८   ति पिण्डक मानिकानां भू प्रतिपादि

१९   ताः [ता] सम्प्रदत्ता लिख्यन्ते पिखु

२०   ग्रामे मा १० शाफना दुलके⁷ मा २०

२१   पागुमके मा ५ पोग्रामे मा २ खू

२२   ल्प्रिङ्ग्राम मा ६ भूयो मा १५ वि⁸

२३   [ङ्] शतिक यैते⁹ अथान्या इचतुर्विशतिकया

२४   यच्च के···अत्र विशति मानिकया

२५   ···६ मासवद···शेषाः श्रृह्वलिकया¹⁰

२६   ···मा···वाराहस्वामि प्रभृतिभिः···

२७   योक्तव्या पालन योज्या देश

२८   ···किन स्तम्भलिखित ॥¹¹

There are 2 or 3 lines more which are not readable.

1. BLI गहनंयं । 2. DV omits श्री । 3. Gn कुग्रामे, etc, BLI omits ता । 4. BLI धर्म; DV उमसोमऋसोम; Gn उमसोमाऋसोम etc. 5. BLI ····सोम etc. 6. DV डु । 7. Gn साफन etc; BLI सामन्त । 8. BLI लपेङ । 9. BLI ····यैति । 10. BLI शेषाः । 11. BLI omits lines 27 and 28.

CV. Chaṇḍeśvara base Inscription

(BLI 11; Gn LIX; DV 113; HJ 113) On the pedestal of the image of Chaṇḍeśvara given above. The inscribed part is about 30 cm wide and 6 cm long. There is no date. There are only two lines in the inscription, which constitute a verse in Śārdūlavikriḍita.

१ ॐ सम्यग्धर्मपदानुरक्त मतिमद्वर्णाश्रमोद्वासितो आचार्यो भगवत्प्रनदंन
इह श्रद्धान्वितो चीकरत्

२ ⋯पाति गुणानु रक्षित जने श्रीजिष्णु गुप्ते महीम् शम्भोरावरणं सुरासुर
गुरो स्संसार पाशच्छिदः ॥

1. Gn reads परम⋯⋯ instead of मतिमद्वर्णा श्रमोद्वासितो which is also DV's reading. 2. Gn कृत्वा पाणि⋯नु⋯ी⋯श्री । 3. Gn omits शम्भोरा ।

CVI. Thankot Inscription

(L 16; Gn LVI; DV 115; HJ 114) A slab of stone standing on the street at Narayantol in the village of Thankot. On the top of the stone is represented in relief a chakra flanked by śankhas. Date: Samvat 59 Kārtika śukla 2. The stone is not well preserved. The inscribed part is 43 cm wide and 100 cm long. As Gnoli says 'The date Samvat 57 still visible at the beginning of the last line, and the name of the king Bhīmārjunadeva are erroneously read by Levi, 500, and the ruler's name as Mānadeva.'

The verse in 1 to 4 lines is in Sragdharā metre.

१ ॐ तर्जन्या कर्णकण्डुमुपशमन सुखोन्मीलिता घर्षणस्य

२ श्री निःसंगोपगूढ स्तन कलशयुगं स्पर्श रोमाञ्चितस्य

३ माया सुप्तो स्थितस्यस्फूट जलधि जल क्षालिताङ्कस्य शौरेः

४ भूयात्पर्यस्तहस्त स्थगित मुखशशि श्रेयसां जृम्भितं व:

५ स्वस्ति मानगृहा त्सिङ्घासना ध्यासि कुलकेतु भंट्टारक श्रीभीमा [र्जु]

६ न देवस्तत्पुर: सर: कैलास कूट भवनात्सोमान्वय भूषणो

७ भगवत्पशुपति भट्टारक पादानुगृहीतो वप्पपादानुध्यात: श्री

८ जिष्णु गुप्तदेव: कुशली थेञ्चोग्रामनिवासिन: कुटुम्बिनो यथा

९ प्रधानङ्कुशलमाभाष्य समाज्ञापयति विदितम्भवतु भवतां

१० अस्मत्प्ये प्रपितामह मानगुप्त गोमि कारित पुष्किरिणीमु

११ द्विश्य ग्रामस्योत्तरेण पर्वतभूमि इचोख्परानाम घेय चैलकर

१२ स्प्रतिमुच्य दत्ता तस्याश्च कालान्तरेण शासनान्तर्भवि मभूत

१३ [द] वेत्य प्रपितामह कृतज्ञतयास्माभिरिदं शिलापट्टक शास

१४ [नञ्चि] रतरकाल स्थितये दत्तं सीमा चास्योत्तर पूर्वेण पूर्वे

१५ ण शिखरो पर्यधोगोमिखातक मनुसृत्य पश्चात्पानीय

१६ पात: पूर्व दक्षिणैनैव येब्रंखरो दक्षिणेन थम्बिदुल् ततोनुसृत्य

१७ दक्षिणैनैव सुरिसिवत्ती दक्षिणेन नदी दक्षिण पश्चिमेन श

१८ लङ्घा पश्चिमेन खातक स्ततो नुसृत्य पहञ्चो ततो लुम्बङ्चोत्तरे

१९ ण तत्पर्वत शिखर मूर्धनि खातक स्ततो यावत्स एवोत्तरपूर्व

२० खातक इति अन्यश्चास्माभि: प्रयोजनान्तराराधितं भंवतां ग्राम

२१ णिवासिनां कुटुम्बिनाम्प्रसाद विशेषो दत्तो दक्षिण कोलिग्रा [मे]

२२ गोयुद्धे गोहले गोहले यद्देयमासीत्तस्यार्धम्प्रति मुक्तम् सितु

२३ करेच येन कार्षापण न्देयन्तेनाष्टौ पणा देया येनाष्टौ

२४ पणा देयं तेन पण चतुष्टयं मल्लकरे च पण चतुष्ट

२५ यन्देयमिति यस्त्वेतामाज्ञामुल्लङ्ध्यास्मत्प्रसादोपजी

२६ व्यन्यो वा कश्चिदन्यथा कुर्यात्कारयेद्वा तम्वयन्न म

२७ र्षयिष्यामो भविष्यन्द्भिरपि भूपतिभि: पूर्वराज [कृ]

२८ तज्ञतया धर्मापेक्षया चेदं शासनं प्रतिपालनी

२९ यं दूतकश्चात्र युवराज: श्री विष्णुगुप्त:

३० संवत् ५० ७ ......शुक्ल दिवा द्वितीयायाम्

1. DV कण्डूमू but the other letters in the line read by him are correct. Gn तर्ज-कर्णकण्ड-प-ह्र सुखोन्मीलिता········, L श्राज्ञाकरण कण्ठ····सुखे···ा···ा···· 2. Gn reads after युग letters स्थान····, L युगस्सागरो···· 3. L omits स्थित; Gn स्थित····जलधि etc upto शो। 4. L स्थगोप। 5. L omits भूयात्पर्य। 6. DV correctly reads but Gn····त्पर्या····सुख। 7. DV reads मुखशशि। 8. L reads श्रीमानदेव। 9. L काचण्णस्त। 10. L न कुटुम्बिनो should be in the 8th line but he puts it on the 9th. 11. L स्वप्रपितामह्। 12. L साघच्च। 13. Gn नैल्यकां; L स्तरवरंनामयाचेलक। 14. शासनं तदुडमस्यत्त-त्य beginning from the upper line. 15. L reads beginning from the end of the upper line पूर्व पूर्वम्। 16. L पञ्चपानीयंयता। 17. L धारिग्मदेल। 18. L वास्तरिसिवत्ती। 19. L लम्पञ्चो। 20. L तुपर्वंत। 21. L सववोनर। 22. Gn सि, L सिंह, DV सि and ends the line but joins it with कर of the next to make it one word but there is another letter after सि in the same line which DV did not notice. 23. L उल्लंध्या; Gn डल्लंध्या। 24. L पूर्वंराजाज्ञातया। 25. L reads the year figure as 500.

CVII. Maligaon Stone Inscription

(Gn LVII; DV 116; HJ 115) A slab of stone in a place called Maligaon, Kathmandu (now in the National Museum). The top of the stone which is now badly damaged is decorated with a chakra and two śankhas. Date: Samvat 59 as read by Gnoli and 57 as read by DV. The inscribed part is 39 cm wide and 62 cm long. As for the date DV is correct.

१ [ॐ स्वस्ति] कैलासकूट भ [वना] द्·······

२ ···········वय··············

३ ·······················

४ ·······················

५ ·······················

६ ·······················

७ ·······················

८ ....
ε ···मा·· कारेण······
१० ··व केवलमि····भिः···हित····
११ ···व्यवस्थेय मुपदा···त ··पत्याबुपरते नष्टे प्रब्रजितेपि वा पतितेपिपत्या[1]
१२ दृष्टे योषितामपरः पति इत्येव······मादिभिः कारणैरपरैरपि का[2]
१३ रणान्तरे विवाहात्पतन काल सङ्ग्रहणेनापर[3]ं पतिमुपयाता[4] नि
१४ रपत्या योषितो ज्ञाति भिः व···या···यदि परिभ्रश्यान्यत्पत्यन्तर
१५ मुपाददत एवं द्वितीयं सङ्ग्रह [मुप] याता निः [पु] त्रवत्यो भविष्यन्ति तां मा
१६ प्चोकाधिकारोयं यथाव्यवस्थम्प्रवर्तंयितव्य स्तास्वप्य तासु यतीसारूप्य
१७ कन्तन्नाम्ना परिभाषिताञ्च धनं तम्माप्चोक वृत्तिभुजा ग्राह्यं ततोपि पुरुषप
१८ रितोष मभावयित्वा बहुशोपि व्यपेतलज्जाप्रखलस्वभावा श्चारित्र धर्मौ पग
१९ ता युवतयः सन्तोषहीना प्रथमे विरक्ता रागानुषक्ताः पुरुष भजन्ते*
२० तापि यदि पुत्रवत्यो भविष्यन्ति नैव माप्चोकाधिकार भागधेया
२१ यास्त्वेतामतीतानेक नरपतिकृत व्यवस्था नुगामिनी मस्मद्व्यवस्थामन्य
२२ था कुर्यात्तं वयमत्यर्थं न मर्षयिष्यामो भाविभिरपि भूपतिभिरिदमस्म
२३ त्कृतं देशपीडापरिहारनिष्ठं शासनमात्मीयमिव पूर्वराजगुरुतया
२४ सम्यगनुपालनीयमिति समाज्ञापना संवत् ५० ७ फाल्गुन शुक्ल
२५ सप्तम्यां दूतकोत्र श्रीयुवराज श्रीधर गुप्तः

*Metre upajāti of Indravajrā and upendravajrā, a mixture of the two.

1. DV correctly reads but Gn has त-रिप-य-ष्टे-प्रश्रवि-पि-पति-पि ।
2. DV is correct but Gn leaves out the का of the end····मादि-कारणैरपरै··· 3. Gn संग्रह्यंयेनापरं । 4. DV puts न्य in the next line, which is wrong.

CVIII. Inscription of Bhimārjuna and Visnugupta at Yangahiti

(Gn LXI; DV 117; HJ 116) A slab of stone in the courtyard of a water conduit called Yangahiti in the south of the city

of Kathmandu. The top shows a chakra flanked by śankhas.
The inscribed part is 43 cm wide and 75 cm long. Date:
Samvat 64 Phālguna śukla dvitīya.

१   ॐ अनन्तनागाधिपभोग भासुरे जलाशये शान्ततमम्मनोहरं

२   मुरारिरूपं यदशेत देहिनां शिवाय तद्वो विदधातु मङ्गलं*

३   स्वस्ति मानगृहात्सकल जन निरूपद्रवोपायसम्बिधानैक

४   चित्तसन्तानो लिच्छविकुलकेतु भट्टारक महाराज श्रीभीमार्जुन

५   देवस्तत्सहित: श्रीमत्कैलासकूट भवनाद् परिमिता भिमत

६   नृपति गुणकलापाविष्कृत मूर्तिरनववदात् ज्ञानमयू

७   खापसारित सकलरिपु तिमिर सञ्चयो भगवत्पशुपति भट्टार

८   क पादानुगृहीतो वप्पपादानुध्यात: श्रीविष्णु गुप्त: कुशली भवि

९   ष्यतो नेपाल भू भुजो यथाहंस्प्रतिमान्यान् दर्शयति विदितम

१० स्तु भवतां सकलजगद वसानोदयैक कारणस्योदारतरम

११ हिमावाप्ति निधान भूतस्य भगवतो विष्णोर्जलशयनरूपनि

१२ ष्पादन योग्य वृहच्छिलाकर्षण व्यापार परितुष्टैरस्माभिर्दक्षिण को

१३ लीग्रामस्य पूर्वमेव द्रङ्ग चतुर्भागित्वेन प्रविभक्तस्यै तत्सीम निवा

१४ सिनाम्पदक केयूर नूपुरा न्वर्जयित्वान्यै: प्रसादाभरणपरिभो

१५ गै: प्रसाद: कृतो येषाञ्चैतत्स्थान निवासिनाम्प्रसादाभरणानि पूर्व

१६ प्रभृत्यैव विद्यमानानि तेषामयमधिकोस्मत्प्रसादो ये वा पुनरे

१७ तद्द्रङ्ग चतुर्भागिसीमाभ्यन्तर वर्तिन इचौर परदार हत्या राजद्रोहका

१८ पराधम वाप्न् यु स्तेषामेवामुनापराधेन दोषवतां यदात्मी

१९ यमेव गृहक्षेत्रगोधनादि द्रब्यं [त] देव राजकुला···मेतद्वो

२० षाभिशप्तानां ये दायादास्तेभ्यो·······न्यायेनायमल्पमपि·····क्

२१ ष्टव्य मित्येष च भवता······समत्कृत प्रसादोप [कारा]

२२ र्थो भविष्यद्दभिरपि भूप [तिभि:]······स्वकृत निर्विशिष्ट ष्टादिनां

२३ मन्यमानै···नुपालनीय:······रनियमास्तैरपि नैष···

२४ मल्पापि [वाधा] विधेया यदि पुनरे तदाज्ञा रतिक्रमेणान्यथा प्र [वति]

२५ ष्यन्ते नि [तरामे] ब ते न मर्षयितव्या इति प्रति[पालना]
    संवत् ६० ४

२६ फाल्गुन शुक्ल द्वितीयायाम् दूतकश्चात्र श्रीयुवराज श्रीधरगुप्त:

*The metre is Vaṁsasthavila.

1. DV रनवदात ।   2. Gn राजकु····रे ।   3. Gn·······न्यायेनायमपि;
DV as in our text. 4. DV तिक्रमेणदान्यथा; Gn ····नान्यथा । 5. Gn
प्रति[पालना] ।

CIX. Bhṛṅgāreśvara Temple Inscription

(Gn LXII; DV 118; HJ 117) A slab of stone placed in
front of the western gate of the temple of Bhṛṅgāreśvara in the
village of Sonaguthi about 2 miles from Patan. The top of the
stone has a floral design. The inscribed part is 42 cm wide and
56 cm long. Date: *Samvat 65 Phālguṇa śukla dvitīyā*.

१   ॐ सम्यक्प्रभाव गुण विस्तर मन्त्रभाजां न ज्ञेयता मुपगतो नृसुरा
     सुराणाम्

२   तोयाशये भुजग भोगवर प्रसुप्तो विष्णुः सवो दिशतु दिव्य सुखानि
     नित्यम्*

३   स्वस्ति मानगृहादमलिनकुशलविपाकोपनत सम्पल्लिच्छवि कुलकेतु
     भंट्टार

४   क महाराज श्रीभीमार्जुनदेवस्तत्सहितः कैलासकूट भवनादतिमात्र
     वस्तुपरि

५   प्रापणोत्सवोपगत हर्षाभिनमस्यमान चरणयुगलो भगवत्पशुपति भट्ट

६   रकपादानुगृहीतो बप्पपादानुध्यातः श्रीविष्णुगुप्तः कुशली भविष्यतो
     नेपाल

७   [भूभु] जो यथाहं स्प्रतिमान्यानुदर्शयत्यस्तु वः समधिगतमसुरासुरं
     नमस्कृतात्य

८   ······गुणसमधिरूढ प्रसाद वेगेरस्माभिराश्चर्यं भूत

९   ······[रू] पनिष्पादन योग्य शिलाकर्षणम्प्रतिनियुक्तै भ ़ङ्गार
     ग्रामपाञ्चा

१० [लिकें]········परया तुष्टया कशष्ठी विष्टि भारा नयन प्रति रा

११ ········मप्रवेशेन प्रसादः कृतो माप्चोक वस्तुना य

१२ ···त··यस्ततोपि पाञ्चालिका····वप्रति···या···गृ

१३ हीतव्य···न्य···विचारणीयमत्वाधिकरण···णान्न···वक्ता

१४ ···मन्त्रेण सर्वंकार्याणामेवास्मरण मित्येव···प्रसादो दत्त श्चौर परदार ह

१५ त्या राजद्रोहिकापराधांश्च प्राप्नुवतो यदचिन्त्यङ्क्रू···लीप्रतिवद्धगृह क्षेत्र

१६ गवादिना स्वद्रव्येणैव···जयितव्य स्तद्दायादेभ्यो नात्रापहारः कर्तव्य

१७ वः प्रसादो दत्त एवं वेदिभि रेतेष्वधिकारेष्वधिक्तैर्तेषा मल्पापि बाधाविधे

१८ [या] ये पुनरे तदाज्ञा समतिक्रमेण प्रवर्तिष्यन्ते तान्वयन्न मर्षयिष्यामो येपि मदू

१९ द्वम्भूजो भविष्यन्ति तैरप्येते धर्माधिकारोपयोगपरितोषकृताः प्रसादविशे

२० षाः स्वकृताः इव मन्यमानैरस्माभिर्यथानुपाल्यन्ते तथैव नुपालनीया इति प्रति

२१ मानना संवत् ६० ५ फाल्गुन शुक्ल द्वितीयायाम् दूतकश्चात्र श्रीयुवराज श्रीधरगुप्तः

*The metre is Vasantatilakā.

1. Gnoli does not read सम्यक् and then keeps space vacant after स्तर upto सुरा । 2. Gn omits तोयाशये and also after वर upto दिव्या । 3. Gn विशालो । 4. Gn स्था । 5. Gn भ । 6. Gn नम्नसी for मनस्य । 7. Gn गुणो for युगलो । 8. Gn न्तृङ्मरि for भृङ्गार । 9. DV हीत for Gn's ष्प···न्य··· 10. DV प्राप्नुवतो but Gn वतो वि···· ये····ङ्ररग् । 11. DV is correct but Gn does not read. 12. Gn reads भूपा but DV reads भुजो which is correct. 13. Gn reads पालना; DV reads प्रति मानना and this is correct.

CX. Changu Temple Stone

(DV 119; HJ 118) A slab of stone inside the temple of Changu Narayana, which talks of Vishnugupta as a ruler (*rājā*); The inscribed part is 48 cm wide and 12 cm long.

१ ॐ निर्भेदं यद्विकारैः समनुगतमिवोपाधिभेदोपचारादज्ञान भ्रान्तिभाजा मविषयमबहिः साधनाधीनतृप्ति

२ भक्तिश्रद्धाप्रसादस्थिरकरण मनोभावनाभ्यासगम्यम्पायात्तद् भूतभर्तुः
सकलगुणगणातीततत्त्वम्पदं वः

३ याङ्कीर्तेः केतुभूतां सरितमिह पुरानीतवान्भोगवर्मा द्वारे दोलासुरेन्द्र
क्षितिधर शिखराध्यासिनः शार्ङ्गपाणेः

४ दृष्ट्वा कालेन जीर्णा विषमगिरितटेष्वध्वनौ विप्रकर्षात्संस्काराधानवित्त
व्यय विधुरतया छिन्न वारि प्रवाहाम्

५ भूयः शैलेन्द्र कुक्षेरमृतरसपयोवाहिनीमापशान्तामाकृष्यातिप्रयत्ना-
त्सकलजनहिताधान निम्नान्तरात्मा

६ राज्ञे श्रीविष्णु गुप्त क्षितितलशशिने कल्पयामास पित्रे···ी···प्रणाली
द्वितय······विष्णुगुप्तः ॥*

*The metre is Sragdharā.

CXI. Tebahal Inscription

(Gn LXIII; DV 120; HJ 119) A slab of stone attached
on the southern wall, which is a water reservoir in the
large quadrangle of Te-Bahal to the right of the temple of
Sankaṭā (it is very close to the New Road) in the eastern side.
The inscribed part is about 23 cm wide and 26 cm long. The
inscription lacks date. The characters seem to belong to the
later Lichhavi period. There are only two lines, and the object
is a gift of a Buddhist layman.*

१ रत्नत्रयम्भगवदार्य्य मुदार वर्णं मुद्दिश्य सत्व परिभोगनिमित्तमेतौ[1]

२ कूपञ्जल द्रवणिका ञ्च शुभाय पित्रोः शाक्यो यतिर्विहितवान्प्रियपाल
नामा

1. Gn, DV तां ।

*The metre is Vasantatilakā.

CXII.

A seal discovered in the excavation site at Dhumvārāhi,
a suburb of Kathmandu in the north east.

१ धर्मा हेतुप्रभवा
२ हेतु स्तेषान्तथागतो ह्वाव
३ दत्तेषाञ्च यो निरोध: एवं
४ वादी महा श्रमण:

CXIII.

A seal discovered at the excavation site of Dhumvārāhi.

ये धर्म हेतु प्रभवा हेतु स्तेषा न्तथागतो ह्वावद तेषाञ्च यो
निरोध एवं वादी महा श्रमण

CXIV. Inscription of Chobar

(HJ 105) Chobar is the name of the gorge cut by the
river Bagmati through the rocky plateau, near which a shrine
of Gaṇeśa amidst a cluster of houses is situated. Here a site
known as charghare (four houses) bears a large stone rock-like
in appearance on which the following lines are engraved. But
the letters are heavily damaged, and it is difficult to assign a
meaning to them. Perhaps this is a charter, as names of two
offices of State occur and it could be guessed that their entry
was barred in a certain locality. The inscription also does not
show any date.

१ ······लाल······कुप···
२ ······भी अदृश्य वी······ण···
३ ······भोल्ल भु······
४ मंन···री···सर···सित···कुलकेतुना······राजा

५   प्रजाहितायविधानसम्प्रत्य [स] चात्र पार्थिव···

६   ···नमि भवतु [का] मपराधीनादपि···माता स्व···

७   ···दि···विज्ञ···म···वहुमानाद्य···

८   ····पर शोल्ल लिग्वल···पू···

९   ······म···वद···न प्रवेष्ठव्य···श्रीवर्मरेव

१० ···   ···पाञ्चालि···ता माज्ञापयत

११ ···   ···म्भूभुजे···श्रीजेन···

१२ ···   ···   ···धर्मलोकस्य तथा

१३ ···   ···   कोत्नारां···

१४ ···   ···   ···

CXV. Yampibahi (Patan) Inscription

(Gn LXIV; HJ 120; DV 122) A water conduit slab of
stone being a reservoir (now not in use) placed in the quadrangle
of the Karunachok in Yampibahi (old monastery) in the north
east of the city of Patan. The inscribed line is just one and is
about 40 cm wide and 3½ cm long.

१   ॐ महाप्रतिहार वार्त्त सुजातप्रभु¹ विहारस्य

1. DV प्रभ; Gn प्रभु ।

CXVI. Luñjhya (Patan Palace) Inscription

(Gn LXVII; DV 123; HJ 123, Sans. San.) A slab of stone
in the courtyard of Luñjhya (golden window), a part of the old
palace, in Patan. The top of the stone shows a chakra flanked
by two śankhas. The inscribed part is 33 cm wide and 45 cm
long. The date is *Samvat 67 Pauṣa śukla pañchamyām* (5).

१   [ॐ स्वस्ति] कैलासकूट भवनाद् भुवनप्रकाशाज्ज्योत्स्ना वमृष्ट
    हिमवच्छिख

२ [राग्र] दीप्ते: आसागर प्रसृत शुभ्र यशो ध्वजानां राज्ञाङ्कुलाम्बर
   शशी भु

३ [वि लि] च्छवीनाम् ।। व ल्गद्वीरपदातिकुन्तविशि ख प्रोताश्वनागा
   कुले शक्त्यान्य

४ स्पृहिणीयया रणमुखे संज्ञावशेषा द्विष: कृत्वा लोक हितोद्यम प्रभ

५ [बया] कीर्या दिशो भासयन्नन्योन्या विहता न्प्रजा सुविदध द्वर्मार्थ
   कामान्मुदा*

६ भगवत्पशुपति भट्टारक पादानुगृहीतो वप्पपादानुध्यातो भट्टारक

७ महाराजाधिराज श्रीनरेन्द्रदेव: कुशली इहत्यान्भूमिभुजो वर्तमाना

८ न्भविष्यतश्च प्रतिमान्यानुदर्शयति विदितमस्तु भवतां कस्मिश्चिद्वस्तुन्युप

९ कृतमवेत्या तत्प्रत्युपकारोत्कण्ठित मतिभि रस्माभिर्यूपग्राममद्रङ्गस्य स

१० वंतल सहितस्यभट्टामाप्चोकाधिकारियो: प्रा [व] ल्यादवश्यं जनस्य
   महती

११ पीडेत्यन योरे वाधिकारयोरप्रवेशेन प्रसाद: कृतस्तदेवं विदितार्थै रे

१२ तदधिकार द्वयाधिकृतै रन्यैर्वास्मत्पाद प्रतिबद्ध जीवनै रल्पापि वाधा न का

१३ र्या यस्त्वेतामाज्ञामनाद्रत्यान्यथा कुर्यात्कारयेद्वा तस्यावश्यमस्मदस्ती
    व्रतरो

१४ दण्ड: पतिष्यत्यस्मदूर्ध्वम्भाविविभिरपि भूपतिभिस्सुकृतकरणैकसाधना

१५ मूर्जिताम्प्रतिजन्म राज्यश्रियस्समनुवुभूषद्भिरिह कीर्यांघुरारोग्यकल्याण

१६ राज्यश्री समुदय मोहमानै: प्रेत्य च शाश्वतन्दिव्यमिच्छद्भि: सुखमनु

१७ भवितुं दिक्षु चाभित शरदाप्यानोडुराजामल किरणमाला बभास्यमान
    प्रालेयम

१८ हीधरोत्तुङ्ग शिखरामलं यशस्तन्वद्भिरा चन्द्रार्कं स्वप्रतिपादितानां
    शासनानां स्थिति

१९ मिच्छद्भि: पूर्वभूपतिषु सगौरवैर्भर्त्वेयमाज्ञा सम्यक्प्रतिपालनीयापि
    चेत

२० त्प्रत्युपकृतन्न बहुमन्यमानै रस्माभि: पुनरप्येषां पीटल्जाधिकार म्प्रति-
    मुच्य

२१ प्रसादीकृत मेबमथँ विदित्वैं नदधिक्रितैर्नं कैश्चिदेतद्गता पीडा कर्तव्या
    यस्तु कु

२२ र्यात्सोस्माभि नं मृष्यते तथैव भूपतिभिरप्यनुमोदनीयं चिरस्थितये
    चास्य

२३   प्रसादस्य शिलापट्टक शासनेन प्रसाद: कृत:इति⁴ स्वयमाज्ञा दूतकश्चात्र

२४   [कुमारा] मात्य प्रियजीव: संवत् ६० ७ पौष⁵ शुक्ल पञ्चम्याम्

1. Gn, DV दिप्ते: ।   2. Gn reads भावद्धि and thinks that it is
a mistake for भाविभि or भविष्यद्धि: ।   3. Gn reads दिप्यम् and a
mistake for दिव्यम् । 4. DV कृत: इति, Gn कृत इति । 5. Gnoli
reads the year symbol as 69.

*Metre: Śārdūlavikriḍita.

CXVII. Yangahiti Inscription of Narendradeva

(Gn LXVI; DV 124; HJ 120) A slab of stone standing
in the water conduit of Yangahiti, Lagan Tol, Kathmandu.
The top of the stone shows in relief a chakra flanked by two
śankhas. The inscribed part is about 40 cm wide and 32 cm
long. Date: *Samvat 67 Bhādrapada śukla dvitīyā*. Inscription is
well preserved.

१   ॐ स्वस्ति कैलासकूट भवनाच्छरदाप्यानशशाङ्क्रामल मयूरवानिकरा
    व भाष्यमति हिमव

२   दुस्तुङ्ग शिखरा वदातयशो मालानतं सिताशेष दिङ् मण्डलो य एष शौर्य्-
    न्नीति गुणैगुणै

३   रकलितं रान्मानमुद् भासिभि: शक्त्या वाहुवलं मति स्मृतिमतीं शास्त्रा-
    गमै भूरिभि: मर्यादास्थि

४   तिभिर्दिशोपि यशसा राज्यश्रिया मेदिनी जत्या लिच्छविराज वङ्शमन¹
    घयोलङ्क्रोत्युच्चकै:

५   भगवत्पशुपति भट्टारक पादानुगृहीतो बप्पपादानुध्यातो महाराजाधिरा

६   ज श्रीनरेन्द्रदेव: कुशली भविष्यतो नेपालराजान्सम्यक्प्रतिमान्यान्
    दर्शयति विदित

७   मस्तु भवतां यथा दक्षिण कोलीग्राम द्रङ्गस्य सर्वंतलग्रामै: सहितस्य
    पूर्वराजभिमनिश्व

८   रे भुवनेश्वर देवकुलं यथा कल्पिताग्रहारादि प्रत्यायम्पालनोप भोगाय
    प्र [तिपादित] म्

९ केनापि च हेतुना श्रीभुमगुप्तेनाक्षिप्तं राजकुल भोग्यमभूत्तदिदमधुना पूर्वमर्यादा

१० स्थितिप्रवर्तनादृतमनोभि रस्माभि कृताभि प्रजानां श्रेयसेस्यैव सर्वतल ग्रामसहि

११ तस्य दक्षिणकोलीग्रामद्रङ्गस्य तदेव भुवनेश्वर देवकुलं यत्रतत्रावस्थित क्षेत्रवा

१२ टिका गृह पण्याकारे य्यथापूर्व भुज्यमानसीमभिस्त्रिभि: कङ्छोबिल्वमार्ग हुस्प्रिन्रदुङ्ग्रामैरेभि

१३ रग्रहारत्वेनोत्सृष्टे श्चाट भटा प्रवेश्यै: सर्वकोट्टमर्चादा स्थिति मवभिश्च सहितम्प्रतिमुक्त

१४ मित्येवञ्च विदितार्थे रप्ये तदग्रहारत्त्रय निवासिभिर्यथा कलिपतं पिण्ड-कादि प्रत्यायम

१५ स्योपनयद्भिर कुतोभयैर्राज्ञाश्रवण विधेयै भंवितव्यम्भूयोपि श्रनेनैव न्यायेन शीताद्याम्

१६ शिवगल्हदेव [कुले] यथा पूर्वकल्पितक्षेत्रपिण्डकादिप्रत्यायम्पालनो पभोगायैव सर्वत

१७ ल[ग्रा] म सहितस्यैवास्य द्रङ्गस्य [प्र] ति [मु] क्तमेवं विदितार्थेन हीनानवमन्यमानैरन्योन्य

१८ प्रीतिदृढीकृतं स्नेहानुवद्धे र-नू···पुरुषे स्तलं समेतँस्त दुभयमेव प्रतिपा

१९ पालयद्भिसततमस्म···र्वतित व्यन्य कैश्चिदस्मत्पादोपजीविभिरन्येर्वैवा स्वल्पा

२० पि पीडा कार्य्या यस्त्वेतामाज्ञामुलङ्घ्यान्यथा कुर्यात्कारयेद्वा तस्य वयं राजशासन व्यतिक्रम का

२१ रारिण स्तीव्रं दण्डम्पातयिष्यामो भाविभिरपि भूपतिभि रिह यश: कल्याणायुरारोग्य राज्य

२२ श्रियां वृद्धिमहिमानै रमुत्र च स्वर्गे शाश्वती स्थितिमिच्छद्भि: पूर्व-राजकृतेषु प्रसादेषु पा

२३ लनादृतं भव्यैय्यश्चिरस्थितयेचास्य प्रसादस्य शिलापट्टक [शासनेन प्रसाद:] कृतं इति

२४ समाज्ञापना दूतक श्चात्र कुमारामात्य प्रियजीव: संवत् ६० ७ भाद्रपव शुक्ल द्वितीयायाम्

1. DV वंश । 2. DV कुल; Gn तल । 3. Gn रस्माभि; DV सततञ्च ।
4. DV पण्या कारैं; Gn धण्याकारैं: । 5. DV प्रवेशैं; Gn स्नेहानुग्रहै ।
6. Gn दृढ़ि; DV वृद्धि । 7. DV समेतैंस्त दुभयमेव; Gn पुरुषैंस्त····
त्रयमेव । 8. Gn पालयद्दिः सततमस्य । 9. Gn reads वृप्निमीह and
takes it as a mistake for वृद्धिम् । But वृद्धि can be easily read.

CXVIII. Deopatan Inscription

(Gn LXV; DV 125; HJ 124) The pedestal of a linga situated
in the private garden of a house in Deopatan, near the western
gate of Paśupati temple. The inscribed part is about 75 cm wide
and 21 cm long. Date: 69 *Jyeṣṭha kṛṣṇa divā* 7. According to
Gnoli 'The characters of this inscription are not very carefully
carved and are in a poor state of preservation.' But this is not so.

१   संवत् ६० ६ ज्येष्ठकृष्ण दिवा सप्तम्यां परम भट्टारक श्रीनरेन्द्रदेवस्य
     साग्रंवर्षशतं समाज्ञापयत: चुहुङ्गपेड्याय···[1]

२   नर्प्रिग्रामस्य[2] दक्षिण तस्तिलमकस्य च दक्षिण पूर्वत: क्षेत्रं····
     शालङ्क्रा व।स्तव्यव्राह्मण विश्व सेनस्य पल्या सुवर्णं[3]

३   गोमिन्या ७ प्रत्याय ्महाबलाढ्यक्ष[4] प्रसादविलेख्यं रामस्वामिना दूतकेन
     दानपाशुपताचार्य्यदक्षिणतिलडुकस्य

४   तेनापि दान श्रृह्ल्लिकपाशुपतानां ग्लान भैषज्यार्थं[5] दत्तं वर्षकं स्तत्रैव
     ग्रामे···म्पिडकं विशतिकया धान्यमा

५   १४ पु ७ ग्रस्य[6] करणीयम्···धान्यकुडा १ गिच्छिजानामिलगतिवल[7]
     वाहिकगुप्त···शारिकावास्तव्य[8] ग्रामात्य भगवचन्द्र

६   तत्रैंव निवासिन चन्दकस्य ग्रत्रं साक्षिक ज्ञेय चुहुंग्रपेडा[9] नियुक्तश्च
     धनवृद्धिसहितेन ॥

1. Gn ग्रामेज्ज्याय···· । 2. Gn कुटुम्बि etc. 3. Gn तस्य प्रसादाधिशासन
स्यपत्त । 4. Gn गोमिन्या । 5. Gn नैसस्यारिदत्त । 6. Gn प्रत्यस्य ।
7. Gn शि for गि and onwards च्छि जानामि···· । 8. Gn
ऐवनिवासिचन्दस्य । 9. Gn ज्ञेयाबुडग्रामे ।

CXIX. Kasaitol Inscription

(Gn LXVIII; DV 126; HJ 125)   A slab of stone standing in front of a mound close to the temple of Nārāyaṇa in Kasaitol (Deopatan, Paśupati).   Its top is decorated with a chakra at the centre.   Date: Samvat 71 Kārtika śukla dvitīyā.   The inscribed part is 44 cm wide and 36 cm long.

Lines from 1-10 are worn away.

११   ······भगवत्पशुपति भट्टारकपादानुगृहीतोवप्पपादानु

१२   ध्यातः परम भट्टारक महाराजाधिराज श्री नरेन्द्रदेवः कुशली······

१३   वृत्ति भुज····धिक्रत····भविष्यत इच··यथा [हंङ्कुशलमभिधाय]

१४   समाज्ञापयति विदितम्भवतु भवतां स

१५   ···नव [गृह]···स्थिति मर्यादो [त्पन्न] त्व [ञ्चाट भटानाम्]

१६   प्रवेशश्च प्रसादः क्रत स्तदित्थं···थंम्वेदिभि भंवद्भिरन्यैर्थाधि··धि

१७   ······रसमत्प्रसाद प्रतिबद्ध जीवनैः कैश्चिदपि नवगृहम्प्रविश्या

१८   ल्पतरापि वाधा न कर्तव्या यस्तित्त्वमामविलङ्घनीया मास्माकीनामाज्ञा मना

१९   दृत्यान्यथा कुर्यात्कारयेद्वा तं वयं राजाज्ञा प्रतीपगामिनामत्यर्थन्न मर्षयि

२०   ष्यामो येपि चास्मदूध्वंम्भूपतयो भवितारस्तैरपि सम्यक्प्रजानुपालना

२१   तसुचरितमभीष्टाना म्सम्पदां कारण मन्यमानैरिह कल्याणरायुरारोग्य

२२   राज्यश्रिय मुपचयायाद्यमुत्रापि चाभ्युदयाय धर्मगुरूतया पूर्वैंराज प्र

२३   सादानुवर्तनम्प्रतिसततमवहित मनोभि भाव्य ञ्चिरकालस्थितये चास्य

२४   प्रसादस्य शिलापट्टक शासनञ्च प्रसादीक्रतमिति स्वयमाज्ञापि चात्म

२५   दिह यात्किञ्चिन्महत्कार्य मूत्पद्यते तच्च स्वयम्पाञ्चालिकैं निर्णेतुन्न शक्य [ते] त

२६   दा तदन्तरासनेन विचारयितव्यं याश्च गौष्ठयो नवगृह प्रतिवद्धाश्च

२७   चाटभटानाम प्रवेश्या एव याचव्यवस्थातान्रशासने लिखिता भूत्तये

२८   ब व्यवस्थया वृजिकरथ्या निवासि मधुसूदन स्वामी पाञ्चालिक सामान्य इति

२६ [दूत] कोत्र दण्डनायको नृपदेव: संवत् ७० १ कार्तिक शुक्ल द्वितीया-
याम्

1. DV सर्व after कुशली, Gn leaves the letters even thereafter
unread. 2. Gn ˙˙˙धिकृत˙˙˙च˙˙˙क˙˙˙ण । 3. Gn reads onwards as
˙˙˙यसायु˙˙˙इ˙˙˙ 4. Gn च्चर˙˙˙˙˙˙सु˙˙˙तो˙˙˙स्थिति: प˙˙˙ञ्चहृततत्त्व˙˙˙
5. DV न्यतरान्यतराधिका; Gn प्र˙˙˙प्रसाद˙˙˙चस्त˙˙˙इ˙˙˙थमेवेदिमिभवत्प
6. DV राधिकृतैस्तथान्यैरसभ etc. 7. Gn इतसुचरितम । 8. Gn ˙˙˙य
˙˙˙ञ्चि˙˙˙रह । 9. Gn याश्चाव्यस्था । 10. Gn ˙˙˙वस्तव्या˙˙˙इका ।
11. DV दूतकश्च । He omits त्र. So does Gn.

CXX. Naksal Road Inscription

(Gn LXIX; DV 127; HJ 126) On the front of the water
conduit tank meant for storage attached to the wall before the
temple of Bhagavatī at Naksal on the way to Pasupatinatha.
The inscribed part is about 49 cm wide and 25 cm long. Date:
Samvat 78 Kārtika śukla navamī.

१ ॐ शौर्योत्साह पराक्रमा वयनय त्याग प्रतापा दिभि:
   श्लाघ्यै: स्वामिगुणै रनन्य सुलभ ै: संस्पर्धयें वान्विते

२ पृथ्वीं [पातिसनरे] न्द्र देव नृपतौ वंशक्रमा भ्यागतां
   संत्यक्त्वना स्वसुखेद्यमे परहित व्यापार निम्नात्मनि

३ तत्पादाव्जप्रसादादुपनतविभवोविष्णुदेव: कृतात्मा
   लोकस्य ब्राह्मणादे स्त्रिषवण विधिव न्मार्जनादि प्रपूर्य्यं

४ पाषाण द्रोणमेनां सुविहित सलिलोद्धार यन्त्रोदपानम्
   कृत्वा तत्पुण्यवीजाढ्यहुतर सुकृतारम्भमाशस्त भूय:*

५ संवत् ७० ८ कार्तिक शुक्ल नवम्याम् प्र युगादौ

*Metre: Śārdūlavikrīḍita and the later portion Śragdharā.

1. Gn पृ[थ्वीं] पा[तिनरे]न्द्रदेव । 2. Gn reads निन्मात्मनि and
thinks that it is a mistake for निम्ना । 3. Gn घ्र: [तत्पादाव्ज] ।

4. DV reads onwards प्रयुगा दौ while Gn omits. The
letters are quite illegible, but can be made out.

CXXI. Gairidhara (deep water conduit) Inscription of Patan

(Ben 3; Gn LXX; DV 128: HJ 130) A slab of stone lying
at Gairidhara, Patan (now in the National Museum). The top
of the stone shows a reclining bull. Date: Samvat 82 as read by
Gnoli and 83 as read by DV, which is correct. The inscribed
part is 40 cm wide and 70 cm long.

Bendall could not read upto 6th line.

१ स्वस्ति कैलासकूट भवनाद्·······[भग

२ वत्पशु] पति भट्टारक पादानुगृहीतो वप्पपादानु [ध्यातः]

३ पर[म भट्टा] रक महाराजाधिराज श्रीनरेन्द्रदेवः कुशली

४ ·······न सर्वाधिकरणाधिक [कृता···]

५ ······वर्तमानान्भविष्यतोपि यथाहं ङ्क्ञशल

६ [माभाष्य] समाज्ञापयति विदितमस्तु [भवतां यथा]

७ महाप्रतिहार चन्द्रवर्म विज्ञापितैरस्माभि [स्तत्प्रतिमान्य]

८ ·······वाग्वती पूर्वकुले भगवद्व ज्रेश्वर मण्ड

९ ल्यां·······सर्वाधिकरणानामप्रवेशेना·······प्र

१० ·············गण प्रसादीकृत मनेनास्यास्मदनु

११ ज्ञातेनात्मनः श्रेयोभिवृद्धयेधार्मिकगणानामतिसृष्टम्

१२ प्रतिपालनम्प्रतिज्ञान कर्मयोगरतैः शीलाचार

१३ परवैंस्तव्यन्तै रपियथा काल मनतिक्रम्य देवाना [म्]

१४ स्तपनगन्धपुष्प धूपप्रदीप वर्षवर्धन वर्षाकाल

१५ वा दित्र जपकादिका कारणपूजा कर्तव्या मण्डल्याञ्च

१६ उपलेपन सम्मार्जन प्रति संस्कारादिक ङ्कृ त्वा यद्यस्ति

१७ परिशेषन्तेन द्रव्येण भगवन्तं बज्रेश्वर मुद्दिश्य

१८ पाशुपतानाम्ब्राह्मणनाञ्च यथासम्भवम्भोजनाङ्कर

१९ णीय स्तदान्यच्च कालान्तरेण यदि कदाचिद्दानपति

२० त्वेन प्रार्थयन्ते ग्रापत्सु तत्कालम्बुध्वा दानपतीनां

२१ धान्यानाञ्चतु विशतिर्मानिकादेया ततोधिकन्दानप

२२ तिभिर्नग्राह्यमयदि चात्र कार्य्यमुत्पद्यते परमासने

२३ न विचारमात्रङ्करणीय न्न तु द्रव्यस्याक्षेप स्तदेव

२४ मवगत्य सर्वाधिकरणाधिकृतैरन्यैर्वा न कैश्चिदय

२५ मस्मत्प्रसादोन्यथा कर्तव्यो ये त्वस्मदाज्ञा व्यतिक्रम्य वर्तन्ते

२६ वयन्तेषान्न मर्षयामो येप्यस्म ढू ध्वम्भवितारो राजा

२७ नस्तैरपि पूर्वनृपतिकृत प्रसाद प्रतिपालनाद्

२८ तैनान्यथा करणीयो स्वयमाज्ञा दूतश्चात्र भट्टार [15]

२९ क श्रीयुवराज स्कन्ददेवः संवत् ८० ३ भाद्रपद शुक्ल [16] [17]

३० [ष] ष्ठयाम् २० [18]

1. Gn's actual reading starts from the 8th. Ben drops 7 lines and starts also from the 8th. 2. Gn इ···· 3. Gn ····य. 4. ··········· 5. ····पशुपतौ etc. 6. Ben ····लेभगवढ्ज्रेश्वर प्रण । Also see DV filling the gap to some extent. 7. But Gn····सर्वाधिकरा- णानामा प्रवेशेना, Ben ग्रप्रविधातव्य नुप्र etc. 8. Gn reads ग्रनेनास्य···· ····न्तु । 9. Also see DV for correct reading, where Gn agrees but Gn omits ज्ञात । 10. DV is correct, but Gn प्रतिज्ञा··· ····कमयोगर । Ben reads योगुर for योगुर and the rest as in Gn. 11. Also DV but Gn न यश्चि···कालमनति क्रम्यप्रधान । 12. Ben omits स्नपन । 13. Also DV but Gn ····काल । 14. Ben मन्त्रजपकादिप्रकरण before पूजा etc. 15. Ben करणीय; DV करणीयो; Gn करणीयम् । 16. Ben omits स्त्री and reads [क] । 17. Gn reads 82, DV reads 83 correctly. 18. Ben has only the last letter म् ।

CXXII. Inscription of Anantaliṅgeśvara

(DV 129; HJ 128) This stele with the inscription of the time of Narendradeva lies near the temple of Anantaliṅgeśvara situated on a hill being the lower part of the inner range of the mountain skirting the valley, to the immediate south of Bhadgaon. The date is missing in particulars but the year 80 is distinctly visible.

The inscribed part covers a space of 34 cm wide and 92 cm long. The top shows in relief a sitting bull.

१ ॐ स्वस्ति कैलास शृङ्गा भान्नयनोत्सव कारिण: कैलासकूट भवनात्

२ रम्याज्जगति विस्तृतात् राज्ञां मणि लिच्छवि वङ्शजातां योभूद्गुणैं
स्सर्वंजनाति गण्यै:

३ शक्तित्रया पूरित मण्डलश्री: शशीव संलक्ष्यतरो नृपाणाम् सविनयनयप

४ राक्रमालङ्कृ त मूतिर्भगवत्पशुपति भट्टारक पादानुगृहीतो बप्पपादानु-
ध्यातो भ

५ ट्टारक महाराजाधिराज श्रीनरेन्द्रदेव: कुशली नेपालसीमान्त: पातिन:
सर्वाधिकाराधिकृ

६ तान्वर्तमानान् भविष्यतश्च समाज्ञापयति विदितमस्तु भवतां हंसगृह
द्रङ्गस्य···पश्चिमको

७ ···ग्राम सहितस्य चाटभटप्रवेश: शरीरकोट्रो भयानेक मर्यादोपपन्न:
कश्चित्प्रसा

८ दशासनपट्टकोभूत्स च पूर्वराजा [ज] विभ्रमतो नष्टोधुनास्माभि
श्चिरन्तन ब्यवस्थानुपाल

९ न ज्ञातादरै: स एव प्रसाद श्चिरस्थितये शिलापट्टका भिलेख्येन प्रसादी
कृतोत्र

१० च मर्यादा कुलपतिना देया कार्तिकशुक्लैकादशशम्याम्मार्ग संस्कारा थ॑न्त

११ ण्डुल मानिका ४ द्वादश्याम्भगवतो लोकपालस्वामिन: प्रतिष्ठादिने तन्नै

१२ व ब्राह्मणजनस्य शान्त्युदकम्पणाना म्पुराणम् २५ द्रङ्गसीमाभ्यन्तरस्था

१३ नाम्ब्राह्मण प्रमुखानाम्मा चाण्डालेभ्यो घृतासन सामतादि भोजनम्

१४ स्तम्भानामेकैकस्य संस्थापनार्थम् तण्डुलमानिका ५४ गोयुद्धपताका वस्तु

१५ पुराण २५ क्रियाकरणम्भगवतो लोकपाल स्वामिन: पावनार्थन्धान्य
मानिका:

१६ ४० देवस्थापकस्य मुक्तिका धान्यमानिका······दक मुक्तिका धान्य-
मानिका:

१७　२४ देवभृत्या नान्दशानामेकतो भुक्तिका धान्यमानिका १४० दासीनां
विंशती

१८　नामेकतो मानिकाशतत्रयं षण्णुत्तर····त···मानिका शतद्वयं चत्वारिंश द्मा

१६　निकाधिकं भास क्षेत्रेणैव········च यत्पूरणीय स्मानिका

२०　शतं त्रिशदुत्तरं तत्कुलपते······ ··न्देव भृत्यानाम्पुरान १२०

२१　दासीनाम्पुराण ८० मृत्तिका········का ४ पण पुराण ६०

२२　अङ्गनशोधनार्थन्तन्डुल मा········शोधनार्थङ्क्रोङ्क्रोग्राम पाञ्चा

२३　लिकाना न्तण्डुलमानिका········१ माघशुक्ल द्वादशबाम्

२४　द्रङ्कसीमाभ्यन्तरस्थानां········यथाग्रयफा

२५　लगुन मासेन क्षेत्रमणि·······ज्येष्ठ शुक्लेका द

२६　श्यां वराहयात्रायां सीमाभ्यन्तर········

२७　सीनान्तण्डुल मानिका···········

२८　मण्या तन्धि············

२६　अर्चना निमित्तम्········

३०　का: १२ इन्द्रो············

३१　यज भवन············

३२　दक्षिण············

३३　··············

३४　··············

३५　पालनीयं········

३६　·············

३७　पूर्वराज प्रसाद········पालनपरैरेव···

३८　शास्त्रानुशीं········यतः पूर्वदत्तां द्विजातिभ्यो य [न्नात्रक्ष] युधिष्ठिर

३६　महीं महीभुजाँ श्रेष्ठ दानाच्छ्रेयोनुपालन मिति संवत् ८०·······

४०　कृष्ण दिवा दशम्याम् दूतकश्चात्र श्रीयुवराज···देवेति

CXXIII.

On a small bowl-shaped stone lying in a courtyard near the
temple of Bhairavanatha in Bhatgaon.*　The date is Samvat 88.

१　ॐ सम्वत् ८० ८ पौषशुक्ल द्वितीयायाम्···उमा तेजसा ल

२   लित महेश्वराय ॥ पुण्यवाप्तयेता

३   म्र कलस दत्तम् ॥ ......

*Also published by M. Khanal in Madhyakalin Nepala ka Abhilekha (inscriptions).

CXXIV. Baṭuka Bhairava Temple Inscription

(Gn LXXI; DV 130; HJ 131) A slab of stone, inscribed part of which is about 40 cm wide and 54 cm long, is lying in the courtyard of the temple of Baṭuka Bhairava at the end of Lagankhel in Patan southern extremity of the city. The top shows in a relief a dharmachakra with two deer one on each side. Date: Samvat 89. The stone is much damaged except for a few letters here and there and the date figure at the end without its month and fortnight (lunar).

१   ......प्र...सरङ्ग-मौपौतशि...तौ-स-भ

२   ......न...बलैं-म्- स्थितं यस्य वः पायात्

३   ......र...सरङ्ग...स्म...दूराद...राजनि

४   ......धि धरणिमण्डल...स-भा-द...स्थि-राज्य

५   भद्राधिवास शिल...वा...

६   ...पला...जि...कृत...

७   प्रसम्क......

८   ...पतिना......

९   भट्ट......

१०   बे......

११   ......

१२   ......

१३   ......

१४   ......दोप-रिभि

१५   ......त्रभ त्त्र...

१६   ......स्मदूर्ध्वं भ

१७   ...यत...एवं स्थित मित्यस्म

१८　···द्रक्षासंविधानं···शासनं पूर्वं नृपतेः

१६　···ति-स्म महीपति···पुण्य--निष्ठानां स्थैर्यंम्प्र

२०　···दा···दूतकश्चात्र राजपुत्र जनार्दन वर्मा

२१　संवत् ८० ९······दिवा त्रयोदश्याम् ॥

CXXV. Balambu Vihara Stone

(DV 131; HJ 132) A fragment of a stele now deposited in
a Vihara at Balambu. Its other fragment which should be the
upper part of the stone is not available. The date is *90 Vaiśākha
śukla dvādaśyām.*

A few lines in the beginning are lost.

१　भवद्भिः परि[पालनीयो]······[1]

२　इत्येवं विदितार्थे [रस्म] त्पादोपजीविविभि [रन्यैर्वायं प्रसादोनान्य][2]

३　था करणीयो यस्त्वेतामाज्ञा मुत्क्रम्यान्यथा कुर्यात्कारयेद्वा तमह्

४　मत्यर्थन्न मर्षयिष्यामि ये वास्मद्ध्वर्म्भवितारो भूमिपतय

५　स्तैरपि पारम्पर्य मेवं स्थित मित्यस्मत्प्रसाद प्रतिपालन सं

६　विधान परैरेव भाव्यमिति स्वशासन चिरस्थितयै लोक

७　द्वयविशुद्धये रक्षितव्यं नृपैर्यत्नात्पूर्वं भूपतिशासन

८　मिति स्वयमाज्ञा दूतकश्चात्र रुद्रचन्द्र गोमीति

९　संवत् ८० वैशाख शुक्ल दिवा दशम्याम्

1. DV does not give the first line.
2. The conjectural reading (also of DV) might not be incorrect.

CXXVI. Chyasaltol Inscription

(Gn LXXII; DV 132; HJ 134) A slab of stone, about
42 cm wide and 44 cm long, standing with its face towards **a**

small temple of Ganeśa at Chyasaltol, Patan. The stone lies in
such a position as to make it difficult to get the tracing. The
first few lines can only be read but they are all destroyed. The
top of the stone shows in relief a reclining bull. Date: *Samvat*
95 Pauṣa śukla daśamī.

१ ॐ स्वस्ति भद्राधिवास भवनात्······[1]

२ ···गृहीत वप्पपादानुध्यात···

३ ···कुशली ··वर्तमान···

४ ···   ···

५ ···   ···

६ ···   ···

७ ···   ···

८ धिकारी ···भूमिकरल···[2]

९ ···वर्तमान भविष्यतश्च भूमुजो [कुश]

१० [ल] माभाष्य समाज्ञापयति भवतु [भव]

११ [तां य] थैषाप्रज्ञणि गुल्मकोमालिहि···माशी···

१२ ···ञ्चाट भटानाम प्रवेशेन···

१३ ···सन्तुष्टे[3] प्रसाद:कृत एव मधिगतार्थैं

१४ [र] स्मत्यादोपजीविभिरन्यैर्वा न कैश्चिदयम्प्रसा

१५ [दो] न्यथा करणीयो य: ममाज्ञामुल्लङ्घ्यान्यथा [कु]

१६ र्या त्कारयेद्वा सोस्माभिर्न मर्षणीयो ये चास्मद [र्वं]

१७ [भ] वितारो भूमिपालास्तैरपि पूर्वराजप्रसाद सं

१८ रक्षण प्रवण मानसैरे व भाव्यमिति स्वयमाज्ञा

१९ दूतश्चात्र श्रीयुवराज शौर्यदेव: संवत् ६० ५

२० पौष शुक्ल दिवा दशम्याम् ॥

1. Lines 1-14 are not clearly readable in the plate except
a few letters here and there but these allow conjectural
decipherment. 2. Gn, DV करल । Lines 4 to 7 are totally
unreadable. 3. Gn, DV तश्च···कुश, DV तुष्ट: without सन् ।

CXXVII. Yanmugal or Yanamugal Inscription

(Levi 20; Gn LXXIV; DV 133; HJ 136) A slab of stone, about 42 cm wide and 80 cm long, placed in a small street known as Tah Galli, within an area called Yangu Bahal or Yanmugal tole, near the Patan Durbar, a little to the east. The date is illegible.

१ [ॐ स्वस्ति भद्राधि] वास भवनाद प्रतिहृत शासनो भगवः [त्पशुपति भट्टारक पादानुगृहीतो]

२ [वप्प] पादानु ध्यातो लिच्छवि कुलकेतुः परसमाहेश्वर पर [म भट्टारक महाराजा थिराज]

३ [श्री न] रेन्द्रदेवः कुशली गुल्लंतङ्ग्रामनिवासिनः प्रथानपुरस्सरा न्सर्वं कुटुम्बिनः [कु]

४ [श] लभाभाष्य समाज्ञापयति विदितम्भवतु भवतां यथायंग्रामो [भगवत्पशुपतौस्व]

५ [कारित] महाप्रणालीनाम शाठ्येन सर्वेंतिकतंव्यानामनुष्ठानार्थं विष्टघा ज्ञानु [विधायित्वे]

६ न चाटभटानाम प्रवेश्येन शरीर कोट्ट मर्यादोपपन्नः सर्वकर [णीयप्रति]

७ मुक्तः कुटुम्बी वहिर्देंशगमनादि सर्वविष्टिरहितो गुर्विणी मरणे गर्भोद्धरणा [य]

८ [प] णशतमात्रदेयेन सक्षतगोष्ठापमृगापचारे सपणापुराणत्रय [मात्र देयेन च]

९ युक्त इ्चौ परदार हृत्यासम्बन्धादिपञ्चापराधकारिणां शरीरमात्रं राजकु [लाभा]

१० व्यन्तद्गृहक्षेत्रकलत्रादिसर्वंद्रव्याण्यार्यसङ्घस्येत्यनेन च सम्पन्नः श्रीशिवदेव वि [हा]

११ [रे] चतुर्दिशार्यं भिक्षुसङ्घायास्माभि रतिसृष्टः सीमा चास्य पूर्वोत्तरेण विहार

१२ स्य प्रणालीभ्रमस्ततो दक्षिण मनुसृत्य गोमिभू ध्ञ्चोप्रदेशे वाग्वती नदीम

१३ नुसृत्य गोत्तिलमक संगमस्तत उत्तरङ्कृत्वा श्रीमानदेव विहार खर्जूरिका [वि]

१४ [हा] रक्षेत्रयोः संधिस्ततः पश्चिमञ्जत्वा खारे वालगञ्चो ततः पश्चिमनु
[सृत्य]

१५ [म] ध्यम विहारस्य पूर्वदक्षिणकोणपाश्वलिमार्गेणोत्तरञ्जत्वा प्रणाल्याः
पू [र्वौं]

१६ [त्त] रानुसारेण कुण्डल क्षेत्रस्य दक्षिणपूर्वंकोणो महापथस्ततो मार्गानुसा
[रे]

१७ णोत्तरञ्जत्वाभयरुचि विहारस्य पूर्वप्रा [कार] सात पूर्वोत्तर मनुसृत्य
वार्तक

१८ ल्याण गुत्तविहारस्य दक्षिण पूर्व प्रा [कार] स्ततः पूर्वोत्तरमनुसृत्य
चतुर्भा

१९ वदादुन विहारस्य पूर्वदक्षिणकोण तदुत्तरं पश्चिम रानुसृत्वोत्तरप

२० श्चिमकोणो वृहत्पथ स्ततपूर्वोत्तरञ्जत्वा कम्विलम्प्राततः उत्तरपूर्वंमनुसृत्य

२१ श्रीराजविहारेन्द्र मूलकयोः पानीयमार्गसंघात [खातक स्तस्योत्तरपूर्वेण]

२२ [वृ] ह्न्मार्गस्य दक्षिणवाटिकाया दक्षिणाल्य नुसारेण पूर्व दक्षिणञ्चा
नुसृत्यप

२३ थस्ततो यावत्स्वल्पप्रणाल्यां परिगे स्पुल्ली पाश्वें मार्गस्ततस्तमेवमार्ग
दक्षिणे

२४ [ना] नुसृत्य सएव विहारस्ततः प्रणालीभ्रम इत्येतत्समीप परिक्षिप्तेसि
न्नग्र[हा]

२५ [रेय] दि कदाचिदार्यसंघस्यशवचं कार्यमुत्पद्येत तदा परमासनेन विचा
[रणी]

२६ [यमित्येव मवगतार्थेरस्म] त्पादोपजीविभिरन्यैर्वायम्प्रसादोन्यथा नक
[र]

२७ [णीयो यस्त्वन्यथा] कुर्यात्कारयेद्वा सोस्माभिस्सुतरान्न मर्षणीयो

२८ [ये चास्म दूर्ध्वंम्भवितारो भूमिपा] लास्तेर्ण्यु भय लोक निरवद्य
सुखार्थिभिः पू

२९ [वंराजवि] हि [तोयं विशिष्टः प्रसाद इ] ति प्रयत्नत [स्सम्यक्परि]
पालनीय एव यतो [ध]

३० मंशास्त्रव [च] नं [वहुभि] वंसुधा दत्ता [राजभि] स्स
[गरादिभिः। यस्य यस्य यदा भूमिस्त]

३१ स्य तस्य तदा [फलम्]

३२ संवत् [१००] ३ ज्येष्ठ [शु] क्ल सप्तम्याम्

1. L ··देव । 2. L पशुपतं··· रितु: । 3. L reads कुटुम्बि । 4. L puts
this at the beginning in continuation from the end of the
last line. 5. L देर्यैनमुक्त । 6. L कुणल । 7. Gn, DV लट् ।
8. L has ····त्य । 9. L आर्यवयम् । 10. Gn reads···3 while DV
reads [100] 3.
Levi omitted 30-32 lines.

CXXVIII. Vajraghar Inscription

(BLI 13; Gn LXXIII; DV 134; HJ 137) A slab of
stone standing just outside the southern gate of the temple of
Paśupatinātha, before a house named Vajraghar but now kept
in the National Museum. Date: *Samvat 103 Jyeṣṭha śukla 13.*
The inscribed part is 38 cm wide and 86 cm long. Gnoli says
'As BLI's reading is extremely fragmentary and erroneous, I
have omitted to annotate all his reading. My reading is
confirmed by the inscription no. 20 of Levi. Instead of *Samvat
103* BLI reads *Samvat 143.*' But we have our own rubbing,
which is read without difficulty in full except in cases as done
by Levi.

१ ॐ स्वस्ति भद्राधिवास [भवनादप्रतिहतशासनोभगवत्प]शुपति
भट्टारक पादानु

२ गृहीतो बप्पपा [दानुध्मातो लिच्छवि कुलकेतु: प] रम माहेश्वर
परमभट्टा

३ रक महाराजाधि[राज श्रीनरेन्द्रदेव: कुशली]···ञ्चगर्तग्रामे प्रधान-
पुस्सरा

४ न्सर्व कुटुम्बिन: कुशल [माभाष्य समाज्ञाप] यति विदितम्भवतु भवतां
यथाय

५ ङ्ग्रामो भगवत्पशुपतौ स्वकारित महाप्रणाली नाम शाठ्येन सर्वेतिकर्त-
व्याना

६ मनुष्ठानार्थ विष्ट्याज्ञानुविधायित्वेन चाटभटानामप्रवेश्येन शरीर कोट्ट
मर्या

७ दोपपन्न: शरीर सर्वकरणीय प्रतिमुक्त: कुटुम्बी वहिर्देशगमनादि सर्ववि

५   ष्ठिरहितो गुर्विणीमरणे गर्भोद्धारणाय पणशतमात्रदेयेन सक्षत गोष्ठापमृ

६   गापचारे सपणपुराणत्रयमात्र देयेन च युक्तश्चौर परदारहत्या संवन्धादि

१० पञ्चापराधकारिणाँ शरीरमात्रं राजकुलाभाव्यन्तद्गृह क्षेत्र कलत्रादि
    सर्वद्रव्या

११ ण्यार्यसंघस्येत्यनेन च सम्पन्न: श्रीशिवदेवविहारे चतुदिशार्यभिक्षु-
    संघायास्मा

१२ भिरति सृष्ट: सीमा चास्य पूर्वोत्तरेण श्रेष्ठि दुल्मूर्ध्नि प्रीतु ब्रुमध्यमाली
    तस्या किञ्चित्पू

१३ र्वेण वृहदालया दक्षिणमनुसृत्य चुह्वङ्गभूमिम्पूर्वदक्षिणेन वेष्टयित्वा
    ह्रुप्रिङ्ग्रामी

१४ मार्गस्तन्दक्षिणमनुसृत्य सरलवनगामी मार्गस्तम्पश्चिममनुसृत्य ह्रु प्रि-
    म्पाञ्चा

१५ लिकक्षेत्र पश्चिमकोणाद्दक्षिणपश्चिममनुसृत्य श्रीखर्जुरिका विहारस्य
    सर्वो

१६ परिप क्षेत्र पश्चिमाल्या दक्षिणङ्गत्वापृच्छि वूदक्षिणेश्वराम्बु तोर्थं
    क्षेत्राणां सन्धि:

१७ ततश्च दक्षिणमनुसृत्य शशिक्षेत्रपूर्वदक्षिण कोणात्किञ्चित्पश्चिपङ्गत्वा
    मित्तम्ब्रूपू

१८ र्वाल्या दक्षिणमनुसृत्य तत्सर्वदक्षिणाल्या पश्चिमङ्गत्वा किञ्चिदुत्तरञ्च
    तत: पश्चिम

१९ मनुसृत्य च निव्रू दक्षिणपश्चिमकोणाद्दक्षिणङ्गत्वा लोप्रिङ्ग्रामेन्द्र-
    गौष्ठिक क्षेत्र पूर्व

२० दक्षिणकोणात्किञ्चित्पश्चिमङ्गत्वा ह्रु प्रिम्पाञ्चालिक क्षेत्रपश्चिमाल्या-
    दक्षिणमनुसृत्य

२१ ……भूमेरुत्तर पूर्वकोणो ह्रुप्रिङ्ग्रामी बृहत्पथस्तम्पश्चिम मनुसृत्य
    ह्रुप्रिलो

२२ प्रिङ्ग्रामे स्तित्स्रोतो धोनुसृत्य मेकण्डिदुल् तिलमक सङ्गम स्तत्पश्चिमोर्ध्व
    मधिरुह्य कन्दर

२३ ……नुसारेणोत्तर पश्चिममनुसृत्यपानीयपातोयावल्लोप्रिङ्ग्रामिनमार्ग…

२४ [नुसृत्य]…शिखर क्षेत्र सर्वदक्षिणाल्या पश्चिमङ्गत्वा लोप्रि………
    तक्षेत्रन्तत:

२५ प[श्चिमम] नुसृत्योत्तरञ्च बृहदारामस्य पूर्वमुखे महापथस्तत [उ]
    त्तरङ्गत्वाबृह

२६ दा [राम] स्य पूर्वोत्तरकोणा दघोवतीर्यं बनपर्यन्तमुपादाय फंशिन्प्रल-
ल्स्रोतस्तदु

२७ त्तरमनुसृत्य स्रोत·········मतस्रोतोनुसाण ब्रह्मतीर्थंसंवेद्यन्नदी वाग्वती-
पूर्व

२८ मनुसृत्य [उत्त] राङ्कत्वा कन्दराग्रानुसारेण श्रेष्ठिदुल्मूर्ध्नि संवप्रीतुब्रू-
मध्यमालीत्यं

२९ [तत्सीम परिक्षिप्तेस्मिन्न] ग्रहारे यदिकदाचिदार्यसंघस्याशक्यहृक्कार्यं
मु [त्प] द्येत

३० तदा परमा [सनेन वि] चारणीयमापणकरोधिकमासतुलादण्डादिश्च
पूर्व एवा

३१ र्यंभि [क्षुसंघस्ये] त्येवमवगतार्थं रसमत्पादोपजीविभिरन्यैर्वायम्प्रसादो-
न्यथा न

३२ कर [णीयो यस्त्वेता] माज्ञामुल्लङ्घ्यान्यथा कुर्यात्कारयेद्वा सोस्मा
[भि] स्सुतरा न्न मर्षणीयो

३३ ये चास्म [दूर्ध्वम्भवि] तारो भूमिपाला स्तैरप्णु भयलोक निरवद्य
सुखार्थिभि: पूर्व

३४ राज विहितोयं विशिष्ट: प्रसाद इति प्रयत्नतम्यक्परिपालनीय एबं
यतो

३५ धर्मशास्त्रवचनम्बहुभिर्बंसुधा दत्ता राजभिस्सगरा दिभि: यस्य यस्य यदा
भूमि

३६ स्तस्य तस्य तदा फल मिति स्वयमाज्ञा दूतकश्चात्र भट्टारक श्रीशिवदेव:

३७ संवत् १०० ३ ज्येष्ठ शुक्ल दिवा त्रयोदश्याम्[4]

1. DV ष्ठ, Gn श्रेष्ठी but also says it is perhaps श्रेष्ठी । 2. Gn
ध्नि; DV reads ध्नि । 3. Gn, DV प्रि··· स्ति । 4. Gn and DV
read 103, which seems correct. BLI reads 143.

CXXIX.

(L 17; Gn LXXV; DV 136; HJ 139) A piece of stone in a
street corner in the village of Sanku about 6 miles north east of
Kathmandu. The inscribed part is 26 cm wide and 4 cm long.

The characters belong to the later Lichhavi period (according to Gnoli after Narendradeva) but it might as well belong to any time in the post-Amśuvarmā period. It is a two-line inscription which begins with Buddhist Mahāyāna invocation.

१ देय धर्मोयं श्रीधर्मराजिका मात्ये षु ¹
२ सांघिक भिक्षुसंघस्य ········

1. L, Gn, DV मात्य ।

CXXX. Chikandeo Stone

(DV 137; HJ 138) A flat stone supporting the pedestal of an image called Balarama or Chikandeo (Oil God). The inscribed part is 72.5 cm wide and 12 cm long. The stone is damaged. The date symbol in the first line is also not clear but DV reads 109.

The first line is completely destroyed.

१ ··········सप्तम्याम्भट्टारक महाराज [धिराज]····देवस्य राज्यम्
संवत् १०७ शुक्ल द्वितीया ········
२ ·······संसृष्ट्वानालवर्मणा भये······गीताद्या म नाभर····
३ ·······रस्य भवति तदाभक्षामवं ग्राम प्रदेश त्र····पिण्डकं
४ ·······द्रव्यं····६ मानिका······ मानिकात्रयम्······

CXXXI. Nala Inscription

(DV 138; HJ 140) An ancient water tank of stone attached to the wall near the temple of Bhagvati at Nala, 2 miles north west of Banepa. The date is 118 *Jyeṣṭha śukla daśamī*. The inscribed part is 36 cm wide and 7 cm long. The record belongs to the reign of Śivadeva II.

१ ॐ संवत् ११८ ज्येष्ठ शुक्ल दशम्याम् राजाधिराज श्रीशिवदेवस्य
राज्यम्

२ उपरिमनालङ्क ग्रामस्योपभोगम् तत्रैव ग्रामाधिवासी हुंध्र वशीलस्य

३ तद्भ्राता हूं श्रणङ्कशील सहितेन पुण्याधिकार प्रणाली कृतम् ।

1. DV भो[गा]र्थम् ।

CXXXII. Lagantol Inscription

(Gn LXXVII; DV 139; HJ 141)   A slab of stone leaning
against the wall of a small temple of Viṣṇu situated in Lagan
tol, Kathmandu. The top of the stone is decorated by a relief
showing a reclining bull. Date: *Samvat 119 Phālguṇa śukla
daśamī.* This inscription is now lost but a rubbing published by
BLI serves the purpose and confirms the existence of the
inscription wherever it might be.

१ ॐ स्वस्ति श्रीमत्कैलास भवनाल्लक्ष्मीलतालम्बन कल्पपादपो

२ भगवत्पशुपति भट्टारक पादानुगृहीतो बप्पपादानुध्यात: परम भट्टार

३ क महाराजाधिराज श्रीशिवदेव: कुशली वैद्यग्रामके प्रधानाग्रेसरान् सकल

४ निवासि कुटुम्बिनो यथाहंङ्क शलमभिधाय समाज्ञापयति विदितमस्तु भव

५ तां यथायङ्ग्राम: शरीरकोट्टममर्यादो [पपन्न] इचाट भटानाम प्रवेश्येना
चन्द्रार्का

६ वनिकालिको भूसिच्छिद्रन्यायेनाग्रहारतयामातापित्रोरात्मनश्च विपुलपु

७ ण्योपचयहेतो रस्माभि: स्वकारित श्रीशिवदेवेश्वरं भट्टारक न्निमित्ती-
कृत्य

८ तद्देवकुलखण्डस्फुटितसंस्कार करणाय वशपातुपताचार्येभ्य: प्रति

९ पादित: तद्देवमवगतार्यं भंवद्धि: समुचित देयभागभोगकर हिरण्यादि

१० सर्वप्रत्यायानेषामुपय [च्छ] द्विरेभिरेवानुपाल्यमानैरकुतोभय: स्वक

११ र्मानुविधायिभिरिति कर्त्तव्यता व्यापारेषु च सर्वैष्टामीषामाज्ञा श्रवण-
विघे

१२ यैर्भूत्वा सुखमत्र स्थातव्यं सीमा चास्य पूर्वेण वृह्मार्गे दक्षिणपूर्वतश्च

१३ शिवी प्रणाली तामेव चानुसृत्य स्वल्प: पन्था दक्षिणइच्च तेह्व पश्चिमे

१४ नापि तेह्लु उत्तरस्यामपि चिशिमण्डातिलमकः उत्तरपूर्वतश्चापि सहस्र

१५ मण्डलभूमिस्ततो यावत्स एव वृह्न्मार्ग इत्येव सीमान्त भतेस्मिन्न प्र

१६ हारे भोट्ट विष्टिहेतोः प्रतिवर्ष भारिकजनाः पञ्च ५ व्यवसायिभिर्ग

१७ ह्रीतव्या ये त्वेतामाज्ञां व्यतिक्रम्यान्यथा कुर्युः कारयेयुर्वा तेस्माभिर्भूशन्न

१८ क्षम्यन्ते ये वास्मद्दूर्ध्वम् भूभुजो भ [विष्यति तैरपि प] र स्वहिता
       पेक्षया पूर्वराज

१९ कृतोयं धर्मसेतुरिति तदा [वगत्य]॰॰॰र वा॰॰॰संरक्षणी

२० यस्तथा चोक्तं पूर्वदत्तां द्विजातिभ्यो यत्नाद्रक्ष युधिष्ठी [र महीम्महीम्]

२१ तां श्रेष्ठ दानाच्छ्रेयोनुपालनं षष्टि वर्ष सहस्राणि स्वर्गे मो [दतिभू]

२२ मिदः आक्षेप्ता चानुमन्ता च तान्येव नरके वसेत् इति स्वयमा

२३ ज्ञा दूतकश्चात्र राजपुत्र जयदेवः संवत् १०० १० ६ फाल्गुन

२४ शुक्ल दिवा दशम्याम्

1. BLI मर्यादो [पयुक्त] । 2. Gn म् मूभुजो । 3. BLI has included
the letters of the 24th line into the 23rd.

CXXXIII. Sonaguthi Stone of Śivadeva II

(Gn LXXVIII; DV 140; HJ 142)   A slab of stone, about
47 cm wide and 74 cm long, standing to the left of the western
gate of the temple of Bhṛṅgāreśvara situated in the village of
Sonaguthi. The top of the stone has a beautiful floral design.
Date: *Samvat*   125 as read by Gnoli and not 121 as read
by DV.

Gnoli has failed to decipher many letters in this inscription
because of the damage, and also due to bad rubbing. But others
show much improvement.

१ [स्वस्ति कैलास] कूट भवनाद् व्याहत शासन स्सु विहित गुण वर्ण
       श्रम स्थिति लिच्छवि कुल

२ केतुर्भगवत्पशुपति भट्टारक पादानुगृहीतो बप्पपादानुध्यातो परम
       भट्टारक

३ महाराजाधिराज श्री शिवदेव: [कुशली] नेपालान्त वर्त्तिन्य: समधि-
करणा नामसमद्पाद*

४ प्रसादोपजीविन्याश्च यथाहं‌ङ्कुशलभाष्य समाज्ञापयति विदितम्भवतु
भवतां

५ ·······मपरिमित जलाशयो द्वेशतया·······पाञ्चालिकानां

६ ···क्षेम जीवेन विज्ञापितेरस्माभिश्च प्रसादानु वर्त्तिभि धर्माधिकार[तया]

७ ·····द्युपयोगायासौ ब्राह्मण पुरस्सराणाञ्च पाञ्चालिकानां प्रकामोपभोगनि

८ मित्तमाज्ञानुक्रम ध्याय भृङ्गारेश्वर देवकुलस्थितये सर्व···तिलमक····

९ ·······प्रवर्त्तनीया स्युरिति तद्देवकुल पाञ्चालिक···गोल·····ग्राम

१० ·······पानीय···प्रणाली तिलमकस्य·······तालपत्र

११ ·······भृङ्गारेश्वरपाञ्चा [लिकानां]···क्षेत्र·······

१२ ·······मुपभोगत्वादस्य···राय·······

१३ ·······दस्माभिरपि निर्वा·······

१४ ·······विचारयितव्यास्तेपि द्रव्यमपि·····

१५ ·······द्विपणा पुराणम्·······

१६ ·······कृत·······

१७ ·······पिण्डक मानिका नि·····

१८ ·······पणां पुराणत्रयं दण्डनीया विदित्वैव भवद्भिरपि·····

१९ ·······कर्त्तव्य: कारयितव्यो वा ये त्विमामाज्ञामु [ल्लङ्घ्या]न्यथाकुर्यु

२० र्वाकारयेद्वा भृषन्न मर्षयितव्याम्·······भावद्भिरपि·······

२१ ···भि: पुरातनराज···यं···द·····

२२ ·······नीय···श्रूयते बहुभिर्वंसुधा दत्ता राजभि:

२३ सगरादिभि: यस्य यस्य यदा भूमिस्तस्य तस्य यस्य तदा फलम् पूर्वदत्तां

२४ द्विजातिभ्यो यत्नाद्रक्ष युधिष्ठिर महीम्महीभुजां श्रेष्ठ दानाच्छ्रेयो-
नुपालनम्

२५ ·······स्वयमाज्ञा दूतकश्चात्र राजपुत्र जयदेव:

२६ संवत् १०० २० ५ भाद्रपद शुक्ल पञ्चम्याम्

*Gn omits नेपालान्त and then after करण keeps the place vacant.
**Gn यथाहि ।

1. Gn भवनाद्···विहितगुण-स्थि-लिच्छवि । 2. DV नेपालान्त वर्तिन:, Gn कुशली····वर्तिन्य: समधिकरण···· 3. Gn मपरिमित जलाशयो वेशतया । 4. Gn ····ताय । 5. Gn प्रकामपभोग । 6. DV omits this word. 7. DV is correct but Gn reads ····प्र-ते ौ यस्मादिति । 8. Gn कुल ग्रागुलस्यादिग्राम । 9. DV is as above, although the unreadable portion marked is incorrect, but Gn reads ····यू····ही···· लीतिलमकस्य । 10. DV as above but Gn omits तिलमकस्य । 11. DV omits द्रव्यमपि; Gn ····ा····यसोपि···· 12. Gn ····द्वि रांणां···· 13. Gn ····न···य···नि । 14. Gn ··· प····दण्डेन य···श्चित्त···· मि··· 15. Gn राज-इ-ह-इ-यरस्तम्···· 16. Gn reads 125 and DV 121 but the former is correct as the symbol for 5 is evident.

CXXXIV. Inscription of Gorkha

(DV 141; HJ 143) A slab of stone at the entrance of the cave of Gorakhnath. The inscribed part is 30 cm wide and 70 cm long. The stone is much damaged. It is a charter. The date is just 122 without other particulars. But the reading of the date figure is doubtful.

१ ॐ स्वस्ति कैलासकूट [भवनाद्]········
२ ····[पादा] नुध्यात········परम
३ [भ]ट्टारक महाराजाधिराज [श्रीशि] बदेव: कु[शली]····
४ ·········समाज्ञाप
५ यति विदितम्भबतु भवतां···········
६ वज्रभैरव भट्टा[रक]········
७ कारण पूजा···········
८ ·········भूमि·······
९ समापन्न···········
१० ···पण········
११ वं भोग दत्तं···········
१२ वादित्रञ्च प्रत्ये[क]······
१३ ···क्षेत्र········
१४ ········क्रत····मतो-दान···

१५ ······कृत ······प्रतिदिन······
१६ ······प्रतिदिन······दान······
१७ ······मिमूल्य······पशा······
१८ पणद्वयं प्रत्येक············
१९ ग्राहक············
२० ततो द्वादश············
२१ मानिका: पा······
२२ स्फटिक व······
२३ द्वादश मानिका······वादित्र······पणपुराण······
२४ पञ्चरङ्ग चित्रकर्मण······मानिका त्रयं······
२५ प्रतिमानिका······
२६ पणपुराणा-पञ्च······मानिका
२७ करण············
२८ वेद्यानि भगवतो दत्तानि······
२९ पूजास जल······
३० हेतो······रकल्पना······
३१ रिति संवत् १०० २० २······

CXXXV. Thimi Inscription (II)

(L 19; Gn LXXXII, DV 142; HJ)　A slab of stone, about
40 cm wide and 16 cm long, near an ancient water conduit
situated outside the village of Thimi which is situated midway
between Bhadgaon and Kathmandu. This inscription does still
stand. Gnoli says 'A reading of the rubbing reproduced by Levi
confirms his transcription. The date of inscription is illegible.'
He also thinks that as Jayadeva is a witness, the record must
belong to the reign of Śivadeva II. He is correct. I have based
my reading of the text on my own rubbing.

Some lines in the beginning are worn away.

१ ······हिरण्यादिप्रत्याम······
२ ······पश्चिमे नि······
३ ············

४ ····गामी····भूतो तस्मात्····[1]

५ ·······तदियमेतत्कोट्टमर्यादावन्ध·······[2]

६ ·······तश्च पश्चिमेन च तदेवं·····[3]

७ ·······तदन्तरेणापि ते माप्रहरणस्य····

८ ·······खातम्पल्ली ततो याव च्चैव····[4]

९ ····ग्र····क····विष्टिमनुष्य सम्बन्धेन प्रतिवर्षं यत्पुराणशतं देयं[5]

१० ····तेभ्य एव ग्रामीणैर्दातिव्यम् राजकुलीय व्यवसायिभिस्तु न कदाचिद [न्यथा]

११ [कर्त]व्यं ये तु केचिदस्मत्पादप्रसादोपजीविनोपरेचान्यथा कुर्यु: कारयेयु [र्वा]

१२ ··तेतितरान्न क्षम्यन्ते भविष्यद्भिरपि वसुधाधिपतिभिरात्मन:करुणाति-शयं

१३ पूर्वपार्थिवप्रणीतोयं दान धर्मसेतुरिति तद्गौरवात्सम्यगेवानुपालनीय स्तथा [चोक्तं]

१४ पूर्वदत्तां द्विजातिभ्यो यत्ताद्रक्ष युधिष्ठिर । महीं महीभुजां श्रेष्ठ दाना-च्छ्रेयोनुपा

१५ लनम् ॥ षष्टि वर्ष सहस्त्राणि स्वर्गे मोदति भूमिद: । आक्षेप्ता चानुमन्ता च ता····

१६ नरके वसेत् । इतिस्वयमाज्ञा दूतकश्चात्र राजपुत्र जयदेव: ॥

१७ सं[वत्]····आश्वयुजि कृष्णषष्ठयाम् ।

1. Gn, DV ····गामी····   2. Gn, DV ····यमेत···   3. Gn, DV चतदा····   4. Gn, DV ततोयाव····   5. Gn, DV omit देयं ।

CXXXVI. Another Inscription of Balambu

(Gn LXXVI; DV 143; HJ 145) A slab of stone, about 50 cm wide and 84 cm long, standing in the open ground on the right bank of a rivulet Indramatī also called Mulakhu near the dilapidated temple of *Mahālakṣmī pīṭha* in the village of Balambu. Date: *Samvat 109* as read by Gnoli and 129 as read by DV, but the symbol 100 and 20 are hardly legible while 9 is clear. The inscription is, however, well preserved. As it belongs to the time of Śivadeva II the year can be between 109 and 139.

१ ॐ स्वस्ति श्रीमत्कैलासकूटभवनात्सम्यग्वि रचित सकलवर्णाश्रम व्यवस्थ: समस्त सामन्त शिर[1]

२ सा रवरिक्रत चरणनरवमयूखसमूह भगवत्पशुपति भट्टारक पादानुगृहीतो वप्प[2]

३ पादानुध्यातो लिच्छविकुलानन्दकेतु: परमभट्टारकमहाराजाधिराज श्रीशिवदेव: कु[3]

४ शली नेपाल भुक्तौ यथास्वमधिकारान् घिष्ठित: सर्वराजा [ज] पुरुषां तटवृत्ति भुजश्च यथार्हङ्कू[4]

५ शलमभिधाय समाज्ञापयति विदितमस्तु भवतां यथा पुत्तिनारायण देवकुल प्रतिवद्धदा[5]

६ वाकोट्टाभिधानोग्राम: पूर्वयावद्राजकुलेनविच्छेदक्रमेनोपभुज्यमान इत्यवगम्य[6]

७ स्माभिरिदानी मयङ्ग्राम: कोट्टमर्यादोपपन्नश्चाटभटानामप्रावेश्येन फलन्जु विष्ढ्या च विनिर्मुक्त:[7]

८ सतलशीताटीद्रङ्जनिवासिनां पालनोपभोगार्थप्रसादी क्रुतोस्य च देवकुल स्यरवण्ड स्फुटित सं

९ स्कार कारण पूजादिकमेभिरेव कर्तव्यं कारणपूजा व्यवशिष्टेन च द्रव्येण भगवत: श्रीपशुपति भट्टा[8]

१० रकस्य प्रतिवर्षमस्मत्पुण्याधिगम निमित्तं शोभनच्छत्रारोपणा करणीया तमुद्दिश्य शोभना यात्रापिक

११ रणीया तदुपयुक्त शेषमपि प्रत्यायजात मेतैविभज्य स्वयमुप भोक्तव्य मेष च ग्राम: फवद्रङ्ग्राम[9]

१२ स्य दक्षिणपश्चिमेन गंप्रोन्द्रिङ्ग्रामस्यापि पश्चिमोत्तरेण गणिदुङ्ग्रामस्य चोत्तरपूर्वेतोनुपुनग्रा[10]

१३ मस्यापि दक्षिणपूर्वेणामीषा ञ्चतुण्णङ्ङिग्रामाणांसीमा सत्वौमालम्ब्वा संझके प्रदेशे समावास

१४ यितव्य: सीमा चास्य प्राक्तनी आराम खर प्रदेशे शोभानाम्लाम्र वृक्ष
दक्षिणपश्चिमत: पाण्डुर

१५ मृत्तिका स्त्रोतसश्च दक्षिण पश्चिमेन यावद्धिमनदीस्त्रोत उत्तीर्य किञ्चि-
दारूह्य स्वकीयां च सीमा

१६ नां वेष्टयित्वा गवां लवणदानस्व दक्षिणालिका समीपे आम्रवृक्ष
स्तत्पश्चिम तो लुन्जु स्त्रोतस

१७ मुत्तीर्य दायम्म्वीगम्प्रोद्धिन्दावा कोट्टु सीमा मध्ये त्रिसन्धि[11] संज्ञक:प्रदेश-
स्तस्योत्तरत: पुत्तिनदी[12]

१८ तस्या एवो परिष्ठा द्यवत्पुत्तीर्यवदुनदीसंगमस्तमुत्तीर्य किञ्चिदारूह्य च
प्राच्यां दिशिभूचन[13]

१९ क्षेत्रस्योत्तरत: सीम्नो यावत्सलम्बुराज वासकस्योत्तरेण न [द्या] स्त्रोतो
वृहत्साल वृक्षस्तत्पूर्वदक्षिण

२० त: पाश्वृक्ष स्तत्पूर्वतोपि राजवासके पानीयारोपित एवोपभिधिसि—
खोट्टु क्षेत्रो त्तरेणाम्रपादप

२१ स्तत्पूर्वतोपि गोल्लंस्त्रोतसो[14] धस्ताद्यावद्गौतमाश्रम सरित्सङ्गमस्तस्य
चाधस्तादुत्थिमनदी सम्वैद्यस्ताम

२२ वतीर्यारूह्य च दण्डङ्गं वृहत्पथस्य त्रिसन्धि संज्ञकात्पश्चिमेनारूह्य
किञ्चित्पलानास्य च दक्षिणतो

२३ वृहद्नं तद्दक्षिणतोपि वस्तुं क्षेत्रं तस्यैव दक्षिणेन चम्पक वृक्षस्तद्
दक्षिण पश्चिमतश्च स

२४ एषा शोभना म्लाम्रवृक्ष इत्येतत्सीमान्त: पातित्यस्मिन् ग्रामे[15] समतप्रति-
वद्ध जीवनोपभोगिभि रन्यै

२५ र्वान कैश्चिदल्पापि पीडा कर्तव्या कारयितव्या वा ये त्वेता मास्माकी[16]
माज्ञा मवज्ञाया न्यथा कुयुं:कार

२६ ये युर्वा तेस्माभिर वश्यन्न क्षम्यन्ते येचास्म दुर्द्धम्भवितारौ मेदिनी नाथ
स्तैरपि पूर्व पार्थिव

२७ कृतोयं विशिष्ट: प्रसाद इति स्वहितोदयापेक्षिभिस्तद्गौरव [वा][17]
न्नित तरान् संरक्षणीयो यथो स्तथा चो

२८ क्त म्पुरातनानां पृथिबीश्वराणा ञ्जगद्धिताया विरतो द्यमाना ये
सर्वदाज्ञामनुपालयेयुस्ते

२९ षां नृपति भियताभि वृद्धि[18] इति स्वयमाज्ञा दूतकश्चात्र श्रीजयदेवो
भट्टारक: संवत्

३० १००······६···दिवा पञ्चम्याम्

1. Gn भवनाद्···· 2. Gn···चरण····भगवत्पशुपति etc. 3. Gn कुला····
4. Gn भु···सराज···इनु···य । 5. DV पुत्तिनारायण but Gn भवतां····
6. Gn ग्राम···ज्यामान; Gn also reads नोज्ञा for कोट्टा in the
beginning; DV omits यावद् before राजकुलेन । 7. Gn झलन्दु but
DV फलन्दु । 8. Gn कर्मेभि-कारणपूजा-वशिष्टेनेदप्र-ण । 9. Gn एष्टमपि ।
10. Gn दिङ्ग्रामस्य । 11. Gn कोट्टसी····त्रिसन्धि । 12. Gn स्योत्तरतः ।
13. DV reads किशि । 14. Gn गोलण, DV is correct. 15. Gn सा····
स्मिन् । 16. DV मवधूया; Gn मवज्ञाया । 17. Gn रक्षणीयोयथा ।
18. Gn नृपश्री नियता-इ-इति । 19. Gn 109....; DV १२६····
पञ्चम्याम्; but the symbol for 20 or any figure is completely
effaced.

CXXXVII. A Slab of Stone of Narayanachaur (Naksal)

(Gn LXXXIV; DV 144; HJ 148) The stone is one of the
two inscriptions found at a site called Narayanachaur in the
Naksal area of the city of Kathmandu. Naksal is the north-
eastern part of the suburb of the city. The stone is much
damaged in the middle portion. The symbol for the year is
missing. The inscribed part is 47 cm long and 37 cm wide.

Lines 1 to 8 are totally damaged.

१   ॐ स्वस्ति कैलासकूट भवनाद्········

२   ···महाराजाधिराज श्रीशिवदेवः कुशली[1]····

Lines 3-8 are not at all legible.

६   ········[यस्त्व] समाज्ञामतिक्रम्यान्यथा कुर्युः कारयेयुर्वस्माभि

१० ····भूपतिभिः पूर्वेराजकृत प्रसादानुपालनस्य ब्यवहित

११ ···दृढ़···या इति स्वयमाज्ञा दूतकश्चात्र भट्टारक श्रीजयदे

१२ [व]···पौषशुक्ल पञ्चम्याम्

1. DV has read these two lines.

CXXXVIII. Inscription of Musubahal (Kathmandu)

(HJ 127; DV 135)   The periphery of a mandala at the top.
The lines are two. The inscribed part is 86 cm wide and 3 cm
long.

१   ······सर्वसत्व हिताय·········
२   तस्य संस्कार पूजार्थम् भिक्षुणीसंघ र्मापतपणाः पुराण सहिता····प्रकल्च-तत्

CXXXIX. Chyasaltol Inscription

(L 18; Gn LXXIX; HJ 134; DV 145) A slab of stone
standing in the courtyard of an ancient water conduit called
Nayohiti at Chyasaltol, Patan. Date: Samvat 137. The inscribed
part is 55 cm wide. The first 11 or 12 lines of the inscription
are lost and not readable.

About 11-12 lines in the beginning are destroyed. Gnoli
starts from the 12th line.

१   ···············वप्प
२   पादानुगृहीत············महाराजाधिराज परमेश्बर श्रीज
३   यदेव: कुशली···········
४   ···········
५   ···········
६   ···········
७   ···········
८   ···········
९   ···········
१० ···········
११ ···········
१२ ······दक्षिणेन···तंर्वाटिकायाश्च दक्षिण·······
१३ ······पश्चिम·······
१४ ·······[द]क्षिण··स्थान सहस्र····दि···नम

१५ स्तन्·······नदीमुत्तीर्यं यावच्च··· पश्चिमतः पानीयपात····

१६ र्वमनुसृत्यदक्षिणापिर्णंपश्चिमेन··· ण्णङ्कक्षेत्रेण किञ्चिद्दक्षिणेन पश्चिम
   शङ्कर

१७ ····टार्वे शिरसा पश्चिमतः उत्तरङ्कंवा अपोवतीर्यं नदी लङ्घयित्वा
   नवगृहमण्डल

१८ ····पश्चिमोत्तरङ्कत्वा महापथेन च पश्चिमंगत्वा शिलासङ्क्रमस्य
   पश्चिमतः रेटा पाञ्चाली

१६ ···न च पूर्वोत्तरङ्कत्वा लोप्रिपाञ्चालिवाटिका पश्चिमोत्तरङ्कत्वा
   दोला-शिखर

२० ···पूर्वेणोत्तरङ्कत्वा पुनुपाञ्चालिका क्षेत्रस्य च पश्चिमोत्तरङ्कत्वा लोप्रि-
   पाञ्चालिका क्षेत्र

२१ स्य पश्चिमेनोत्तरंगत्वानारायणादेवकुल दशमीगौष्ठिक क्षेत्रस्याप्यु-
   त्तरङ्कत्वा

२२ लोप्रिग्रामेन्द्र गौष्ठिक क्षेत्रस्योत्तरं गत्वोमातीर्थं क्षेत्रस्य चोत्तरंङ्कत्वा
   ततो यावत्स

२३ पुष्पवाटिका विहार क्षेत्रस्य सीवावधि रित्ये तत्सीम···

२४ ल प्रासादमण्डलाभ्यन्तरे च कोट्टमर्यादास्माभिः प्रसादीकृता···जान

२५ ध्रिरस्मत्पादप्रसाद प्रतिवद्धजीवनें रन्यैर्वा न कैश्चिदयम्प्रसादो व्यति-
   क्रमणीयो

२६ ···नामास्मदीयामाज्ञमवबूय्न्यथा कुर्वीरन् कारयेयुर्वा तेस्माभिनं··

२७ नराधिपतिभिः पूर्वंमहीपाल कृतप्रसाद परिरक्षणैकतानें····

२८ तितरान्न मर्षणीयाः स्वयमाज्ञा दूतकोप्यत्र भट्टारक श्रीविजयदेवः सं

२६ वत् १०० ३० ७ ज्येष्ठ शुक्ल पञ्चम्याम्

CXL. Mīnanātha Water Conduit Stone Inscription

(Gn LXXX; BLI 14; DV 146; HJ 152) A slab of stone
standing near the courtyard of a water conduit close to the
temple of Mīnanātha or Manjughosa, Patan. Date: *Samvat 145*
as read by Gnoli and 148 as read by DV, but the year symbol
indicates 100 40 8. Some portions of the inscription in the
beginning are worn away and illegible. The inscribed part is
41 cm wide and 48 cm long.

Many lines in the inscription are totally lost due to damage.

१   ....र्णंद....मपूर्वो....[1]

२   ....ज्य....

३   ....स्तस्यान्तरेप्यमुं जानद्भि रस्माकमन्यथा....निरूप्य....[2]   [3]

४   ....रूयमपल....दत्तमाद्यप्रसादं विशुद्धमनसा....शासन....[4]

५   ....षा....यूपग्रामे....लिम प्रतिपादित स्त....कुर्पासद-[5]   [6]

६   त्पुरोरशनस्तस्यान्तरे चाग्रत वने मत्तिकां चोत्पाट....[7]

७   ....विघ्नमिममपराधं कृत्वा प्रपलायित: कोट्टस्थानम्....[8]   [9]

८   ... निवेद्य यथापूर्वमनुष्ठातव्यं तिलमक समीपे च ..क....[10]

९   रात्रौ दिवा वाविशत् कंश्चित्तत्परिपन्थिभिरन्यैर्वा न विरोधनीयस्तद्वि-
      रोधक....

१०   ....प्राप्तिरेव गृहीत्वा राजकुलमुपनेतव्या: तिलमक सम्बद्धं कार्यञ्च
      यदुत्पद्यते [तदन्तरास]

११   [ने] नैव विचार्य निर्णेतव्यं तिलमकश्च सप्तधा विभज्य परिभोक्तव्यो
      गीग्वल्पाञ्चालिकै रे [को भा]

१२   गो ग्राह्यो जाञ्जैपाञ्चालिकैरेको भागस्तेग्वल्पाञ्चलिकैरेको भागो[11]
      यूग्वल्पाञ्चालिकै स्त्रयो [भागा]

१३   ....हलपाञ्चालिकै स्त्बेको भाग इत्येव मवगतार्थैर्भवद्भिरनुमन्तव्यमेतत्[12]
      ....शासनं प्रदा....[म][13]

१४   नागपि न लङ्घनीयो ये त्वेतामस्मदीयामाज्ञामतिक्रम्यान्यथाकुर्यु:
      कारयेयुर्वा [तेस्मा]

१५   भिदृढन्न क्षम्यन्ते ये चास्मद्दूर्ध्वमवनिपतयो भवितारस्तैरपि पूर्वराजस्थिति[14]
      परिपाल [न]

१६   व्यवहित मनोभिर्भव्यं तथा चाह। ये प्राक्तनावनिभुजां जगतो[15]   [16]
      हितानां धम्म्याँ स्थिति स्थितिकृताम

१७   नु पालयेयु: लक्ष्म्या समेत्प सुचिर न्निज भावयैव प्रेत्यापि वासवसमा
      दिविते बसेयुरिति स्वयमाज्ञा

१८   द्तकश्चात्र युवराज श्रीविजयदेव: संवत् १०० ४० ८ पौषशुक्ल दिवा[17]
      तृतीयस्याम् ॥

1. Lines 1 & 2 are not available in BLI.   2. स्त्रस्वान्तरे etc.

3. निरुप्य is missing in BLI. 4. BLI प्यमुपलपनंचकुमार्या प्रसादं
वि·····सास·····; Gn रूपयमपलद·····तमा-प्रसादं वि·····शसु । 5. BL यूपग्रामे
युथिमा; Gn onwards ग्रामाम् । 6. Gn adds आ before कु; BL
blank after दित । 7. Gn चाप्रतवनेपत्तिकाचात्पाट; BL reads
ङ्त्यारगन । 8. BL पिघं·····मपराधं । 9. Gn adds ौ but BL omits.
10. BL omits; Gn [ग] ह्याञ्जापाञ्चालिका etc. 11. BL गढ्या
साञ्जापाञ्चा etc. 12. BL omits ल्ल । 13. BL, Gn and DV omit
प्रदा । 14. BL स्मामि etc. 15. BL adds ौने before व्य whereas
this should go as न at the end of the upper line. 16. BL
त्यथा । 17. BL just दूतक ।

CXLI. A Water Conduit Inscription near Jaisideval

(Ben 4; Gn App. 2; DV 147; HJ 153) The inscribed lines are
on the reservoir of a deserted water conduit of stone, which
lies a little further to the east of Jaisideval. The date is 151.

१   ॐ संवत् १०० ५० १ वैशाख शुक्ल द्वितीयायाम्
२   लञ्जग्वल्पाञ्चालिकानां नित्योपभोगार्थम्
३   प्रतीतलम्भस्य भार्यया भोजमत्या दत्तम्
४   जलद्रोणेन सह·····मा २

CXLII. The Paśupati Stele of Jayadeva II

(BLI 15; Gn LXXXI; DV 148; HJ 155) A slab of stone,
about 109 cm wide and 98 cm long, standing near the western
gate inside the temple precincts of Paśupati. The top of the
stone is decorated with fully blown lotus with 8 petals. Date:
Samvat 159 as read by Gnoli but seems to be 157 as read by
DV. Gnoli says: 'The inscription consists of 34 stanzas. The
metres used are: stanzas 1, 3, 5, 19, 20, 23, 30, 32, sragdharā;
stanzas 2, 4, 6, 7, 12, 15, 17, 21, 25, 27, 33, 34, śārdūlavikridīta;

stanzas 8, 11, 16, vasantatilakā; stanzas 9, 24, 31, upajāti of indravajrā and upendravajrā; stanzas 10, 18 anustupa.'

१ ॐ व्यक्षस्त्रचब्ययात्मा त्रिसमय सदृश त्रिपती स्त्रिलोकी त्राता त्रेतादि-
हेतुस्त्रिगुणमयतया व्यादिभिर्वर्णितोलं । त्रिस्त्रोतो धौतमूर्द्धा त्रिपुर-
जिद जितो निर्व्विबन्ध त्रिवर्गो यस्योत्तुङ्ग

२ स्त्रिशूल स्त्रिदशपतिनुतः स्त्रि दरित्रोटनो नः । राजद्रावणमूर्धपङ्क्ति
शिखर व्यासक्त चूडामणि श्रेणीसङ्घृति निश्चलात्मकतया लङ्काम्पुनानाः
पुरीं········द्व न्ध्यपराक्रमा

३ ·······सङ्घताः श्रीवाणासुरशेखराः पशुपतेः पादार्णवः पान्तु वः ॥
सूर्याद् ब्रह्म प्रपौत्रान्मनु रथ भगवाञ्जन्म लेभे ततोभूदिक्ष्वाकुश्चक्रवर्ती
नृपतिरपि ततः श्रीविकुक्षिर्बभूव ।

४ जातस्तस्मात्ककुत्स्थः पृथुरिति बिदितो भूमिपः सार्व्वभौमो भूतोस्मा
द्विश्वगश्चः प्रवल निजबल व्याप्त विश्वान्तरालः ॥ राजाष्टोत्तर
विङ्शति क्षितिभुजस्तमा द् व्यतीत्य क्रमात्संभूतस्सगरः पतिः

५ ···सागरायाः अभूद क्षितेः । जातोस्मादसमञ्जसो नरपति स्तस्मादभू-
दङ्शुमान् स श्रीमन्त मजीजनन्नरवरो भूपन्दिलीपाह्वयं ॥ भेजे जन्म
ततो भगीरथ इति ख्यातो नृपोत्रान्तरे भूपालान्प्रविल [ङ्घ्य]

६ ····रघुर्जातो रघोरप्यज· । श्रीमत्तुङ्गरथ स्ततो दशरथः पुत्रैश्च पौत्रे-
स्समं राज्ञोष्टावपरान्विहाय परतः श्रीमानभूल्लिच्छविः ॥ अस्त्येव
क्षितिमण्डलैक तिलको लोक प्रतीतो महानादि [त्य]

७ प्रभवः प्रभाव महतां मान्यः सुराणामपि । स्वच्छं लिच्छविनाम विभ्रदपरं
वंशः प्रवृत्तोदय श्रीमच्चन्द्र कलापधवलो गङ्गाप्रवाहोपमः ॥ तस्मा-
ल्लिच्छवितः परेण नृपतीन् हित्वा प

८ रान्द्वादशः श्रीमान्पुष्पशराकृतिः क्षितिपतिर्ज्जातः सुपुष्पस्ततः । साधं
भूपतिभि स्त्रिभिः क्षितिभृतां त्यक्त्वान्तरे विङ्शति ख्यातः श्रीजयदेव
नाम नृपतिः प्रादुर्ब्बभूवा परः ॥ एकादश क्षिति

९ पती [न] परञ्च भूपं हित्वान्तरे विजयिनो जयदेवः नाम्नः स्रीमान्व-
भूव वृषदेव इति प्रतीतो राजोत्तम सुगत शासन पक्षपाती ॥ अभूत्ततः
शङ्करदेव नामा श्रीधर्म्मदेवो प्युदपादि तस्मात् ।

१० श्रीमानदेवो नृपतिस्ततोभूत्ततो महीदेव इति प्रसिद्धः ॥ वसन्त इव
लोकस्य कान्तः शान्तारिविग्रहः । आसीद् वसन्तदेव स्माद्रान्त
सामन्त वन्दितः ॥ अस्यान्तरेप्युदयदेव इति क्षितीशाज्जातस्त्रयो

११ दश इतश्च नरेन्द्रदेव:। मानोन्नतो नतसमस्त नरेन्द्र मौलिमालारजो-
निकर पाङ्शुल पादपीठ: ॥ दातासद्द्रविणस्य भूरिविभवो जेता
द्विष्टसंहते: कर्त्ता बान्धवतोषणस्य

१२ विधिबत्पाता प्रजानामलं हर्त्ता। संश्रित साधुवर्गं विपदां सत्यस्य वक्ता
ततो जात: श्रीशिवदेव इत्यभिमतो लोकस्य भर्त्ता भुव:॥ देवी बाहु-
बलाढ्य मौरवरिकुला श्रीवर्म्मं

१३ चूड़ामणिख्याति ह‍र्षित वैरिभूपतिगण श्रीभोगवर्म्मोद्भवा। दौहित्री
मगधाधाधिपस्य महत: श्र्या दित्यसेनस्य या व्यूढा श्रीरिव तेनसा
क्षितिभुजा श्रीवत्सदेव्योदरात् ॥

१४ तस्माद्भूमिभुजोप्यजायत जितारातेरजय्य: परं राजा श्रीजयदेव इत्यवगत:
श्रीवत्सादेव्यात्मज:। त्यागी मानधनो विशालनयन: सौजन्यरत्नाकरो
विद्वान्सत्कविराश्रयो

१५ गुणवतां पीनोरुवक्ष: स्थल: ॥ माद्यद्दन्तिसमूह दन्तमुसल क्षुण्णारि
भूभृच्छिरो गौडो ड्रादिक लिङ्गकोसलपति श्री हर्षदेवात्मजा। देवी
राज्यमती कुलोचित गुणैर्युक्ता प्रभूता

१६ कुलैर्येनोढा भगदत्तराजकुलजा लक्ष्मीरिव क्षमाभुजा ॥ श्रङ्गश्रिया परि-
गतो जितकामरूप: काञ्चीगुणाढ्यवनिताभिरुपास्यमान:। कुर्व्वन्सुराष्ट्र-
परिपालन कार्यचिन्तां य: सार्व्वं

१७ भौमचरितं प्रकटीकरोति ॥ राज्यं प्राज्यसुखोर्जित द्विजजन प्रत्यर्पिता-
ज्याहुति ज्योतिउज्जर्ति शिखा विजृम्भणजिता शेष प्रजापद्रुतं। बिभ्रत्कण्ठक
वर्जित निनिजभुजा षष्टम्भ विस्फूर्जितं

१८ शूरत्वात्परचक्रकाम इति यो नाम्ना परेणान्वित: ॥ स श्रीमान् जयदेवा-
ख्यो विशुद्धवृहदन्वय: लब्धप्रताप: सम्प्राप्त बहुपुण्य समुन्वय: ॥ मूर्त्ती-
रष्टाभिरष्टौ महयितुमतुलैं:

१९ स्वेदेलैंरष्टमूर्त्तं पातालादुत्थितं किं कमलनभिनवं पदमनाभस्य नाभे:।
देवस्यास्यासनायोपगतमिह चतुर्व्वक्त्रसादृश्य मोहाद् विस्तीर्णं विष्टरं
किं प्रविकसित सिताम्भोजमम्भोज

२० योने: ॥ कीर्णा किम्भूतिरेषा सपदि पशुपते नृत्यतोत्र प्रकामं मौलीन्दो:
किम्मयूखा: शरदमभिनवां प्राप्यशोभामुपेता: भक्तया कैलासशैला
ढिमनिचयरुच: सानव: किं

२१ समेता दुग्धाब्धेरागत: किं गलगरसहजप्रीतिपीयूष राशि: ॥ राज्ञ: देवं
वन्दितुमुद्यतो द्युतिमतो विद्योतमान द्युति: किं ज्योत्स्ना धबला फणाबलि-
रियं शेषस्य सन्दृश्यते ।

२२ अन्तर्दूर रसातलाश्रितगतेर्देव प्रभावश्रिया किं क्षीरस्नपनं विधातुमुदिताः
क्षीरार्णवस्योर्म्मयः ॥ विष्णोः पातालमूले फणिपतिशयनाक्रान्ति लीला
सुखस्था दाञां प्राप्योत्प

२३ तन्त्यास्त्रिपुर विजयिनो भक्तिततोभ्पर्च्चनाय । लक्ष्म्याः संलक्ष्यते
प्राक्करतल कलितोत्फुल्ललीलासरोजं किं वेतीत्थं वितर्कास्पदमतिरुचिरं
मुग्धसिद्धाञ्जनानां ॥ नालीनालीकमेत्तन्न खलु समुदितो राजतो [13]

२४ राजतोहं पद्मापद्मासनाज्वे कथमनु हरतो मानवा मानवाभे । पृथ्व्यां
पृथ्व्यान्न मादृग्भवति हृत जगन्मानसेम अनसे वा भास्वान् भास्वान् विशेषं
जनयति नहि मे वासरो वा सरोवा ॥ इतीव

२५ चामीकर केशराली सिन्दूर रक्त द्युति दन्त पङ्क्त्या राजीवराजीम्प्रति
जीवलोके सौन्दर्य्यदर्प्पादिवसप्रहासः ॥ एषा भाति कुलाचलैः परिवृता
प्रालेय संसर्गिभिर्व्बेंदी मेरूशिलेव काञ्चन मयीदेव

२६ स्य विश्रामभूः । शुभ्रैः प्रान्तैः विकासिपङ्कजदलैरित्याकलय्य स्वयं रौप्यं
पद्मचीकर तपशुपतेः पूजार्थमत्युज्ज्वलं ॥ राज्ञः ॥ यं स्तौति प्रकट
प्रभाव महिमा ब्रह्मा चतुर्भिर्म्मुखैं र्यञ्च श्लाघ

२७ यति प्रणम्य चरणे षड्भिर्म्मुखैः षण्मुखः । यन्तुष्टाव दशाननोपि दशभि
र्व्वक्त्रैः स्फुरत्कन्धरः सेवां यस्य करोति वासुकिरलं जिह्वा सहस्त्रैः
स्तुवन् ॥ ख्यात्या यः परमेश्वरोपि वहते वासो

२८ दिशाम्मण्डल व्यापी सूक्ष्मतरश्च शङ्करतया ज्ञातोपि संहारकः । एकोप्यष्ट [14]
तनुः सुरासुर गुरूर्व्वीतत्रपो नृत्यति स्थाणुः पूज्यतयो विराजति गुणैरेवं
विरुद्धै रपि ॥ राज्ञः ॥ तस्येदं प्रमथा

२९ धिपस्य विपुल ब्रह्माञ्जतुल्यं शुभं राजद्राजतपङ्कजं प्रवितत प्रान्त-
प्रकीर्णैर्दलैः । पूजार्थम्प्रविधाप्य तत्पशुपतेर्यंत्रापि पुण्यम्मया भक्तया
तत्प्रतिपाद्य मातरि पुनः संप्राप्नुयां निर्वृ ंति ॥

३० राज्ञः ॥ किं शम्भौरूपरि स्थितं ससलिलं मन्दाकिनीपङ्कजं स्वर्गाद्
भिन्ननवाम्बुजे क्षणधिया सम्प्राप्त मम्भोरुहं । देवानां किमियं शुभा
सुकृतिनां रम्याविमानावली पद्मं किं करुणाकरस्य करतो

३१ लोकेश्वर स्यागतं ॥ राज्ञः ॥ श्रोतः स्वर्गापगायाः किमिदमवतरल्लोक-
कल्लोलरम्यं किं ब्रह्मोत्पत्तिपद्मं तलकमलवर प्रेक्षणायोपयातं । सम्प्राप्त
ञ्चन्द्रमौलेरमल निजशिर इचन्द्रविम्बं

३२ यद्वीक्ष्य शङ्खां वहति भुविजनो विस्मतोत्फुल्लनेत्रः । श्रीवत्सदेव्या
नृपतेज्जनन्या समं समन्तात्परिवारपद्मैः । रौप्यं हरस्योपरि पुण्डरिकं
तदादरैः कारित मत्युदारं ॥ पुण्यं पुत्रेण दत्तं शशिकर विमलं

३३ कारयित्वाञ्ज मुख्यं प्राप्तं शुभ्रं शुभञ्च स्वयमपि रजतैं: पद्मपूजां
   विधाय । सर्वं श्रीवत्सदेवी निजकुल धवलाञ्चितवृत्ति दधाना प्रादा-
   त्कल्याण हेतोश्चिर मवनिभुजे स्वामिने स्वर्गताय ।। क: कुर्या¹⁵

३४ त्कुलज: पुमान्निजगुण श्लाघामिति ह्रीच्छया राज्ञा सत्कविनापि नो¹⁶
   विरचितं काव्यं स्ववंशाश्रयं । श्लोकान्पञ्च विहाय साधु रचितान्प्राज्ञेन
   राज्ञा स्वयं स्नेहाद्भूभुजि बुद्धकीर्तिरकरोत्पूर्वामपूर्वामिमां ।। योगक्षेम
   विधान बन्धुर

३५ भुज स्संवर्द्धंयन् बान्धवान् स्निह्यत्पुत्र कलत्र भृत्यसहितो लब्ध प्रतापो
   नृप: दीर्घायुन्नितरामय वपु न्नित्य प्रमोदान्वित: पृथ्वीं पालयतु प्रकाम
   विभवस्फीतानुरक्त प्रजाम् ।। संवत् १०० ५० ७ कार्तिक शुक्ल
   नवम्याम्¹⁷

1. N. Nath (S.S.I. p. 1) व्यम्बकत्रयाव; Gn स्त्रय····त्रोटनोत:; DV
स्तादरि etc. 2. Also see DV but Gn भूपालान्···· 3. NN भू
पालाञ्चरघुर भूज्जातो रद्धोप्याज: । 4. Gn महा···· but DV is correct.
5. Gn····but DV प्रमव which is correct. 6. Gn परो; DV परो ।
7. Gn पतिञ्चपरञ्चभूप । DV पतिनपरञ्चभूप···· Gn's first ञ्च is
actually न and it also makes no sense in having two ञ्च in
two words coming one after the other in the same context.
8. BLI एकादशक्षिति····[त्यक्त्वान्तरे] । 9. BLI जातस्त्रयोदशततश्च, NN
reads इतश्च, Fleet follows BLI (CIII.3, p. 186). 10. BL यम्वत ।
11. BLI राज । 12. BLI श्रीयाय । 13. BLI समुदितम । 14. BLI
ख्यातो । 15. Omitted by BLI. 16. BLI भाविरितो । 17. BLI
reads 153, Gnoli 159, but DV with 157 is correct.

CXLIII. Naksal Nārāyaṇa Chaur Inscription

(L 21; Gn LXXXIII; DV 149; HJ 157) A slab of stone
standing in a locality called Narayana Chaur in Naksal part of
Kathmandu. The stone is now deposited in the National
Museum. The date is illegible. Lines 1-9 are completely lost.

Lines upto 18 are also almost unreadable except a few letters. The inscribed part is about 28 cm wide and 122 cm long.

(L omits lines upto 19. The lines 1-9 are worn away.)

१० ⋯⋯⋯⋯पाञ्चा[1]⋯⋯

११ श्रवद⋯⋯⋯⋯⋯

१२ ⋯⋯⋯⋯⋯मदुवे

१३ ⋯⋯⋯⋯⋯⋯धिकरण ि र⋯⋯

१४ ⋯⋯⋯⋯दान⋯प्रयग⋯⋯⋯

१५ ⋯⋯⋯दा⋯ि⋯नि⋯ि⋯

१६ क्ष⋯य⋯स्य⋯⋯स ⋯

१७ ⋯प्र⋯पह⋯⋯शि⋯शि⋯शि⋯ते

१८ त्रयथायुक्त विचारणीय[2]⋯⋯⋯⋯दिव⋯िततपूर्वंपा⋯दौ[3]

१९ वारिकैर्यथायुक्त विचारणीय⋯दश[4] पणं [पु] राणा⋯मध्यकहृ⋯श्री
पूर्व्वाधिकरणस्य देया[5]

२० य⋯⋯⋯वप⋯⋯पुत्रककार्येण[6] श्रीपश्चिमाधिकरणस्य श्रीपूर्व्वाधिकरणस्य[7]
दक्षिणगत⋯त्र.घे

२१ करणस्य⋯चरण⋯पुरो दौवारिकेणापि यथाशास्त्रानुगतं विचारणीयं[8]
तथा

२२ कदृतोन[9]⋯[10]⋯⋯[11]भट्टाधिकार प्रभृतीनां सर्व्वाधिकाराणाम प्रवेश[12]

२३ सीमनि समुपस्थित कार्याणां च स्वयं पाञ्चालिकानामेव न्यायावलोकन
पश्चिमे[13]

२४ न-र्यकात्परि⋯यांकुसविवर्त क अपरिहारगे⋯पणे[14]⋯प⋯

२५ को दोलने[15] पणपुराणाः[16] पञ्च । निबन्धलंघने[17] पणपुराण चतुष्टयं ।
साक्षिनिदेंशे[18] पणपुराण[19]

२६ द्वयं सार्द्धं । मुद्रयाप्युद्गारे[20] विशतिपणाश्चात्रोपस्थित[21] साक्षिणां दण्ड:[22]
पणशत् चतुष्टयं लिखित[23]

२७ भाश्रन्ते[24] पणशतम् ॥ संप्रतिपत्तौ पणापुराणाः[25] सद्विपणः[26] । प्रीवन्तेणे
पणपुराणाः पञ्चवि[27]

२८ शतिः अयक्षिकाङ्क्ता दशपणपुराणाः साद्धं च उत्तमकायेे । मध्यमा वरकायेषु
च षट् पणपुराणाः

२९ संद्विपणाः सपणं पणपुराणा त्रयमिति निर्णिण्क्त व्यवहार भग्रस्य सपणं
पुराणशतं पञ्चासत्प

३० ञ्चर्विंशतिं श्च पणपुराणाः कलिपतो दण्डः । व्यवहार परिनिष्ठित जातं
द्रव्यस्य षड्भागं पाञ्चालिकानाँ दातव्यं

३१ यस्तु द्रव्यं न्न प्रयच्छेत्स्वस्थान वास्तव्य स्यान्य स्थानीयस्य च धारण
कस्यात्रैव रोधोपरोधो भवेत् । यस्तु कुदृ

३२ ष्टमिति कार्यमस्य ततो रोगमाचौदौवारिकस्यावेदनीयं तेनापि श्रीम-
त्पादीयान्तरासन करणे यथा

३३ मासं रोपणीयः सगर्भनारीमरणे पणशतमेकम् । आत्मघातकाना मुच्छि-
ष्टदत्ताम् सकलह मरणे

३४ दौवारिकस्यावेद्यं मृतशोधनं तदर्थमागतस्य तस्य सद्विपणाः षट्पणपुराणा
देयाः । सक्षत गोरूप वि

३५ वासे सपण पुराण त्रयं यथाधिकारिणां देयं । प्रासादरथंचित्रणे सिन्दि-
दौवारिकस्याशीतिः पण

३६ पुराणाः देयाः रथोत्तोलने प्रासाद संस्कारे च सर्व्वंपरिच्छदने प्रतिवर्षं
वेत्र दौवारिक स्याशीतिः पणः

३७ पुराणाः एवं चेलकरस्य च षट्पणपुराणाः सद्विपणः । २२ घटिका क्रये
दौवारिकेण पञ्चभिः

३८ पणपुराणे र्देया मणिडपीयात्रायां शाचेलंपट्टोयुगमुत्तमञ्च पञ्चाभरणकम्
प्रतिवर्ष स्थानदौवा

३९ रिकस्य पणपुराण सहस्रमेकं पाञ्चालिकैर्देयं । ताम्रकुट्टशाला मानेश्वर ।
साम्वपुर ह्यप्रिग

४० पुठम्प्रङ्ग जमयम्वी पुंदृत्रग्रामाणां द्रङ्गत्व मात्रमेव प्रसादीकृतमत्र शिला-
पट्टकोत्कीर्णाः श्रीस

४१ ङ्घादि प्रसाद विशेषाः समाविष्टा इति । परिगतार्थैर्यथोपरि लिखित
   नियोगा धिकृतैस्तदधि

४२ कारिभिः स्वव्यापार व्यपदेशेन मनसापि प्रसादात्ति क्रमसाहसाध्यवसायो
   न कर्तव्य इत्यादि ज्ञात्वा

४३ येन्यथा कारिणस्तेषामतिदारुणंदण्डं पातयिष्यामो भाविभिरपि नरा-
   धिनाथैः पूर्व्वनृपक

४४ त प्रसाद पालन परैः प्रजाप्रमोददान ज्ञंस्सुतरां न मर्षणीया स्तथा च
   पालनानुशन्सा श्रू

४५ यते । ये शीतांशुकरावदातचरितः सम्यक्प्रजापालने नो जिह्माः प्रथमा-
   वनीश्वर कृतां रक्षन्ति धम्म्यां स्थिति

४६ तेवज्ञांविजितारि चक्रुश्चिराँ संभुज्य राज्यश्रियं नाके शक्रसमान मानवि
   भवास्तिष्ठन्ति धन्याश्चिरम् सीमा

४७ चास्य स्थानस्योत्तर पूर्व्वस्यां दिशि अजिकाविहार पूर्व्वं द्वारा द्वात्रि-
   ङ्कान्ठको ततो दक्षिणाभिमुखेन महापथानु

४८ सृत्य मणिनागाट्टिकस्योत्तरतो बृहद्ग्रामं यावत् ततोत्तर पश्चिमाभिमुखेन
   वलसोक्षि देवकुलस्य दक्षि

४९ ण तिरस्मिमनुसृत्यवोद्विषय अरघट्टस्योत्तरेण माशानुसृत्य पश्चि
   [मा] भिमुखेन लंखुलउट्टणे ततस्ता

५० त्मनट्टणकमनुसृत्य नडपटा वाटिका मनुसृत्य पश्चिमाभिमुखेन महाप्रति-
   हारस्य गृहमंडलस्य द

५१ क्षिणस्य कण्ठानुसारेण महारथ्यायां स्तम्भितशिला ततस्तेन रथ्यामूलस्य
   यद्दुद्द्वारं प्रविश्य दक्षिणं गृहमादाय पश्चिमके

५२ धंभागमाक्रम्य दक्षिणगृहाग्रतः पश्चिममनुसृत्य द्वार गृहमण्डल प्रविश्य
   दक्षिणं गृहमादाय पश्चिमक

५३ च्छं लङ्घयित्बा यावीग्रामं मध्येन तवंचेषानुसारेण पश्चिमाभिमुखेन
   मार्गस्ततस्तन्मार्गेण उत्तरमुखा

५४ नुसारेण द्रमकुटीमार्गस्ततः पश्चिमाभिमुखेन परिक्रम्योत्तरामुखमनुसृत्य
   पोन्दिमण्डपिका समी

५५ पेन उडणेहुशस्ततस्तन पश्चिममवतीर्य ताम्रकुट्टशालागमन मार्गानुसारेण [76] [77]
जरिखसंक्रमाभिमुखेन [78]

५६ ताम्रकट्टशाला लखमक स्ततोत्तराभिमुखेन मानेश्वर राजाङ्गणाली [79]
दक्षिणेन प्रेक्षणमण्डपी पृष्ठत: पूर्ब्बो

५७ त्तरं गत्वा पूर्ब्बद्वारेण प्रविश्य राजाङ्गणमध्येन पश्चिमद्वारेण ततस्चोत्तरं [80]
गत्वा प्रवर्द्ध मानेश्वरस्याग्रत: [81]

५८ पश्चिम मार्गमनुसृत्य यावत्वोत्तरितोकारित प्रणाल्यग्रत: व्यति य मस्ता [82]
तद्दक्षिणेन साम्वपुर

५९ वाटिका [या] श्चार्द्ध तत: ......मार्गस्योत्तल्या: पश्चिम (म) नुसृत्य [83] [84] [85]
दक्षिणमनुसृत्य दक्षिण यष्टि [86]

६० गामी पश्चिमद्वारेण......जीववर्म्म विहारस्य दक्षिण......हृद्वाटिकाया [87] [88]
दक्षिणाली

६१ पश्चिमा......(तिल) मकादुत्तर पश्चिमेन......मनुसृत्य कम्प्रोयम्बी [89] [90]

६२ मार्गेणोत्तर......[भट्टा]रक प्रतिबद्ध क्षेत्रखण्ड......विहारभूमे: प [91] [92]

६३ शिचमाल्याब [तीर्य] बृह्नदीमध्यानुसारेण......मान-नति मध्या [93]

६४ दुत्तरमनुसृत्य......दीपेका ततो दक्षिणमार्ग......ग्रामगामी मार्ग तिविद्धा यथा [94] [95]

६५ स्ततो......थ मार्गा नुसारेण विङ्वोचामण्डपि पश्चिमे यकुस्ततो काम [96]
स्वामि कार्त्ति [97]

६६ के[य]......करगोष्ठिभूमे: पूर्ब्बं तश्चेव सप्तमी गोष्ठिभूमे पू (वं)...... [98]
बिहारभूमे

६७ पश्चिमालीमा......रपाञ्चालिभूमेश्च पूर्ब्बालीततुनु सारेण श्रीतुकाण- [99] [100]
पूर्ब्बालीततो

६८ नुसारेण तैत्तिरीशाखा गोष्ठिभूमे पश्चिमाली ततोनुसारेण...... [101] [102]

६९ नुसारेण अष्ट......गर्त्तभेगस्तत: पूर्ब्बानुसारेण कङ्ध्वावत्तिखा ततोनुसारेण [103]

७० ......मार्गस्ततो नदी प्रोल्लंघ्य वातं कुटी पूर्ब्बं पङ्कुटी प्रविश्य सर...... [104]
परिमित:......

७१ सारेण सामन्तः·····गोष्ठिभूमेः पूर्व्वलीतिलमक¹⁰⁵

७२ पूर्व्वली ततो···········

७३ ·····नुसारेण प·····¹⁰⁶·······

7 to 8 lines at the end cannot be read.

1. Gn, DV पञ्च । 2. Gn नायुक्त विवारण । 3. Gn, DV तत । 4. Also see DV. But Gn·····दश । 5. DV but Gn मष्यक दलन·····, L तास·····नदन पणपुराण-काम व्याक···· 6. DV पश्चिमा । 7. DV but Gn कार्य्णे···· 8. L ·····लकोणस्यश्रीपूर्व्वाधिकरण···· 9. Gn नुगत·····; DV विचारणीय·····; L omits विचारणीयतथा । 10. Gn, DV क·····णान । 11. Gn दत्त णोन·····रि etc. He omits धिकाभट्टाधिकारी and other letters are correct. 12. Also DV but Gn सर्व्वाधिकरण···· 13. शि-रि·····प्रज्ञान·····कार्याशां·····न्त; L श्रीत्तिसमकापृस सरेकारे·····णाम् समम्·····कानामेवब्व्याप·····; DV leaves हिचमे । 14. Gn, DV न र्याकिपरि···· ·····र्याकुस·····हार पणेप·····; L ·····मियाकु-प·····तो हार औपणे । 15. Levi कादलने । 16. L ·····प···· 17. Also DV correctly reads but Gn ·····नि-क्षले-ङ्ग·····; Levi नियकाला···· 18. DV but correct Gn यो-इ-नि·····पणपुराणम् । 19. Levi ·····अजति-सेपा । 20. Gn देयसार्धमुद्रयाधाङ्ग; Levi देयं तार-पदप घानाने । 21. DV correct but L and Gn वेत्रो । 22. DV correct but Gn दत्ता; Levi also दत्ताः । 23. DV correct but Gn omits त and Levi reads ·····कान । DV reads लिखित but Gn only लिखि । 24. Gn ना-श; Levi आवने, DV is correct. 25. L ·····दिपा । 26. DV प्री-वणे; Gn क्षिवणे; Levi प्री-श्रावणे । 27. Gn omits पञ्चिर्वि; L just प and DV is alright. 28. L अयत्ति । 29. L स्माय॑ । 30. Gn काये·····प्र-र्ग; L कारे व्यमवरश्राव्य-वाम । 31. DV शर्ति etc. as in our text but Gn शतिपण-स and then as in our text, L सतिपणस पण त्रयेन । 32. DV correctly reads but Gn क्ष । 33. DV but Gn भागस्यगण·····ण·····भवेश्चा·····च for the rest of the line. 34. DV पञ्चा । 35. DV correct but Gn पुराणा ।̐ ि द श्रा, L विंशति-त्रिपणपुराण तेंदत्तां । 36. DV correct but Gn reads जपग्र in place of षड्भाग । 37. L द्रव्यस्य वहु सम्पादनी [यम्] । 38. L कस्यतेन । 39. DV correct but Gn क·····मिति and L परोघो [स] म्वत श्राय । 40. Gn रोगमासौ; L तत्पर मावौ । 41. DV correctly reads but Gn क for न्त । 42. L पादीयोन्तरा-सनकरणे; Gn पाद्‌ीयाकारासनकरणे । 43. Gn

नापृच्छिष्ठहुभाषकण-मरणे, DV is alright except for कानांच्छिस; L घातँकाव्य-विषवृत्तासकल-यं···· 44. Gn निवासे, DV विनाशे, L सङ्कृतगो···· परिवार्य । 45. L सि····पर···· 46. Gn स्नपने, L परिक्षालये । 47. Gn, DV एवञ्चेलकरस्य, L एवं and further as in Gn. 48. L पुराणादेया: । 49. Gn मण्डपायावाया-साचेलपट्टा etc., L श्रारोपेयासाम् । 50. L पासोरिक । 51. Gn, DV शाम्भपुर but L साम्वपुर । 52. L रहास्सिपग । 53. L यथायम्गग जमण । 54. L दान-स्-एस्तराम् । 55. L पालनानुशस्सा । 56. L राजि-आ: । 57. DV, Gn स्थिरम् । 58. L omits श्रव and स्याम् after पूर्व in the next line. 59. DV द्वाराद्रङ्कण्टको; Gn द्वारा····ङ-कष्टका । 60. L वलसैंकि । 61. DV निरश्चिश्रनु and also Gn but L reads तिधि । 62. L श्ररघतस्यो । 63. Gn मोशा but DV is correct, L मार्ग । 64. DV reads मा but there is no such letter. However this letter has been omitted erroneously by the scribe. 65. L लंखुलम् ॥ डडिणि; Gn लंखुलम् ड दृण । 66. L न····पट्टा । 67. Gn omits स्य; L भस्-श्रा । 68. L क्षि-स्य । 69. L स्थवित । 70. L मूलस्यद्वारंपश्चिमेन चे । 71. L omits द्वार । 72. L omits ङ । 73. Gn गोवी; L योवि । 74. L त:-चेवा । 75. DV क्षुम; Gn कुमुढ्रती; L कुमुढ्रती । 76. L यो-तं निमा····पिका । 77. In Gn the last word is स्नान; L धन-ने-च-सने । 78. DV जप्ति; Gn जाप्तिखु; L जप्ति 5 सकम । 79. L क्षुणमृत्तानि । 80. DV ſ····त्तरं, Gn द्वारेणं····; L ſ ो····नरे । 81. L स्याग्रत: । 82. DV ति-य, the rest as above; Gn -ति यमस्ता etc, L यावत्-श्राम्····साकारितष्ट and the rest as in Gn. 83. DV is right; Gn टिका····श्चार्व···· 84. Gn मार्गस्योल्मा, but DV is right, L मार्गस्य···· 85. Gn पश्चिम-स···· 86. Gn, DV omit यष्टि । 87. DV, Gn गामी । 88. DV is right but Gn जातवर्म, L गामीप····विहारस्य····काइ । 89. L पश्चिम । 90. Gn कघप्रायम्मी, L कण्टयम्पी but DV is correct in his reading. 91. DV leaves space vacant up to भट्टारक । 92. DV is correct but Gn ····ण··रकप्रतिवद्धतत्रकुन्चो, L as in Gn but he reads खरो for कुञ्चो । 93. Gn line 63 just नदीमध्ये····मान····, DV's reading after मान is नतिभि-हुडिखुमध्यातिमि हेम्-ी भूमध्य; Levi reads भूमध्य तिमिहृत्ति···· 94. DV is correct but Gn ····दिपेका । 95. Gn दक्षिणमार्ग····, but DV corrected the end portion. 96. DV is correct but Gn ····नुसारेपि 97. Gn स्ततो····पिका, DV fills the

gap but omits some letters like यथा etc. 98. Gn and DV तत्रैव ।
99. DV correctly reads but Gn just मालि । 100. DV correct
but Gn प्रणाली । 101. Gn ⋯⋯एतुरिष⋯⋯ 102. DV correct but Gn
ि मालितत । 103. DV's and my reading same. Gn त्तमा⋯⋯अप्र⋯⋯
त्त⋯⋯म⋯⋯पूर्वानुसारेण च श्रावति । 104. Gn after नदी has पह्लवार्त-दिपूर्व
प-ि ी⋯⋯, DV omits भिसा of the end. 105. DV alright but Gn
ित्प⋯⋯पूर्व⋯⋯विल⋯⋯ 106. DV corrected the two 70-71 lines.
L does not read 70-73 lines. Gn omits the last two lines.

CXLIV. Inscription of Jñāneśvara

(HJ 124; DV 150) A slab of stone lying in a locality (eastern
extension of the city) of Kathmandu called Jñāneśvara. The top
is decorated with a chakra and śankhas. The date is missing as
the inscription is not well preserved. The inscribed part is 60 cm
wide and 76 cm long.

१ ⋯⋯⋯कैलासकूट भवनाद प्रतिहत धर्मशासनो लिच्छवि [कुलकेतु]⋯⋯

२ ⋯⋯⋯परम भट्टारक⋯⋯⋯⋯⋯

३ ⋯⋯⋯निवासिनो यथास्वमधिकरण⋯⋯⋯

४ ⋯⋯⋯यथार्हद्ङ्कुशलमभिधाय समाज्ञापयति

५ ⋯⋯⋯भवतां वर्णोत्तमा भूमिदेवा सस्मार्तं शास्त्राणाम्⋯⋯⋯

६ ⋯⋯⋯रनु पाल्यमान सुप्रक्षौम्मा⋯⋯⋯

७ ⋯⋯⋯पूर्वस्थित्या परिपालन निमि [त्त]⋯⋯⋯

८ अस्माभिस्तत्र वसतां⋯⋯⋯⋯

९ सीमापरिच्छिन्तस्यास्य स्थानस्य पूर्व⋯⋯⋯

१० ⋯⋯⋯विधारणादि पीडा हेतोनं कैश्चिद्⋯⋯⋯

११ ⋯⋯⋯वह्निगतानाञ्च देहिनां धनिक मनुष्यैरपि⋯⋯⋯

१२ ⋯⋯⋯विषादसापराध कारि स्वराज्य⋯⋯⋯

१३ ⋯⋯⋯त पाञ्चालिकं रेब गृहीतो राजकुलस्यार्पणीय —

१४ ⋯⋯⋯पणपुराण एको मध्यकं हंसेषु श्रीपूर्वाधि [करणेषु]⋯⋯

१५ ⋯⋯⋯पूर्वंकार्येषु ब्राह्मणानां मा ४० प्रसादानां वृद्धि⋯⋯⋯

१६ ⋯⋯⋯दक्षिण राजकुलस्य [पू] र्वाधिकरण⋯⋯⋯त्थं

१७ ·······करणीयं·······मात्रं···यकरणत्रयस्य···

१८ ···········न्यपूर्वाधिकरणानाम् यच्च करणत्रयं······

१९ ·········पण···दि···कार्येण·······

२० ·················

२१ ·······स्थानोत्पन्नानि··········कार्याणि······

२२ ·······हंस्य च दण्डाहंस्य उत्तम साहस कार्याणि···

२३ ·······धिकार······पञ्च पणा······

२४ रेवप्ररण···पित्रोदण्ड: शरीरापराधं च प·······
⁴

२५ ·······तेषां पणपुराणा देया······

२६ ·······पाञ्चालिकानां प्रदातव्या यस्तु द्रव्यं न प्रयच्छेत······

२७ ·······पणद्वयम् षट्पणपुरादेया·······

२८ लभ स्वद्वारावगतं दक्षिणराजकुल·······

१९ ·······पणशत मात्रं सक्षेत्रं·······

३० देयं र स्थान चेट्रीना·······

३१ करणिकावाहैरपि पण···पुराणा
⁵

३२ तण्डुलमानिकाद्वयं दातव्यं मानिका····
⁶

३३ ·······मानिका स्वाधिकार सम्बन्धेन पीडा कार्या
⁷

३४ ···कुर्युस्ते स्माभि र्भिविविश्च भूतार्थैः पूर्वराजकुल·······
⁸

३५ ·······पूर्वेषां पृथिवीन्द्राणां प्रजार्थैकरतात्मनां·······

३६ दूतकोत्र युवराजा (ज) श्रीविजयदेवः··········
⁹

३७ ············

1. DV नेपालमण्डलान्तर्गंत । 2. DV कारण । 3. DV हंस-श्रीं । 4. DV रिके । 5. DV पण···· 6. DV omits मानिका । 7. DV मात्रस्य । 8. DV तेस्माभि । 9. DV युवराज ।

CXLV. Taṅgabahāhiti Stone

(DV 152; Gn LXXXV; HJ 148) One of the two slabs of stone lying near the courtyard of an ancient water conduti known as Tangahiti lying in front of the main gate of the temple of Mīnanātha or Manjughoṣa in Patan. The top has a chakra flanked by two śankhas. The stone is much damaged. The inscribed part is 45 cm wide and...cm long.

१ ·····ल···द····रा·········
२ ······श्रीविजय·········
३ हरशा·········परम भ
४ ट्रारक······महाराजाधिराज परमेश्वर श्रीजयदेवः
५ कुशली············(य)
६ थार्हंङ्कुशलमाभाष्य······
७ ···दू·····यि······
८ परिजिह्·········
९ श्रीम·········
१० ण···यदि स्य·········
११ ञ्च द······
१२ ·········
१३ नारीण············

CXLVI. Kumbheśvara Inscription

(Gn LXXXVI; DV 157; HJ 159) A stone forming a slab on the front portion of a platform in the temple of Kumbheśvara in Patan.

१ ॐ स्वस्ति पर मंकारण········भगवतः [प्र] तिष्टानादस्ति परपुण्यमिति मत्वा भगवन्त न्त्रैलोक्यगुरुम्

CXLVII. Vārāhī Image Inscription

(DV 154) The pedestal of the image of Vārāhī inside a small temple of Gaṇeśa in the Mahabauddha quarter of Kathmandu.

१　ब्राह्मणः शक भ [ट्ट¹]·········

२　पुत्रा² न्यजठराग्रेति······

1. DV ट्ट्रस्य ।　　　　2. DV पुंत्रस्य र-स्य कृतिः ।

CXLVIII.　Patan Adalat (Court) Water Conduit

(DV 170; HJ 160) Water Conduit Inscription in front of the old judicial court house at Patan. This inscription on a dilapidated water conduit previously kept stuck to a raised platform in front of the old district court at Patan is engraved on two sides of the sprout with the wide open crocodile bulge. The inscribed part is 7-1/2 cm wide and 39 cm long. Date 170 Kārtika...divā 12.

One side

१　संवत् १०० ७० का [र्तिक]

२　······दिवा दशम्याम्

३　शुद्ध प्र णाल्या······¹

४　·········णाम्

Other side

१　दिवाकरेन² दत्तम्

२　···हितम् ध्वोलवास

३　प्रदेशे महापथे

४　दक्षिणे चुल्लंखूप

५　छिम कलोपिग्राम

६　पाञ्चालिकाणाम्

1. DV ···णा ।　　　　2. DV र ।

CXLIX. Fragmentary Inscription of Bungmati

(DV 164) A fragment of a stone inside the bāhā (within the courtyard of a monastery) of Machhendranatha in the village of Bungmati, about 3 miles south of Patan.

१ ······कदा कारूण्य प्रा॰श्रे॰ष्ठे प्राणिहि
२ ······यश्चावाप्या समस्त भूमिपति ता
३ ······कुलवतां जात्यादि दुःख क्षय···
४ ······नादमुखराढर कामिनी···

1. DV क-कारूण्य····प्राणिहि ।

CL. Gaṇabahal Image Pedestal Inscription

The pedestal of an image in the collection of Gaṇa-bahal, a newly discovered site in southern Kathmandu at its outskirt.

१ ····पूर्वं ङ्गमङ्क्कृत्वा सर्व्वसत्वा नाञ्च श्रनुत्तरज्ञानावाप्तये सं····

CLI. Dvākhābahā Image Inscription

(DV 165; HJ 133) The pedestal of the Buddha image on the Chaitya of Dvākhābahā or Henākara vihāra.

[ये धर्मा] हेतु प्रभवा हेतु तेषाञ्च तथागतो ह्यवदत् तेषाञ्च यो निरोध एवं वादी महा श्रमणः

CLII.

At an unknown site in Patan on a stone.

१ एते द्वे प्रतिमां याग्रहः मण्डल द्वयम् ।

CLIII. Bhwanginanitol (Patan) Inscription

(DV 181; Gn LXXXVI; HJ 158) Water conduit tank attached to the wall of a lane at Bhwanginanitol, Patan. The inscribed part is about 40 cm wide and . . . cm long. No date is visible. The area lies in the eastern extremity of the city of Patan.

१   पौनपान्या भिक्षुणी सद्योभोग दया स्वयम्
२   दत्ता एषाशिलाद्रोणी सत्वानां हितहेतवे ॥

1. DV सु····क्या ।

CLIV.

On a stone reservoir at an unknown site in Patan. This is different from the preceding one.

पौन पान्यां भिक्षुणी सद्यो भोगदया स्वयम्
दत्ता एषां शिला द्रोणि सत्वानां हित हेतवे

CLV. Inscription of Tānābahā (Kathmandu)

(DV 173; HJ 165) On the pedestal of Nārāyaṇa image at Tānābahā in the Makhantol quarter of the central part of the city of Kathmandu.

१   ····श्राषाढ़ कृष्ण सप्तम्याम्····[महाराजाधि]
२   राजपरमेश्वर श्रीमानदेवराज्ये । ····यत परम्य निहिजित
३   यथा मयं संग्राम शत्रो सुख मोचनाय च
४   ····जगतात्मनः चरणराज्ञ····
५   पुण्य स्वस्मृति कृत्यये····

1. DV reads only 2 lines.

CLVI. Lokesvara Pedestal Image of Patan

(DV 172; HJ 167) The pedestal of the image of Lokeśvara inside a small temple in Yangubahi, Patan with date 100 80 Māghakṛṣṇa dvitiya.

१ एतङ्ग्रामलहुग्वले प्रतिवसं हूँधर्मंजीव: स्वयम् प्राकार्षीदवलोकितेश ममलम्पाषाणमत्यद् भूतम् ।

२ सत्वानाम विकल्पमुत्पथगता म्प्रज्ञार्थ¹ चित्तात्मनाम् संसारार्त्तिमलान्धकार गहनान्तिर्मुक्तये सर्व्वदा ॥

३ राज्ये श्रीमानदेवस्य वर्षेशीत्युत्तरे शते । माघक्रृष्ण द्वितीयायाम्प्रतिष्ठास्य गुणोदघे:

1. DV ताम्प्रा-न्ध ।   2. DV मला-कार ।

CLVII. Chaitya Inscription of Su-bahal (Patan)

(DV 174; HJ 168) A Chaitya in the platform of a water conduit courtyard near Su-bahal in Patan.

१ ....

२ संवत् १८२ आषाड़ शुक्ल त्रयोदश्याम्

CLVIII. Royal Palace Nasalchok (Kathmandu)

(DV 177; HJ 179) On the deserted water sprout (Jaladroni) of a stone to the south west of Nasalchok at the old palace in Kathmandu.

१ ॐ भक्तया विष्णो: समुद्दिश्य..........

२ आषाढक्रृष्णसप्तम्याम् दत्तं ममृतवर्मणा.......पुन: पुनर्दे....

३ संवत् २०७

CLIX. Inscription of Lubhu-Motitar

१   ॐ पञ्चाशता समधिके सम्वत्सरशतद्वये
२   प्रथमाषाढ मासस्य द्वितीया दिवसे शुभे
३   जलद्रोणिरियं शैली पातिता दाक्षिणामुखा
४   श्री मताथ वलीराज्ञा राज्ञा पुण्याभिवृद्धये

CLX. Changu Nārāyaṇa Gate Śivaliṅga Base Inscription

(Gn LXXVIII; HJ 161; DV 180) Around the Jalahari (base)
of Śivaliṅga placed at the entrance door of the temple of
Changu Narayana. The inscribed part is about 85 cm wide and
8 cm long. Date: Samvat $200+70+2$, but Gn reads 172.

१   ॐ संवत् २७२ वैशाखशुक्ल दिवापञ्चम्यां ⋯ राज श्रीबरदेवराज्येलब्धा[1]
    ग्रामनिवासि कंभुसत प्रभिकरन ⋯⋯म्प्रभृति⋯⋯प्रतिष्ठापित भगवतो प्रति व
    लस्वामि

२   ⋯⋯देवस्थापक तेषां कुमारस्वामि⋯प्रदत्तं भुक्ति पुण्य⋯म हुं[2] दीनार
    लम्भेण कारितक मिति⋯⋯मानिका ८० पु ५
३   पश्चिमेन

1. DV and Gn read वल ।   2. Gn मुक्ति⋯म हुं हार, DV मुक्ति⋯
म हुं हार ।

CLXI. Colophon of Sahottaratantra

(DV 190) The colophon of the manuscript Sahottaratantra.
The page giving the colophon is 33 cm wide and 4 cm long.
The metre is Śardūlavikriḍita.[1]

The book was copied, on Samvat 301 Vaiśākha māsa, bright
fortnight (śukla), 7th day puṣya rikṣe (constellation) Sunday and
siddha yoga, by Vaidya Vasuvarmā in Gvala (Deopatan), while

Mānadeva with great fame like the light of the moon, and
pleasing everybody was ruling over the country.

समाप्तञ्चेदं सहोत्तर तन्त्रमिति
राज्ञि श्रीमान देवे पृथुजितयर्‍सि प्रोद्य दिन्दु प्रकाशे ।
काले पुण्यार्ज्जितस्य सकलजनमनो ह्लादिरम्ये वसन्ते ।
वर्षे चैकोत्तरेसिं स्त्रितय शतगते माधवे मासि शुक्ले
सप्तम्यां पुष्यऋक्षे दश (श) तकि रणे वासरे सिद्धयोगे ॥
उत्पत्त्या चम्बु वेलाकुल विविधरुजा ग्राह ···तिरोद्रै
संसारे सागरेसिम व्जगदिद मखिल ग्लानिनं सम्प्रवीक्ष्य ।
तस्माच्छ्री हर्षचन्द्रा निरतिशय घृणा भावितो मोक्तुकामः
प्रीस्या चे······तंप्रालिखत्सु श्रुताख्यम् ॥
श्रीगणदेव देवकुलदूरी ग्वलक निवासिनो वैद्य वसु वर्मणः पुस्तक
मिदं पठित्वार्थमवगम्य सर्वसत्त्वानामुपदेशं विधातुं······

1. Kaiser Library no. 699.   2. The श within brackets has to
be introduced, because there is only one श ।

CLXII. Bhuvaneśvara Stone

(DV 18°; HJ 170)   A slab of stone near a small temple of
Bhuvaneśvara within the precincts of the Paśupatinātha temple.

१   प्रद्युम्न प्राणस्य कीर्ति

CLXIII. A Small Stele in Paśupati Temple Area

(DV 185; HJ 166) One line inscription of another slab within
the confines of the temple of Paśupatinātha.

१   ···लोकोत्तर···हषिखड्गरागभूधर वक···महाभैरव

1. DV···कविक··· ।

CLXIV. Palanchok Wall Line

A slab of stone on a part of a wall in Palanchok temple on an ancient water sprout of stone at Dupet tol in Patan.

ॐ म्रनत देविच एतौ

APPENDICES

I
Lumbini Pillar

The village in the south west of Nepal in the plain of the Terai is known as Lumbini or Rumendei.

१ देवान पियेन पियद सिन लाजिन विसति वसा भिसितेन
२ अतन आगाच महीयते (।) हिदबुघे जाते सक्य मुनीति (।)
३ सिलाविगडभी चाकालापित सिलथमे च उस पापिते (;)
४ हिद भगवं जातेल्यु मिनिगामे उवलिके कटे
५ अठ भागियेच (।)

According to Hiuen Tsang the horse and the capital fell down being hit by lightning.

Sanskrit rendering from Pāli

१ देवानां प्रियेण प्रियदर्शिना राज्ञा विशतिवर्षों भिसिक्तेन
२ आत्मना आगत्य इह बुद्धजातः शावयमुनिः इति ।
३ शिलाविष्कृत गर्दभि च कारिता शिलास्तम्भः च उत्थापितः ।
४ इह भगवान्जातः इति लुंविनीग्रामः ५ द्वलिकः
५ अ्रष्ठभागिकः च

II
Niglihava (Nigalī Sagar) Pillar

The pillar in this area is broken and there are differences about the whereabout of the stūpa. Niglihava lies about 15 miles west of Lumbini.

१ देवानंपियेन पियद सिना लाजिन चोदस वसा (भिसितेन)
२ बुघस कोनाकमनस थुवे दुतियं वढिते (।)
३ (विसतिव) साभिसितेन च अ्रत आगाच महीयिते
४ (सिलाथव) (च) (उस) पापिते (।)

Sanskrit rendering

१ देवानां प्रियेण प्रियदर्शिनी राज्ञाचतुर्दश वर्षाभिसिक्तेन

२ बुद्धस्य कनक मुनेः स्तूपः द्वितीयं वद्धितः

३ विंशति वर्याभिसिक्तेन च आत्मना आगत्य महीयतं

४ शिलासाभा च उच्छापितः

III
Inscription of Musum-bahal

It is a slab of stone by the side of a modern water tap in the vicinity of the temple in a former monastic area called Musumbahal. The inscription is mutilated and is not readable except a few letters.

We do not know as to the lines inscribed. But the following can be made out. The latter part is totally destroyed.

१ ॐ स्वस्तिमानगृहाद् ··········· ··········

२ ··

३ ··

४ लिच्छवीकुलकेतु भट्टारक··········· ······

५ ··· ······················

IV
Sitāpailā Rock Inscription

(Gn App. 3; DV 176)

१ परम स्वामिनः

२ ॐ सम्वत् १०० ८० ४ पशुपतिभट्टारकः

३ चन्द्रेश्वर कारितः णापकः

Gn reads कारिकमितिः णापकः ।

BIBLIOGRAPHY

Bendall: A Journey of Literary and Archaeological Research in Nepal & N. India, 1884-85, Cambridge Univ., 1886

Bhagvanlal: Twenty Three Inscriptions from Nepal, Bombay, 1885

Sylvain Levi: Le Népal etude historique dun Royaume Hindou, III, Annals Musée Guimet, Paris, 1908

R. Gnoli: Nepalese Inscriptions in Gupta Character, ISMEO Roma, 1956

Thomas O. Ballinger: An article in Journal of the American Oriental Society, n. 4, 1958

Sanskrit Sandeśa: A monthly magazine in Sanskṛt published in 1954 (12 issues)

Itihāsa Prakāśa, another Sanskṛt magazine, Kathmandu, 1955 (only 3 issues)

Dhanavajra Vajrāchārya: Lichchhavi Kala kā Abhilekha (Inscriptions), Kathmandu, V.S. 2030

Hariram Joshi: Nepala Ko Prāchina Abhilekha, Kathmandu, V.S. 2030

Shankarman Rajavamsi: Several articles written in 'Ancient Nepal', a quarterly of the Archaeological Department of Nepal, Kathmandu

INDEX

CORRIGENDA AND ADDENDA

Ins. n. VI   P. 10 read in the 3rd line हृयास्प्रिङ् for प्रङ्

,,   IX   P. 11 read in the second line उरूधि: for रूधि:

,,   XII   P. 13 add in the introductory second line *close to Dhando Chaitya* after *reclining*

,,   XIII   P. 14 remove चाक्षय मस्तिवति in the 3rd line

,,   XX   P. 20 last line read ८ for ६

,,   XXI   P. 21 third line with brackets read तेष्टुज्ञ for तेष्ट

,,   XXVI   P. 25 read in the title (*Patan*) in between Khapinche and Inscription

,,   XXXII   P. 33 second line read मि for भि after भू

,,   XXXIII   P. 33 read 462 for 402 in the last line of the introductory portion

,,   XLIII   P. 41 read *Deonanitol stone of Satungal* in place of *Kulachhetol stone of Kisipidi*

,,   XLVI   P. 44 line 1 end with ध्यातो

line 2 begin with भट्टा and end with तुञ्चतु

line 3 start with तुतु and add ब्राह्मण पु

line 4 begin with रस्सरा and delete मनु and put समा at the end.

line 5 ज्ञापयति in the beginning and end with यथानेन

line 6 remove the brackets for सर्वं

line 7 end with केन

line 8 begin with प्रसाद: then
कृतोष्टुनाइत्येव
line 9 टुम्बिनो कस्यचिइ····यत्करं
line 10 भवड्डू: देयं····
line 11 नित्ये व करणीयंमुक्तम्
line 13 There is no vacant space in
the line.
line 14 मापहानिरिति········राजक्षेत्रम्
line 15 दत्तं ···
line 16 add अशीति initially
line 17 put केन at the end
line 20 begin with वं and then (अ)

,,	XLIX	P. 47 in the title add hill between Viṣṇupādukā and stele
		P. 48 line 11 read थंतुरी in place of थंतुरी
,,		P. 48 line 15 read ग्रहितव्यम् in place of गहिमव्यम्
,,	LIV	P. 53 line 6 read सामन्तांशु in place of सामन्ताशु
,,	LV	P. 55 line 14 read घेलन्ति in place of घेलन्ति
,,	LVI	P. 56 line 6 read सामन्तांशुवर्म्मं in place of सामन्ताशुवर्म्मं
,,	LXIII	P. 64 read धिकरणाप्रवेशेन for धिकरणप्रवेशन
,,	LXV	P. 64 line 16 read पश्चिमतश्च for पश्चिमनश्च
		line 18 read गोमी for गोभी
,,	LXVI	P. 68 end of line 8 and beginning of 9 read स्वामिभूमे: भट्टाक्षेत्रम् in place of क्षिप्तम्
		line 18 read त्र for च
,,	LXVII	P. 69 line 5 read मीर्मे for मिर्मे
,,	LXVIII	P. 70 line 1 read स्वस्ति for स्वस्चि
,,	LXIX	P. 72 read धावक for धावके
,,	LXX	P. 73 line 4 read ङ्कुशल for ङ्कुशल
,,	LXXV	P. 80 line 4 read ङ्कुशल for ङ्कुशल
,,	LXXV	P. 80 line 15 read तुञ्चरात्रणाली for शाला- प्रणाली
		line 12 read after नियतम् the word पुष्कलामा

line 14 the last letters are युवरा.
There is no ज, which is pushed to
the next line thus.
line 15 जोदय देव: [सं]वत् 30 etc.
footnote line 7 last letter read
भि: for मि

,,	LXXXV	P. 85 footnote read (तं) at the end
,,	LXXXVIII	P. 87 read in the third line of the intro-duction after Kathmandu the words *Through Tundikhel* which is a parade ground since last century
,,	XC	P. 88 footnote line read the letters with-out *double brackets*
,,	XCIV	P. 91 line 11 within brackets read श्चा in place of श्रव
,,	XCVII	P. 94 line 19 read at the end 8 in place of 9
,,	XCIX	P. 96 line 1 at the end read मयंर in place of भूत्पन्न
,,	XCIX	P. 96 line 3 at the end read व्छिराजेश्वराय line 16 in the beginning read [शैले]श्वर etc.
,,	CI	P. 99 line 22 read at the end वर्तिन: line 23 at the end येतेच line 24 is completely damaged
,,	CII	P. 99 line 8 read मस्मामि in place of मस्सामि and at the end लाम्मो for लाम्भो
,,	CII	P. 99 line 8 read हा(ह)जनि etc. P. 99 add at the end of the record गीनुङ् line 14 तत: एव ह्लागुं in place of ......
,,	CII	P. 99 There is one more line at the end but letters are all damaged.
,,	CIII	P. 100 Intro, add at the end a few more letters are effaced line 4 read भूरि····जाग्रत line 7 read एव ह्लागु in line 14 and vacant add at the end मुदितदान

line 14 read शक्तवाटकरणीयं

line 15 remove the brackets only for
च and स्ता

line 15 brackets only for रण

line 16 read in the appropriate
place कृति····पुरुष····जातीयतु and in
the beginning etc. as in the text.

line 17 कालघरेण for कालघर and
then स: पूज्यते एव द्विमर····

line 19 read व: प्रसाद कृ[त]···द

line 18 read दानी यतं राशिसहितं········

line 20 read दक्षिण कोलीग्रामनिवासिभि:

line 21 read··· ····ष्यते रू·······र्घक

line 22 read त्रिभि: मा···

line 23 read नीयते ·······

,,	CVI	P. 104 line 10 add छठ after ज्ये
		line 19 make मूर्ध्नि in place of मूर्धनि
,,	CXVII	P. 114 line 12 remove र and read हुस्प्रिङ् हुन् ग्रामे
		line 9 read भूमगुप्त in place of भुमगुप्त
,,	CXVIII	P. 116 line 6 read चुहुंगपेडा
,,	CXXII	P. 121 line 40 read भुक्तिका for मुक्तिका
,,	CXXIII	P. 122 add in the title portion of the Inscription *Bhairavanatha Temple Stele (Bhadgaon)*
		P. 123 line 2 laḍita after maheśvarāyah
,,	CXXVI	P. 125 line 11 remove प्र between थैषा and ज्ञणि
,,	CXXVII	P. 126 read in the title portion also Yaṅguvahi after Yanmugal
,,		P. 127 line 18 read गुप्त after कल्याण in place of just गुप्त